STEPFAMILY
THERAPY

STEPFAMILY THERAPY

A 10-STEP CLINICAL APPROACH

SCOTT BROWNING
ELISE ARTELT

AMERICAN PSYCHOLOGICAL ASSOCIATION

WASHINGTON, DC

Published by
American Psychological Association
750 First Street, NE
Washington, DC 20002
www.apa.org

To order
APA Order Department
P.O. Box 92984
Washington, DC 20090-2984
Tel: (800) 374-2721; Direct: (202) 336-5510
Fax: (202) 336-5502; TDD/TTY: (202) 336-6123
Online: www.apa.org/pubs/books
E-mail: order@apa.org

In the U.K., Europe, Africa, and the Middle East, copies may be ordered from
American Psychological Association
3 Henrietta Street
Covent Garden, London
WC2E 8LU England

Typeset in Goudy by Circle Graphics, Inc., Columbia, MD

Printer: Edwards Brothers, Inc., Ann Arbor, MI
Cover Designer: Berg Design, Albany, NY

The opinions and statements published are the responsibility of the authors, and such opinions and statements do not necessarily represent the policies of the American Psychological Association.

Library of Congress Cataloging-in-Publication Data

Browning, Scott.
  Stepfamily therapy : a 10-step clinical approach / Scott Browning and Elise Artelt. — 1st ed.
    p. ; cm.
  Includes bibliographical references and index.
  ISBN-13: 978-1-4338-1009-1
  ISBN-10: 1-4338-1009-3
  1. Family psychotherapy. 2. Stepfamilies—Counseling of. I. Artelt, Elise. II. American Psychological Association. III. Title.
  [DNLM: 1. Family Therapy—methods. 2. Divorce—psychology. 3. Family—psychology. WM 430.5.F2]

  RC488.5.B766 2011
  616.89'156—dc22
                                2011002247

British Library Cataloguing-in-Publication Data

A CIP record is available from the British Library.

Printed in the United States of America
First Edition

DOI: 10.1037/13089-000

To my wife, Joanne Ahearn, the person who gives
true meaning to my life. You offer me so much, from the
deepest love I can imagine to extraordinary assistance as an editor.
Most importantly, I know what it means to be in a marriage
with love and understanding. It has been the greatest gift in
my life to parent with you, love you, and grow old with you.
—*Scott Browning*

To Maria, Dylan, and Caitlin: the most unique, intelligent,
and creative set of stepchildren on the face of the planet.
And to my beloved Maya, you have brought so much joy
and love. You have made sense of everything.
—*Elise Artelt*

CONTENTS

ACKNOWLEDGMENTS

This book is the outgrowth of many years of teaching and conducting therapy with stepfamilies. We must thank various colleagues, students, assistants, and of course the many stepfamilies who have shared their unique perspective and allowed us to try something new to assist them.

Three graduate assistants have been instrumental in assisting in editing, organizing, researching, and keeping this process moving forward. Sara Mack worked before there was a contract to help us reach the point at which our materials were ready to be sent out. Rebecca Shaffer took over when Sara left, and her efforts have been extraordinary. Becca has been a tireless worker and an exceptional editor who is exact, perceptive, funny, and dedicated. We are so grateful to her and will miss her as she moves on to bigger things in her career. And recently, thanks to Amy Roth, who came aboard late and helped in bringing this book to the finish.

To Trish Broderick, we thank you for sitting down with us early in the process and giving us a realistic view of the time and commitment necessary to write a book. You were right. To Meg Mitchell, your enthusiasm in tracking down references is a marvel to observe.

To our editors Susan Reynolds, Tyler Aune, and Jessica Kamish, thank you for your sage advice, your patience, and your belief in this project.

Scott is grateful to his students, both at Chestnut Hill College and in professional trainings, who offered advice and challenges that allowed this model to be refined and improved.

Scott's colleagues at Chestnut Hill College have been supportive of this project for a long time. Steve Berk, Ana Caro, Susan McGroarty, Cheryll Rothery, Steve Simms, and Mary Steinmetz have been generous with ideas, resources, and encouragement. The chair of the department, Joe Micucci, supported Scott's request for a sabbatical that made the concentrated time for writing possible and had excellent advice about the process of writing a book. Scott is also indebted to administration members William Walker, Sister Kathryn Miller, Ken Soprano, Sister MaryJo Larkin, and especially, the president of the college, Sister Carol Jean Vale. Although Sister Carol has been overseeing the tremendous growth of the college, she always had time to ask about this project and show her support, for which Scott is deeply grateful.

Patricia Papernow has supported the teaching methods and the general idea of this book for years. In addition, she read an early version of Chapter 3 and offered exceptionally useful advice. James Bray has been supportive of our clinical theory and gave Scott professional advantages by coauthoring a chapter with him and encouraging the writing of this book. Francesca Adler-Baeder kept the trainings for clinicians interested in stepfamilies going when the Stepfamily Association of America came to an end. In starting the National Stepfamily Resource Center at Auburn University, Francesca provided us with a forum to continue to wrestle with the ideas presented in this book as well as access to herself and her mentor Kay Pasley. Kay Pasley has been a mentor, advocate, friend, and valued editor. It was because of Kay that Scott was invited to the first Wingspread Conference. She also gave him his first opportunity to publish his ideas about stepfamilies, and she supported his application to the board of the Stepfamily Association of America. No person has been more influential in his professional growth or success. Scott thanks Kay from the bottom of his heart. It is his honor to have been guided by her and to count her as a colleague. Scott's parents, siblings, and friends have always been on the sidelines cheering him on. So, Jordice, Karen B., Bill, Debbie, Neil, Josh, Jazz, Richard, Tony, Paul, Dennis, Adam, Bob, Marty, Diane, Karen G., David, Nancy, and John, Scott sends his love and thanks. Finally, Scott thanks his son, Owen, for being patient when he was busy and for giving him a different perspective on the world.

Elise would like to thank the administration and staff of the Canaday Library at Bryn Mawr College, where she spent many hours, for their help and for allowing her to use their wonderful resources in an excellent academic atmosphere. Working for Carson Valley Children's Aid has given her many opportunities to work with stepfamilies, which has provided an incredible, steady learning experience. The agency also appointed her to work in schools as a student assistance program counselor, which has been a most rewarding work experience. She would like to thank Cathi and Ken in the guidance offices of Christopher Dock Mennonite High School and Mary Lou, Cathy, and Anne in Lansdale Catholic High School for their support and respect as a colleague. Lansdale Catholic High School has given Elise the opportunity to work with hundreds of stepchildren over the years.

Marty Keyser has been Elise's mentor, supervisor, and friend, whose brilliant work in the field of family therapy, sense of humor, and charismatic personality have been a constant inspiration to colleagues and clients alike. Elise became a therapist largely thanks to the late Marjorie Bayersdorfer, who was a gifted therapist, an intellectual marvel, and also a mentor. Elise's office mates, Joanne Hostetter and Dr. George Zeo, have listened to her ideas, her reflections, and her personal saga with humor and patience on a steady basis. Elise is deeply indebted and grateful for the presence of these people in her life. Elise thanks her friends for their patience and support and as sources of inspiration: Joan B., Kathy, Bob, Geb, Bette and Alan, Anne M., the late Chuck Corbett, Barbara, Annie and Doc, Marcella, Maureen, Joan L., Elayne, Reidunn and Oivind, Maria, Bill, the late Sean Deibler, Ann T., Vicki and Robert, Sheila, Betty, Holly, her treasured "amoeba," and her family, Ham, Mike, the late Tommy and Mackie Bie, Celia and Dick, Nancy and Katie, as well as her late parents, Margaret and Ted Artelt, her late stepgrandmother Inge and her stepgrandchildren Katherine, Christopher, Erin, and Alexander. Finally, Elise would like to thank David for sharing his children with her and enriching her life in so many ways.

STEPFAMILY THERAPY

INTRODUCTION

Elena, a stepmother, calls; she says that things are getting out of hand with Maria, her teenage stepdaughter. Maria feels that Elena and her (Maria's) father, Joaquin, have too many rules and that all they do is yell at her. Several months earlier, Maria had moved back in with her mother Lucy, who lost custody of Maria when she was younger as a result of drug and alcohol abuse. Social services intervened after Maria was found out after curfew; they took her home to a drunken mother and then placed her unwillingly back in her father's house. Elena is distraught because Joaquin does not come home from work until 7 p.m., so there are 4 difficult hours when she is alone with the girl. Maria throws her belongings everywhere and does not keep her room neat. It smells of stale food and dirty clothes. Elena feels powerless; Maria says, "You're not my mother, and you're not even married to my father!" Joaquin feels he has to be nice to Maria so she will be happy and not want to leave.

A father calls. Martin says his 8-year-old daughter, Tammy, is having trouble sleeping because of recurring nightmares. She lives with her mother, Lorraine, and her stepfather, Jerry, who tells Tammy what to do all the time and gets angry when she does not obey right away. When Jerry's children from a previous marriage visit, they pretend to be nice to Tammy when her mother and stepfather are around but are mean and nasty when they are alone with her. When Tammy tells "stories" about his kids, Jerry is so cold and unsympathetic that she is somewhat afraid of him. Tammy's mother does not stick up for her. Jerry is very possessive and claims not to want the aggravation of having any contact with Martin; on visitation days, Martin must pick up and deliver Tammy around the corner from the house. Tammy feels her mother is just a "clueless doormat." And she desperately wants her parents to get back together.

What is a therapist to do in these situations? Many therapists are taken aback by the chaotic dynamics, the multiple issues, and the sometimes confusing logistics and find it difficult to know where to begin. Because stepfamilies present in many variations—married or cohabiting; gay, lesbian, or straight; and with multiple ethnicities and religions—therapists need to have a starting point, a framework for treatment, and an ability to determine the priorities at hand as they learn more about the family. This book, *Stepfamily Therapy: A 10-Step Clinical Approach*, supplies a model and guidelines to provide therapists with confidence and strategies to tackle the challenging family configurations. Helping family members to examine their negative interactions and to come to the understanding that their feelings can be regarded as somewhat reasonable within the context of stepfamily adjustment provides a remarkable service. Herein is a rationale, supported by research and clinical and scholarly observation, for creating a way to decipher various issues that are idiosyncratic to stepfamilies.

DEMOGRAPHICS

"Stepfamilies are the fastest growing family form in the United States" (U.S. Bureau of the Census as reported in Hetherington & Stanley-Hagan, 1999a, p. 137), whether formed through marriage or cohabitation. In 50% of marriages, either one or both people have already been married (Bumpass, Sweet, & Castro Martin, 1990). Cohabitation is also increasingly common (Cherlin, 2009)[1]. According to the 2008 Census, there were 6.8 million couples living together—an increase of 800% since the 1960s (Deal, 2010). No longer does cohabitation necessarily occur as a precursor to marriage; some couples choose not to marry (Bumpass, Sweet, & Cherlin, 1991) and nonetheless maintain long and fruitful relationships. However, cohabitants who do marry have "higher rates of marital separation and divorce," a statistic that has been called the "cohabitation effect" (Cohan & Kleinbaum, 2002, p. 180). When stepfamilies form through marriage, one third of them do not ever divorce (the divorce

---

[1]Hereafter, we assume that stepfamilies are formed through either circumstance, and we do not make a distinction between the two unless specified (see the section on cohabitation in Chapter 2, this volume).

rate for second marriages is 60%, and for third marriages, the rate is 73%; U.S. Bureau of the Census as reported in Deal, 2010). These statistics speak to the necessity of professionals trained to meet the needs of this growing population.

STEPFAMILY FUNCTIONING

Stepfamily configurations are distinct in important ways: There may be emotional residue from the former partnership; a history of rituals, structure, and expectations for the future; prior systems of parenting and division of household responsibilities; and loyalty issues (see Chapter 2, this volume, for a more in-depth look at disparities between the two types of families: first unions and stepfamilies).

When couples come together for the first time, they begin a life together on fairly equal footing. There are no ex-partners, no shared home experience, and no children. They are learning about each other and the aforementioned factors from the same basic starting point. When a stepfamily forms, one or both partners may have a former significant other, and there must be children; otherwise the partners are referred to as a remarried or cohabiting couple. Questions arise about the relationship between the ex-partner(s). How did the relationship dissolve? Is there residual acrimony between the former partners? Are there roadblocks to collegial communication and functioning? Are there custody and visitation arrangements with which both parties are satisfied? How did they divide household duties? Logistics may present further complications. Where is the new family going to live? How are the financial needs of both of the newly formed households going to be assured?

Often, the prior relationship determines the mind-set of the family members. There are myths, expectations, and hopes that this new relationship will provide a second chance to do things differently and be a success. Partners assume there will be an "instant family" (Visher & Visher, 1979) in which adults and children will come together in a harmonious "Brady Bunch" manner. Patricia Papernow (1993) called these expectations and fantasies the "invisible burden." This burden is outside of awareness and may impinge on the relationship in covert, damaging ways, leading to an undefinable disappointment and lack of fulfillment. For example, a stepmother may be expected to play the role of principal "caretaker and nurturer" simply because she is a woman (Whitsett & Land, 1992). This may be a self-imposed expectation, or a presumption by her husband and family, in both ways implicit. She may wonder why she cannot feel maternal toward her stepson or stepdaughter and chastise herself, even though she has no history with them and possibly no experience being a mother. In addition, children carrying the pain of the transition into the marriage may disrupt the family by ignoring or disrespecting the new interloper, or by eschewing any changes in routines, schedules, and parenting. They may also hold memories of their original parents together, may feel loyalty to each parent, and wish that they would reunite (Visher & Visher, 1979), all of which may promote active or passive sabotage of the newly formed stepfamily.

The case of Elena and Maria, described previously, illustrates many common themes of stepmother families. For instance, research suggests that stepmothers find it more challenging forming a stepfamily than do stepfathers (Coleman, Ganong, & Fine, 2000). For many stepmothers, the stress of their new role, along with potential parenting disagreements, disruption in routines, and other factors that stepchildren bring to bear on a marriage, can negatively impact marital quality (Ambert, 1986). At the same time, an adolescent's need for autonomy from the family can conflict with the stepfamily's tendency to desire more unity as the new family is forming (Bray, 2001). For an adolescent from a single-parent family who is used to more independence and responsibility, adjustment may be difficult; this is particularly true for girls because the stepmother can easily be seen as usurping the girl's place with her father and limiting her freedom. (Hetherington & Jodl, 1994).

Likewise, Tammy's predicament is quite common among children in stepfather families. After a divorce, children show behavioral disturbances as well as emotional upset due to the pain of the transition (Hetherington & Jodl, 1994). Elementary-school-age children, ages 6 to 12, may feel that their behavior was the basis for the divorce and are often focused on getting their parents together again (Visher & Visher, 1996). Early in the remarriage, the relationship between the mother and her children is frequently more conflicted; also, there is often less monitoring and less control of the children (Bray & Berger, 1993; Hetherington & Jodl, 1994).

OVERVIEW OF STEPFAMILY THERAPY

The stepfamily that presents with these and similar issues requires a therapist to immediately put together a plan for treatment while assessing many competing priorities. A key component of our approach to treatment is to understand the stepfamily as comprising *subsystems*, or relationships between individuals within the family. For instance, in the example of Tammy, she and her mother represent one subsystem; Tammy's mother and father represent another; Jerry and his children represent another; and so forth. Being versed in the stepfamily therapy (SfT) approach, the therapist knows that a troubled subsystem has the potential to undermine the entire family system, and the therapist must move to strengthen the family by stabilizing and addressing the difficulties of the various subsystems.

This book describes a 10-step model, which can be grouped into three phases: assessment, treatment, and integration. We provide a detailed explanation of each of these steps in Chapter 3; here, we present a brief overview.

Assessment

During assessment, the therapist determines the type of stepfamily and gathers information through the intake process, which incorporates the information supplied by the couple and the therapist's research-based knowledge of stepfamily functioning. After identifying the various subsystems, a decision can be made regarding a plan for therapy.

Treatment

There are five types of clinical interventions in the treatment phase; these are listed in Exhibit 1.1 and discussed in Chapter 3. After having determined the priorities for treatment, the therapist chooses the subsystem to be seen. The couple subsystem may need to be stabilized before the therapist can move to the other subsystems. The therapist must be aware of any faulty dynamics or *labeling* in whichever subsystem is present and must make an intervention judiciously at the moment that provides the greatest clinical effectiveness. Expressions of empathy are critical to the treatment process.

Often the biological subsystem in a stepfamily (e.g., a mother and her natural child) may become overwrought because individuals' natural connections may be taken for granted. Boundaries may be drawn less clearly in stepfamilies because relationships within the couple subsystem and the stepparent–stepchildren subsystem are being simultaneously established (Hetherington & Stanley-Hagan, 1999b). It becomes vital that the therapist convene the biological subsystem and confirm that the individuals are secure in their affective connection.

As the family members begin to understand how they are interlinked dynamically and how the behaviors of one family member elicit particular responses from the others, the circularity of their communication becomes more apparent. They are then able to expand their understanding of their own family system and the role each family member plays in it.

Integration

The third phase of the SfT model is integration. After the stepfamily subsystems have been stabilized, the family members are ready to come together. This can be the most challenging phase of therapy, both for the family and the clinician. Each family member is a member of different subsystems, and loyalties are tested and divided. A subsystem that appears cooperative and ready to integrate may suddenly refuse to come to the session. A nonresidential biological parent may feel threatened by the perceived newly gained unity of the stepfamily. This phase of the SfT model requires the therapist to demonstrate balance and fairness and an awareness of the likelihood of possible pitfalls or sabotage.

INTENDED AUDIENCE

The SfT model will be invaluable to therapists working in private practice and community mental health agencies and institutions such as schools or hospitals. Graduate students entering the field will gain confidence and learn a proactive therapeutic stance and strategies to tackle the complicated family configurations. SfT is an approach that will help to prevent the usual errors made when family therapists begin to apply to stepfamilies standards of care that they have learned for first-union families. Ancillary professionals, such as educators, school counselors, children and youth workers, and lawyers and mediators, will welcome information and insights that help them to identify when the problem at hand is a stepfamily issue and to pinpoint the locus of conflict (i.e., between which family members), the level of discord, and the pertinent issues. This will aid them in proper referrals, facilitate communication, and give them a sense of appreciation for the frustration and confusion the family is experiencing. In addition, families may be interested in learning about the SfT approach, including those who exhibit a reluctance to seek treatment. In such a case, this book may be useful in elucidating the salient issues and any roadblocks to effective communication.

OUR BACKGROUND

We have been working on the articulation of a therapy directed toward stepfamilies for the past 20 years. Scott Browning initiated the idea of a subsystem approach to stepfamilies, which has evolved from his lectures for trainings at the Stepfamily Association of America, his teaching graduate courses on stepfamilies, and earlier developments of this model (Browning & Bray, 2009). He and Elise Artelt subsequently formulated a 10-step model. Although Scott has long been involved in research, his primary contributions to the field have been made as a clinical theoretician and teacher. His early challenge to the family therapy field (Browning, 1994) highlighted the idea that cardinal family therapy interventions were unhelpful when applied to stepfamilies. Scott was invited to become a board member of the Stepfamily Association of America, and he was asked to become particularly involved in the upcoming efforts to create a training institute to assist professionals in the mental health field wishing to work clinically with stepfamilies. One of the unique features of this training for professionals was a protocol that assisted in forming role-play stepfamilies (*created families*) in an accurate and ethical manner so that trainees could observe people with particular clinical expertise demonstrate clinical interventions with "real" stepfamilies (Browning, Collins, & Nelson, 2004).

Elise Artelt's interest in and experience with stepfamilies began the day she met her stepchildren Dylan, 16, and Caitlin, 13. Finding herself in the position of a residential stepmother and not really having a clue what to do was at once unnerving and bewildering. She got along pretty well with Dylan, but her relationship with Caitlin was challenging at best; trying to get to know each other often seemed like a game of "approach and avoidance." Elise and Caitlin went through an endless struggle those first years, which could have been addressed and possibly assuaged had there been a stepfamily therapist to help them sort through the relationship and avoid needless pain. This experience formed the foundation of Elise's interest in becoming a stepfamily therapist.

STEPFAMILY THERAPY: A 10-STEP CLINICAL APPROACH

The book is divided into eight chapters. A brief overview of each chapter follows.

Chapter 1 is designed to place SfT into the context of the larger field of family therapy. We provide a brief overview of family therapy to examine ideas that continue to be important in any model that addresses the clinical needs of families. We then examine those classic interventions that, in fact, do not serve the clinician in working with stepfamilies. This leads to a discussion of the foundational research that serves to clarify how stepfamilies differ from first-union families. The conclusion is an explication of those theories that have examined treating stepfamilies.

In Chapter 2, we examine the particular attributes of stepfamilies that can lead to vulnerability and the need for clinical intervention. We provide introductory clinical information to assist the reader in articulating the unique needs of stepfamilies and some of the possible approaches that can make clinical work more successful. The chapter ends with an examination of SfT in the spectrum of evidence-supported approaches.

Chapter 3 is in many ways the centerpiece of the book. It fully examines and makes practical the 10-step model. Each step moves the stepfamily through assessment of the problem areas, interventions with the subsystems, and finally, integration of the stepfamily subsystems into a more functional whole. The model is intended to be applied over a relatively brief period, generally 7 to 12 sessions; the steps are provided not as a strict treatment plan but rather as a general outline in which each step is necessary, although not necessarily in a linear fashion.

In Chapter 4, we apply the 10-step model of SfT to the Jones family, a prototypical simple stepfather family presenting for therapy. The therapist guides the stepfamily through the 10-step model while clarifying each step so that the reader understands the application and timing of the interventions. We then use excerpted dialogue from sessions to further illuminate the treatment approach, and discuss common problems (e.g., stepfather and adolescent stepchild conflict) in the context of treatment.

The goal of Chapter 5 is to clarify the clinical model as applied to a step-mother family. The Walker stepfamily is a prototypical stepmother family; they formed following the death of the first Mrs. Walker. We examine the differences between stepfamilies without a nonresidential parent and a former in-law system while the therapist treats the family using the 10-step model of SfT. The chapter includes session dialogues to show how the therapist implements the clinical interventions of the treatment phase. The therapist explains the rationale for treatment of the Walker stepfamily and the overall goals for reducing chaos and moving toward more optimal functioning.

In Chapter 6, we discuss the Coleman family, a complex stepfamily that was formed when two people who both had children repartnered and moved in together. This family illustrates the often extraordinary confusion that a therapist encounters in working with this type of configuration. With a step-mother and a stepfather living in the same household; multiple visitation and custody arrangements; full siblings, half siblings, and stepsiblings coming and going; and a complex array of issues and relationships, the clinician can feel relieved that he or she has the SfT model for treatment. Breaking the family down into subsystems helps the therapist to discern the critical problem areas and the subsystems in distress and to move forward with confidence.

The role of the extended family is critical in understanding treatment issues in stepfamilies. In particular, the role of grandparents and stepgrandparents has only recently begun to be examined in the research literature and as a clinical concern. Although the extended family may offer support in some cases, these family members can also be the source of great stress. In Chapter 7, we examine how various stepgrandparent structures raise particular clinical issues and how those issues may be addressed in therapy. When a new stepfamily is created following the death of one of the parents, one of the most complex issues is determining the role of the former in-laws.

Chapter 8 focuses on diversity. After a brief overview of diversity in clinical practice, we present examples of stepfamilies comprising minority populations to explain the impact of racial, ethnic, and cultural identity in stepfamily therapy. We close the chapter with a discussion of gay and lesbian stepfamilies; the 10-step SfT model is applied to a lesbian stepfamily in an abridged form.

CONCLUSION

It is clear that stepfamilies are unique and that the therapy offered to them needs to be tailored to avoid traps that traditional family therapy might generate. *Stepfamily Therapy: A 10-Step Clinical Approach* is written to provide the clinician or anyone involved in working with stepfamilies a clear understanding of some common experiences of stepfamilies, a treatment rationale and a clear-cut 10-step methodology to assist these families.

1

THE EVOLUTION OF
THE STEPFAMILY FIELD

Since the emergence of the field of family therapy, many individuals have supported the idea that the therapist's ability to understand the systemic functioning of a family is a necessary and sufficient foundation for clinical work with any family (Haley, 1976). According to this unique view, the family, and not the individual, is the client. Despite its utility in family therapy, however, this idea has created precedents that are not optimal for treating stepfamilies.

The family therapy movement represented a radical departure from individually focused treatment (Haley, 1981; Stanton, 2009). A unifying factor across models involved the importance of understanding or observing the family's systemic pressures and patterns. Family therapy can be perceived best as a movement that accepted different theories in regard to the specifics of treatment but was united in conceptualizing the presenting problem in the context of the family. However, to understand how stepfamily therapy (SfT) has evolved, it is necessary to place it within the context of the wider field of family therapy.

This chapter expands on ideas that first appeared in *Stepparenting: Issues in Theory, Research, and Practice*, edited by K. Pasley and M. Ihinger-Tallman, 1995, Westport, CT: Praeger Publishers.

From the beginning of family therapy and for many years, the standard belief was that family therapists did not need to specialize regarding the type of family treated. Don Jackson (1967) stated, "There is no such thing as a normal family" (p. 31). Jackson's statement implied that rather than establishing whether a family was normal or pathological, it was more important to understand that families were systems. A system, as defined by von Bertalanffy (1968), involved the interaction of elements. When the elements, or component parts, interacted, they influenced each other. Solar systems, corporations, and computer networks were systems, and so too, the family was viewed as a system insofar as it included the interaction of elements. Furthermore, the interaction of elements followed specific rules. Given the extraordinary range of relational units that were considered systems, all families were assumed to be equally amenable to the benefits of family therapy.

The pioneers of family therapy established theories based on therapy with a "generic" family to gain acceptance and credibility. There were good reasons to avoid heading in the direction of addressing family typologies (Hoffman, 1981). It might have been destructive to the nascent field of family therapy to dilute the concept of systems thinking by creating separate rules for stepfamilies, single-parent families, adoptive families, and other nontraditional family types. Different proponents of family therapy did not identify their models as more useful for one family type than another. In fact, the early general acceptance of "the family" allowed early theorists to focus on the systemic nature of family.

A brief description of some of the pivotal leaders of family therapy highlights the variety of perceptions that were considered important in treating families. It is helpful to understand that many of the early models appear to use very powerful interventions. According to the prevalent belief in the concept of homeostasis (Bateson, Jackson, Haley, & Weakland, 1956), change was seen as quite difficult to achieve. Therefore, the early models often appear to concentrate on agitating families in treatment. As the field has evolved, theories explaining what helps families to change have become more subtle and focused. As can be seen from the short list of family therapy pioneers included here, some profoundly affected the philosophical understanding of family therapy and how families change, some provided significant technical advances in the field, and some did both.

Nathan Ackerman (1966) was "one of the first to envision whole family treatment, and he had the inventiveness and energy to carry it out" (Nichols, 2010, p. 32). He articulated a model that bridged psychodynamically informed individual therapy and a clear systemic perspective, thus creating a model that postulated that a therapist needs the input of all family members to effect significant clinical change. Ackerman articulated how a therapist could pursue the dynamic issues of the individual while also being aware of the systemic patterns. This model advocated working with both of these considerations in tandem, thereby weaving an understanding of the individual's defensive structure with the family's behavior patterns. Once the family members were able, in Ackerman's view, to see how these defensive features functioned to be part of an unhelpful cycle, that family was far more able to change these patterns.

Ackerman was interested first and foremost in the various compositions, whole families and subsystems, attending therapy sessions. Carl Whitaker (1958; Napier & Whitaker, 1978), in contrast, strongly believed that the entire family must show up for therapy. He believed that if a therapist created a level of anxiety by asking many varied questions, the family would coalesce into a more functional form because they would grow psychologically through the process of therapy. This was a radical notion, one that rejected working toward a specific goal and instead posited the experience of therapy itself as primary. In this approach, the presence of the entire family was clearly justified on a theoretical level. With all members of the family present, no one member could be scapegoated. In other words, the family would be unable to avoid anxious feelings generated by Whitaker's questions by transferring the anxiety to the person missing from the session. Few clinicians work exactly as Whitaker did; ultimately, his influence was philosophical rather than practical. He caused this newly established field to address the question, "How much anxiety is helpful in treating a family?"

Virginia Satir (1964) took a position that aimed not to increase the anxiety of the members of the family but rather to increase their self-esteem. She chose to help them identify their feelings, the role they played, and how these factors might be perpetuating dysfunction within the family. Although Satir did not describe the steps of her technique, it is evident in watching films of her work that she understood how to safely open up family members to hearing each other's concerns, which often resulted in the family being brought closer together through tenderness, a focus on the positive, and an altering of the way in which the family members labeled their own actions.

Murray Bowen (1978; M. E. Kerr & Bowen, 1988) was the quintessential systems thinker who created the most comprehensive theory in family therapy. His explanation of how a system works gave evidence of how family members could shift away from a position of blame. He provided a clarity of thinking that established a thorough understanding of the family's emotional process. Although Bowen's theory had eight interrelated core concepts, it was his idea of *differentiation* that dominated his work. He saw differentiation as how an individual learns to take a position that is independent from the emotional process of her or his family. Because of his belief that one becomes fused within the family system, he recommended a method to gain greater objectivity to understand one's role in the family process and thus be able to avoid becoming co-opted. One tool he used to achieve this was a *family diagram* (basically what is now referred to as a genogram). The family diagram allowed Bowen to both diagnose problems and understand specific patterns in the family. Bowen highlighted the importance of family members becoming less emotionally reactive, which he suggested allowed family members to tolerate greater levels of anxiety. Clearly, this lesson is one of great importance in working with stepfamilies. Although Bowen did not explicitly discuss these ideas in relation to stepfamilies, they are quite useful and applicable to stepfamily therapy.

Salvador Minuchin (1974) brought a clear process to the field of family therapy. His structural approach was specific: One assessed the boundaries and hierarchy of the family to focus the process on a certain series of tried-and-true intervention techniques. Not all of Minuchin's techniques were original (e.g., the reframe), but he articulated how to implement his model with great elegance and precision. The structural model was helped by its use of visual tools to explain the process of therapy to the clinician. Satir and Bowen both used the genogram extensively; Minuchin added a very basic visual tool: the structural map. This allowed a supervisor or teacher to show a student exactly what the end goal would look like. In other words, if the graph indicated that mother and daughter were too close and their relationship was keeping the father estranged from both, then the supervisor could draw a graph with mother and father close and the daughter attached to both in a relatively equal manner. In a sense, the supervisor was encouraging the therapist to "paint by the numbers:" follow the structural map and work to adjust the hierarchy of the family. This was done in order to improve relationships by making the boundaries and hierarchy of the family meet a more functional standard.

Richard Fisch, John Weakland, and Lynne Segal (1982) provided a practical application of the works of both Milton Erickson (Haley, 1973) and Gregory Bateson (1951). The model, usually referred to as the interactional approach of the Mental Research Institute, provided therapists with an understanding of paradox that up to that point had often been misunderstood. Many students learning about paradox would place it in the same light as reverse psychology. For example, "I will tell the clients not to go out so they will rebel against me, and in fact, go out." Although on occasion the intervention worked, often in spite of a naïve therapist, the confusion around the concept made paradox appear to be manipulation. However, in reality, the strength of paradox is putting change squarely into the hands of the client. When implemented well, paradox, the most profound intervention of the strategic schools of therapy (of which the Mental Research Institute is central), is a humane and powerful intervention.

Michael White's narrative approach (White & Epston, 1990) had a seismic effect on the field of family therapy. Interestingly, his influence remains on the larger theoretical issues, rather than on technique itself. Although White created the very interesting techniques of *externalization* and *witnessing,* many of his interventions had come from earlier models. Few therapists still call their theoretical foundation *narrative;* however, many are likely to talk about having been influenced by narrative ideas. In essence, White used the writing of Foucault (1980) to form the foundation of his challenge to family therapy. White's theory was the most popular theory in family therapy that could be labeled a *postmodern* model. His approach presented a clear rationale as to why clinicians had inadvertently misused power in the clinical relationship, and he alerted the field to the critical importance of having the clinician actively engage in understanding the cultural and gender issues at play in every case. In this way, he provided an important correction to some mistakes that were becoming endemic in family therapy. For example, as a field, family therapy was blinded to the manner in which gender, cultural and power issues remained unaddressed in most family therapy sessions. On a practical level, however, White took the family interaction out of family therapy as a result of his profound allegiance to each person's personal narrative. His attention was on the individual, but given his respect for systemic understanding, he conceptualized the person's problems within the family.

Susan M. Johnson (2004) took her work on studying the clinical implications of addressing emotions directly in the clinical setting and combined it with a focus on how attachment concerns play out in couples' relationships. In her emotionally focused model, Johnson was prescient about the shifting importance of a model needing to be evidence supported, and thus she laid out a series of steps that formed guidelines for treatment. Johnson established an explicit process (S. M. Johnson & Bradley, 2009) that could be used as a guide to treatment of couples' problems. In this way, couples are often able to understand how a particular attachment need results in an unhelpful interactional pattern. Thus, when the pattern begins to happen, the need is quickly identified so the real concern comes to the fore rather than just the topic of the disagreement. In essence, she advocated making the pattern the enemy, not one's partner.

The approaches discussed so far all adhere to a systemic perspective but envision various methods to assist families in making clinical change. Instead of recycling each other's ideas, these theorists perceived a unique mechanism within families that encouraged lasting systemic alterations. Their models then addressed the particular concerns that each felt was useful for clinical progress with families.

Newly emerging approaches to family therapy are more focused. Rather than create models that are intended for any and all families, most new approaches are targeted toward a narrower population. This is progress, although it may at times appear to be a tactical retreat by the field. The postmodernist movement made it impossible, or at least unlikely, that theorists would return to a time when factors such as culture, structure, and disability were largely ignored. The field had matured; a correction in the direction of family therapy was inevitable. However, certain realities also served to nudge family therapy toward a practice that saw much more specialization. First, therapists began to note (even before they were told to make their therapy evidence based) that some approaches seemed too blunt for specific problems and populations. Second, particular concerns (e.g., adolescent addiction, impoverished families, eating disorders) began to push theorists and therapists alike toward determining targeted clinical approaches. Third, insurance companies recognized that paying for therapy gave them the right to examine the therapeutic process. Once the veil was lifted, it became all too clear that the different disciplines (psychiatry, psychology, social work, and counseling) had all permitted practitioners to conduct therapy with little focus on verifiable outcomes. Although the debate continues as to how therapeutic outcomes can be measured, clearly more focus on *best practices* was inevitable. Fourth, research, both qualitative and quantitative, increased the awareness that different populations, such as stepfamilies, really do need to be understood and respected, and therapy would likely be more effective if it addressed, rather than ignored, these unique needs.

Many of the standard techniques of family therapy remain useful and transferable across more focused populations. For example, most models of family therapy encourage a method to engage the family, determine the strengths of the family, track the interactional sequences and increase collaboration between the therapist and the family. So although the field of family therapy continues to evolve, certain cardinal precepts and techniques remain.

However, family therapists became increasingly aware that stepfamily cases frequently seemed unusually difficult to resolve. The techniques that they had learned and had applied most often to first-union families did not seem to work as frequently with stepfamilies. A therapeutic impasse is not uncommon when the distinction between the stepfamily and the traditional first-union family is ignored. This impasse occurs because the therapist might make errors simply by not understanding that certain interventions that work well with first-union families aggravate a stepfamily.

The honored role played by the early theorists and pioneers of family therapy in the history of psychotherapy is well deserved. In challenging the status quo of treating the individual client, they achieved an epistemological shift in the understanding of what therapy is and does. The following critique is not intended to question the tenets or efficacy of their theories. Rather, some common family therapy interventions missed the particular needs of stepfamilies while having served first-marriage families well. For example, the following four highlighted family therapy interventions established precedents that caused confusion and inconsistent clinical results when applied to stepfamilies.

COMMON PRACTICES IN FAMILY THERAPY TO BE AVOIDED WITH STEPFAMILIES

An argument made previously (Browning, 1994) is that the generic application of interventions designed for first-marriage families serves stepfamilies poorly. Although keeping a systemic understanding of the stepfamily remains a useful, and in many ways a necessary perspective in conducting stepfamily therapy, the interventions that have been applied to first-marriage families for years need to be avoided.

Inviting Entire Families Into Sessions

Family therapists had long been taught that to conduct effective therapy, the entire family must be present (Bell, 1975). Any missing member posed a significant problem because it was the family that was seen as the client. Therefore, without the entire family present, the client was not present. A systems orientation dictates that the clinician must never lose sight of the family system as a whole. In fact, it was not unusual for family therapists to request that a family leave if all the members could not be present and only return when the entire family was complete. This approach further reinforced the notion that to obtain an honest picture of family rules and patterns all family members were required to be present at the initial session.

Establishing a stepfamily involves numerous changes and adjustments. Stress is created by the increased complexity of the family, conflicting loyalties, and the assumption of immediate love (Pasley & Ihinger-Tallman, 1982; Pasley & Lee, 2010). Although an emphasis on seeing the entire family might allow a therapist to receive information that was previously left unspoken, the benefit of receiving that information will likely be offset by the unnecessary pressure added to the stepfamily by seeing them all together at first. Statements made in the presence of a therapist that are driven by extreme anger and frustration may create an environment that is poorly suited to the development of trust, which is necessary for therapeutic intervention. Clinical experience with stepfamilies has forced therapists to question whether including all members of the stepfamily in the initial session is as useful as it often is with first-union families.

In concentrating on the subsystems, rather than on the entire stepfamily system, during the initial therapy session, the therapist discourages the notion that the stepfamily must be viewed as a single unit. Instead, the therapist will more accurately address the stepfamily's true composition. The therapeutic process is meant to parallel the reality of stepfamily life by stabilizing the subsystems, with the eventual goal of integrating them. In keeping with Heider's (1958) balance theory, the complete system is strengthened by secure subsystems.

Establishing Hierarchical Boundaries

The structural school of family therapy is most commonly associated with the concept of establishing hierarchical boundaries. Although Minuchin (1974) directed greater clinical interest to the nontraditional family form than did other theorists (in part as a result of his work in the inner city), he still instructed family therapists to reinforce appropriate boundaries. The boundaries in stepfamilies in which children are brought in from previous marriages are more complex than those of the traditional first-union family (Bray & Kelly, 1998; Hetherington & Kelly, 2002; Pasley, 1987). Consequently, without an examination of a myriad of contextual variables, any discussion of an appropriate boundary in a stepfamily is unreasonable. This is not to say that stepfamilies never adopt a hierarchical system that is parallel to that of the traditional first-marriage family. In fact, in some stepfamilies, such a system evolves naturally and effectively. For example, in some stepfather families, the new stepfather may, without much discussion or conflict, adopt a role that is indistinguishable from that of a biological father. However, more frequently, stepfathers who attempt to establish such equal parental authority find that neither they nor the biological parent sees the other as working effectively with the child (Bray & Kelly, 1998).

Those therapists who adhered to the structural family therapy model believed that a clear agenda existed when dealing with child-related problems in the family context. That agenda included a commitment to correct dysfunctional hierarchies by putting the parents in charge of the children (Minuchin, 1974). However, because the pivotal research of James Bray and Sandra Berger (1993) advocated that stepparents should adopt the role of a monitor of their stepchildren (for at least the first 2 ½ years) rather than a disciplinarian, therapists are now aware that the inclination to intervene in this manner with stepfamilies would be a mistake.

Adhering to structural theory, a therapist might see a stepfamily and correctly diagnose the presence of a coalition between the biological parent and child. The assumption that follows from the diagnosis would normally be that this coalition developed to redirect stress away from the couple's relationship. Through family mapping, the usual intervention is to identify the coalitions that exist in the family and then to work to strengthen the generational boundaries. Although it is frequently well suited to the traditional first-marriage family, such a move on the part of the therapist can cause a deeper fracture in the structure of the stepfamily.

Enactment and Therapeutic Intensity

Structural family therapy uses two particularly powerful therapeutic maneuvers, *enactment* and *therapeutic intensity* (Minuchin, 1974). The former intervention involves the process of acting out familial transactions during the therapy session, whereas the latter occurs when the therapist delivers a forceful message or strongly confronts the status quo of the family.

In a stepfamily there naturally exists a high level of intensity. This intensity is sometimes so great that to increase it clinically or to enact a problem situation often will produce a reaction that can be too powerful for the permeable boundaries of the system. In such cases, the members of the stepfamily are likely to retreat from family therapy in uncertainty over whether they can trust that their family is capable of tolerating additional stress. The stepfamily may also be concerned that the therapist does not understand the tremendous pressure they are under.

A disturbing fear that exists for many stepfamilies is the likelihood of redivorce. This fear is made more real by the fact that, in most instances, at least one of the remarried parents has already experienced divorce. The need for a sense of stability is often paramount in a stepfamily. Any intervention designed to create a crisis to restructure the family is likely to increase the already present fear of dissolution. Therefore, these interventions are often contraindicated for stepfamilies.

Family Rules

The rules that existed in a previous first-union family are often revised or dropped by the remarried family. Even a rule that is retained from one family to the next is no longer the same rule because the family context is more powerful than the content of the actual rule. A change in family membership shifts the rules by which family members live. That is, out of the original context, an old rule will no longer serve the purpose it was intended to achieve.

A strong focus on family rules can undermine the therapeutic agenda when working with stepfamilies. Whereas working to discover the rules of a traditional first-union family may lead to some revelations that explain behaviors and communication styles in the home, the stepfamily often lives with a necessary double standard regarding rules. For example, a remarried couple feels some relief when they determine that they agree on a rule to apply to a child in the stepfamily. If, however, the rule contains language (e.g., in the "case of emergencies") that could be defined differently by each member of the couple, the clinician must be extremely careful to avoid setting up a couple by acting as if the rule has been definitively determined. The clinician should go over a series of examples to establish that an agreement is strong enough to stand the light of day.

EARLY CLINICAL WORK ADDRESSING STEPFAMILIES

Reviewing the major theorists in the field of family therapy, one is struck by the fact that stepfamily therapy is rarely mentioned. Among the pioneers of family therapy, only Virginia Satir (1967) discussed the remarried family at any length. As we suggested earlier in this chapter, making special provisions for each different family composition would have been seen as negating the general applicability of researchers' theories.

Stepfamily therapy was formed and elucidated by theorists and clinicians who became aware of the glaring void of information that was applicable to this family type. Some had experienced living in stepfamilies and found that they needed to better understand what was happening in their own lives; others found themselves with a number of stepfamilies in their clinical practice and were unsure how to proceed.

As early as the 1950s, researchers recognized the importance of studying this type of family (Bernard, 1956; Bowerman & Irish, 1962; Fast & Cain, 1966), and those working with stepfamilies described them as an exciting and challenging population (Visher & Visher, 1979). However, several questions have continued to both fascinate and perplex researchers and clinicians: Why is the remarried family so often a clinical challenge? Is it simply the structural complexity of these families, or is there an inherent problem caused by the addition of a new authority figure to an already established family system?

In addition, therapists have attempted to treat this unique family type with therapeutic methods that were not specifically designed to be responsive to their special problems. It was not until the late 1970s, when Visher and Visher (1979) authored *Stepfamilies: A Guide to Working With Stepparents and Stepchildren*, that it became clear that therapy with stepfamilies demanded unique skills.

The 1980s produced an explosion of clinical information on stepfamilies. Lillian Messinger (1982) published an edited volume of *The Family Therapy Collections on Therapy With the Remarried Family*. Although his model did not have significant longevity, Clifford Sager and the team at the Jewish Board of Family and Children's Services (Sager et al., 1983) must be acknowledged for creating a very early clinical approach to treating stepfamilies. Visher and Visher (1982, 1988, 1989, 1990, 1991) continued their writings on stepfamily therapy. The 1988 publication was an excellent compilation of theoretical considerations and clinical intervention strategies. Carter and McGoldrick's (1988) work is another example of clinicians who were dedicated to providing colleagues with an understanding of the process of remarriage and to suggesting clinical methods to address the problems that are unique to stepfamilies (e.g., triangulation). Finally, the systemic aspect of the stepfamily was expanded by Ahrons (1979) in her description of the binuclear family system. Her article created a fuller understanding of the dilemmas facing stepfamilies and the complexity inherent in working with the larger family system that exists following divorce.

INTERACTION BETWEEN RESEARCH AND CLINICAL INTERVENTIONS

Researchers and clinicians examine the research literature with a different goal in mind. Researchers, even those not performing a meta-analysis on a particular field of study, are looking at various studies and trying to build a case that the central tendency of the findings is consistent. Clinicians, however, are perusing the literature with the intention of seeking support. They look to research to confirm that the clinical direction they are pursuing is correct or that the actions being taken by this stepfamily are not helping the stepfamily to develop. Clinicians are not worrying about cross-checking all the research findings to be certain that each conclusion has been repeatedly confirmed. Clinicians assume that if the study was published in a peer-reviewed journal, then its findings must hold some weight and could benefit the stepfamily.

Neither party is using research "the wrong way." And even though researchers have a purer idea of how to correctly interpret the findings, they are dependent on clinicians to provide them with interesting phenomena that occur in the clinical arena to investigate. To this end, research serves the purpose of providing foundational information that establishes an "objective" understanding of the population under study, in this case stepfamilies, and also addresses issues that relate directly to treatment concerns. For example, research may suggest that specific areas are crucial for therapeutic intervention because a particular issue can be directly translated into a presumably effective intervention. Second, outcome research can explicitly attempt to determine if the clinical intervention used does, in fact, offer assistance to stepfamilies receiving treatment.

Practice, although seemingly self-contained, is therefore reliant on research to (a) validate the effects of the clinical process and (b) provide clinicians with a wider perspective that can be extremely valuable by placing each person's experience into a wider context (K. Pasley, personal communication, November 2, 2009). When individuals feel "out of synch," as often happens in a new stepfamily, it is comforting for them to know that some of the issues they are experiencing are common among other stepfamilies. Although such information does not make the situation easier necessarily, it tends to calm the panic that the problems might represent individual pathology. In fact, the awareness of similarity to other stepfamilies confirms that this is a unique family form, one that needs to be understood.

Bridging the Gap Between Research and Clinical Practice

Kay Pasley began her work in the late 1970s and continues to be a scholar who has bridged the gap between researchers and clinicians interested in stepfamilies. She, along with a like-minded band of scholars (Marilyn Ihinger-Tallman, Marilyn Coleman, and Larry Ganong), recognized the tremendous necessity of making research findings available and understandable to those doing clinical work with this population. Although connecting research with clinical practice has always been valuable, especially as the importance of evidence-based treatment has crystallized, Pasley was unique in seeking funding and forums for which the discussion across disciplines, particularly on the topic of stepfamilies, was the precise mission.

Possibly the first institutional effort to bring scholars together to share ideas about stepfamilies was a focus group from the National Council on Family Relations that was formed by Pasley and Ihinger-Tallman in 1981. However, in 1987, a significant event for the field occurred when the Johnson Foundation funded a gathering of individuals from multiple disciplines who were all interested in stepfamilies. The conference, titled the Wingspread Conference on the Remarried Family, was spearheaded by Katherine Baker, Carolyn Brandt, Helen Coale, Kay Pasley, and Emily Visher; all but Pasley were noted clinicians. The 3-day conference brought together researchers, clinicians, and public policy scholars interested in establishing a dialogue to address the confusing state of affairs confronting stepfamilies. Stepfamilies were hampered by legal obstacles that had not been anticipated; clinically they were often lumped in with first-union families, deemed less than satisfactory, or ignored by society. The mission of this group of 30 was to determine (a) what knowledge about stepfamilies existed (e.g., the structural variations, the quality of relationships, a model of "healthy" stepfamilies, stages of stepfamily development), (b) what the legal rights and responsibilities of stepfamily members were, (c) what treatment approaches should be investigated, and (d) what the government should pursue in regard to social policy changes to assist stepfamilies.

The Wingspread Conference was a watershed event in the field of stepfamily studies. Out of this work came a commitment to continue a dialogue among various fields, particularly sociology, family studies, and psychology. On a very practical level, the board of the *Journal of Divorce* was asked to enlarge their focus to include stepfamilies. The journal agreed, and its title became *Journal of Divorce and Remarriage*. The conference acknowledged that the remarried family is far more complex than had been assumed. Conference members challenged the research community to continue to look to study areas that provide a bridge between their findings and the clinical work that was needed to assist those remarried families who were confused and frustrated. They also emphasized that there was still much work needed to understand the longitudinal development of stepfamilies, the intergenerational issues, and the complex kinship system.

FOUNDATIONAL RESEARCH ESTABLISHING STEPFAMILIES AS A UNIQUE POPULATION

How are stepfamilies different from first-union families? Stepfamilies are less cohesive and more highly stressed (Hetherington & Jodl, 1994). In addition, Bray and Hetherington (1993) established that stepfamilies follow a developmental trajectory that is distinct. Although the practice of one-to-one comparison of stepfamilies and first-union families may make stepfamilies appear to be a lesser family model, this type of comparison is necessary. As the field grew and become more sophisticated, many studies examined stepfamilies in comparison with each other, but the so called *deficit comparison* was needed to confirm for stepfamilies that their experience of family life was not identical to that of first-unions, and therefore they could be less self-critical about some of the patterns that were emerging.

Another area that researchers quickly determined was unique to first-union families and stepfamilies was the role of the parent and the stepparent (Pasley, 1987). The notion that a stepparent would, in the majority of cases, simply embrace the child with the same love and tolerance as a parent does and that the child would wish to establish a rapid emotional bond with the stepparent was simply unrealistic. However, many stepfamilies felt a pressure to pursue this first-union model, for no other system existed. Coleman and Ganong (1997) provided evidence that it was best for a stepparent to seek a relationship with his or her stepchild that was not modeled on the parent's relationship. Bray and Kelly (1998) suggested that a better approach would be to see the stepparent, certainly for the first few years, as a monitor rather than a parent with equal say in discipline. Findings such as these served to support the stepparent community, which had become increasingly aware of parenting differences but had often blamed themselves, their partners, or the stepchildren.

Research on the perceived empathy between a parent and a child in a stepfamily serves as an excellent example of the importance of thinking systemically. Browning (1987) found that adolescents in a stepfather family perceived that their own mother had become less empathic after she had remarried (all the families in this study were legally married). The mothers reported that they felt the same empathy toward their child as they had always felt. The gap in those two statements can be explained by systemic phenomena. Because the mothers did not feel that they were any less empathic toward their children, it is likely that the presence of the stepfather, combined with the mother's appreciation of this man, and the confusion between the stepfather and the stepchild as to the parameters of their new relationship created a perception of mothers feeling less empathic.

Another finding that would later have important clinical implications was the research that examined role ambiguity. Research by both Pasley (1987) and Fine (1995) suggested that the lack of a defined role for stepparents was a significant problem in stepfamilies. Because of this lack, the determination of such a role is dependent on the expectations of all those involved in a stepfamily. Therefore, although a stepfather may believe that his role is to serve as a disciplinarian, such a belief may cause great distress for himself, his wife, and his stepchild. If stepparents' expectations are not discussed, it is likely that the resulting ambiguity will create interpersonal problems.

Finally, recent research by Coleman and Ganong (in press) has suggested that certain factors appear to be critical in determining how relationships in a stepfamily develop. Their study, which is a qualitative examination of young adults from stepfamilies reflecting on the nature of their relationships with stepparents, suggests that the effort made by a stepparent and a stepparent's avoiding the role of primary disciplinarian have a significant effect of the success on the relationship.

Even though many of the findings appear to paint a negative picture of stepfamily functioning, there is ample evidence that many stepfamilies are in fact positive and fulfilling (Pryor, 2008). One factor that appears to work in the favor of stepfamilies is time. If a stepfamily can remain together, its members have the possibility of transitioning to more positive relationships. Therefore, therapy aimed at helping stepfamilies weather difficult periods and create stable relationships can serve to support the stepfamily over the long haul.

STEPFAMILY ASSOCIATION OF AMERICA

The Vishers—Emily, a psychologist, and John, a psychiatrist—married in 1959. Each brought four children from previous marriages into this union. They believed that as two accomplished mental health professionals they were well prepared to merge these two families seamlessly. They quickly found that attempting to force everyone to feel a spirit of togetherness was impossible, and each spouse needed to seriously examine the expectations that the two had held about the formation of a stepfamily. The Vishers were not only struck by how difficult stepfamily living was, they were also surprised by misperceptions that they heard from teachers, lawyers, and mental health professionals. In 1979, the Vishers launched the Stepfamily Association of America (SAA), an organization dedicated to serving both counseling professionals and the public at large, particularly stepfamilies. The SAA grew to include 1,200 members in 28 states and Canada.

Normalizing Stepfamilies

Importantly, the SAA was always committed to sharing research-based information. The Research Committee of the SAA included short reports for the newsletter that summarized current research findings. Pasley commented (K. Pasley, personal communication, November 2, 2009) that the Vishers were exceptionally skilled at using the growing body of research to help stepfamilies recognize that they were not alone in their struggle. Stepfamily life is varied. Some stepfamilies seem to develop with little distress, although most find themselves having far greater difficulty than they expected. It is this latter population—those who are surprised to discover that even though the couple is deeply in love, relationships with other family members greatly affect the unity of the stepfamily—that benefits from *normalization*. In response to this realization, the Vishers began to form groups for stepfamilies to meet one another and discuss their process of integration. They called these groups *chapters*, and they were formed throughout the country. Members of SAA would receive instructions on how to open a chapter in their town; these instructions provided basic discussion points and the early writings of the Vishers (supplemented with guest authors from the research community) so that each chapter would have the freedom to really listen to members' stories while also having some structure in the way of specific topics that were determined to be trouble spots for many stepfamilies. The model worked brilliantly, and SAA began to mature into an organization that was clearly the primary voice of those living in stepfamilies and those interested in treating stepfamilies.

Interestingly, the chapters did not tend to last more than 4 or 5 years. Usually, one stepfamily would begin a chapter, and other stepfamilies would join, many at a similar developmental level. They would either all evolve together, eventually not needing the meetings, or one or two stepfamilies would not survive the formation process and proceed toward divorce. The stepfamilies that thrived would rarely continue in a leadership position because there was really little benefit for them to reconnect with the very distressing feelings of early stepfamily development, and mature stepfamilies did not tend to need care that differs from that associated with the growing pains of any family. Therefore, SAA found that rather than building on established chapters, this was an organization that needed to constantly find newly formed stepfamilies willing to take on leadership roles. The organization depended on the energy of two or three dedicated people in every community, and thus, the model could not be self-sustaining.

Training Counselors to Treat Stepfamilies

Although the Vishers and the Board of SAA remained committed to the legion of actual stepfamilies, they found that this part of the mission could be reasonably well handled by increasing the presence of SAA materials on the World Wide Web and continuing chapters when possible. As this shift occurred, the primary task of SAA became to disseminate information to clinicians about stepfamilies, and to do this, a model of treatment with specific interventions was required, and research had to be conducted to determine what stepfamilies needed to benefit from treatment. With these goals in mind, SAA formed a continuing education arm that was explicitly geared to offering training. It was through this forum that a number of the leaders of stepfamily treatment connected with one another and formed a community of researchers and clinicians dedicated to establishing the necessary procedures for ensuring the well-being of many stepfamilies in need of guidance and therapy.

On a theoretical level, clinicians who had been working with stepfamilies had noted that specific knowledge, beyond generic family therapy training, was necessary to address the unique needs of stepfamilies (Browning, 1994). The first large-scale study to support this belief was published by Pasley, Rhoden, Visher, and Visher in 1996. That study asserted that clinicians who were not aware of the particular challenges faced by stepfamilies were perceived by stepfamilies that had been in treatment to be less effective than were clinicians who possessed a knowledge base about stepfamilies. Once armed with this clear mandate, one that asserted that clinicians needed special training to provide the best possible treatment to stepfamilies, the SAA set forth to provide that training to professional mental health workers.

THE DEVELOPMENT OF STEPFAMILY THERAPY

The evolution of a theoretical model is dependent on the accumulation of research findings, clinical reflection, and building on earlier models. SfT is no different and owes a great deal to the many sources that serve as its foundation. In essence, the model grew into its current form through years of refinement from clinical experimentation, 20 years of lectures, and a deep respect for the related research findings. Two sophisticated models geared specifically for treating stepfamilies need to be acknowledged and referenced because, although SfT is unique, clinical theory stands on the shoulders of its predecessors. The two models that we discuss briefly are the work of the Vishers as well as the model created by Patricia Papernow.

The Visher Model

Emily and John Visher wrote three books (1979, 1988, 1996) that were explicitly intended to assist therapists working clinically with stepfamilies. The Vishers created a model that was elegant in its simplicity and extremely useful. In their final text, *Therapy With Stepfamilies* (1996), they identified 16 differences between nuclear families and stepfamilies and discussed the clinical implications of each difference.

The majority of the book, however, established eight areas that can cause difficulty in "newly formed remarried families" (p. 70). The eight areas of difficulty outlined were (a) change and loss, (b) unrealistic beliefs, (c) insider or outsider, (d) life cycle discrepancies, (e) loyalty conflicts, (f) boundary problems, (g) power issues, and (h) closeness and distance. As they were in most of their work, the Vishers were gifted at describing the traps of stepfamily living. They opened up topics so that discussions could take place and couples would recognize some of the unintended mistakes that were occurring in their stepfamily and, by doing so, avoid having these particular issues destroy the families. In this way, many of the topics identified by the Vishers were useful for self-help groups and therapists alike because they established a series of issues that could be addressed and often reconciled.

Although the Vishers were dedicated to the improvement of all members of a stepfamily, their most established interventions were aimed at the subsystem they considered by far the most influential in the stepfamily: the couple. With the couple, the Vishers pursued both a sense of normalization and a clarification of each person's expectations. This model emphasized that this couple at the center of the stepfamily is "the couple," in other words, the most important couple in the household and, as such, needs to be nurtured. By forging a clear agenda that included very clear communication, the couple would, in most cases, win the affection of all members of the stepfamily. However, the Vishers were very realistic about the difficulty of coparenting. They highlighted that the couple needs to be aware of all the historical issues of parenting from the prior relationship and during the period of single parenting; then an awareness of the inherent difficulties can be pursued, with the adults recognizing that the process of working as a team will take time. Therapy was primarily focused on assisting the couple in understanding why certain expectations were particularly difficult to achieve.

In time the Vishers were challenged regarding their lack of emphasis on children in stepfamily treatment (Gamache, 1997). However, to their credit, the Vishers examined the developmental level of any child in a stepfamily and worked to address the three issues that they believed were most consistently salient for children and adolescents, "loss, loyalty and lack of control" (Visher & Visher, 1996, p. 150).

The Vishers are the most significant pioneers of the treatment for stepfamilies. They created the SAA, explicated the dynamics of stepfamily life, created a clinical model, encouraged a bond between research and practice, and finally, truly wanted their model to change and improve life for stepfamilies. The two models that follow were explicitly supported by the Vishers during the later years of their lives. Because Papernow and Browning were the primary teachers of the SAA's clinical trainings, the Vishers observed and supported the construction of their two models. Papernow's model and an early form of SfT were designed with the assumption that one was already familiar with the theoretical model and background information provided by the Vishers.

The Papernow Model

In 1984, writing for *Family Relations*, Patricia Papernow cited the gestalt experience cycle as a "model of healthy human process" (p. 356). Papernow found that the gestalt experience cycle helped illuminate the process of adjustment and development in the stepfamilies. She explored this more fully in her book *Becoming a Stepfamily: Patterns of Development in Remarried Families* (1993). When the stepfamily cycle is disrupted at any point, there is unhappiness and frustration. Many stepfamilies work their way through the disruption, some after many years. Others may need to seek clinical help to successfully navigate the distressing interruption in the movement through the cycle.

Papernow's stepfamily cycle is divided into three sets of stages: early, middle, and later. The early stages consist of fantasy, immersion, and awareness. The *fantasy* stage begins with the formation of the stepfamily. Often there are many expectations and hopeful longings that the transition into stepfamily life will be smooth and the forecast for life together, positive. Individuals anticipate that the future will bring what the past could not: healing, nurturance, and understanding. Papernow called these expectations the *invisible burden*, a bundle of aspirations of which the couple is often largely unaware, and when these aspirations are unrealized, they contribute to the couple's anxiety and distress. Not fulfilling these visions, the couple may be confused and mystified about their inability to sail into stepfamily life without any glitches. In the *immersion* stage, the reality of stepfamily structure sets in. The parent–child unit has come into a stepfamily more connected to each other than the adult couple, placing the stepparent in an outsider position and the parent in a stuck insider position. In the immersion stage, the stepparent's feelings of loneliness, resentment, and incompetence may begin to form. The parent may begin to feel torn between the people he or she loves. In the *awareness* stage, the stepfamily members begin to identify the feelings with less shame and blame and to gain more understanding and compassion for each other's very different experiences.

Mobilization and action are the middle stages in the cycle, and as the words indicate, there is more energy as family members begin to assert themselves. Stepparents may begin to voice their experience of feeling alone and excluded. Parents may begin to voice their feelings of being unable to please all the people they love. Children may begin to voice their unhappiness at all the changes in their lives. Many families present for therapy in the mobilization stage when there are arguments and disquiet from conflict. Depending on how constructively the couple can engage, this can create a positive or a negative impact on stepfamily development. In the action stage, the stepfamily members begin to resolve some of their differences and reorganize boundaries. New *middle ground* emerges, a gestalt concept of "shared experience, shared values, and easy cooperative functioning created over time" (Papernow, 1993, p. 39). In a first-time family, middle ground, a concept created by Sonia Nevis at the Gestalt Institute of Cleveland, begins forming from the beginning of the relationship. By the time the children are born, much middle ground has been established, helping to hold a family together. In a new stepfamily, the child's relationship with the stepparent is the most unstable ground. This necessitates effort by all family members to build new middle ground by recognizing each other's needs, negotiating, making concessions, and establishing new rituals and experiences.

The contact stage and the resolution stage, the two later stages, reveal a stepfamily structure that has become stronger and more resilient. Even in the later stages in a healthy stepfamily, parent–child relationships can remain stronger than stepparent–child relationships. However, in the contact stage, intimacy and authenticity have been established in steprelationships, including in both the stepcouple and in some (but often not all) stepparent–child relationships. Often, the stepparent has moved into a role Papernow called an *intimate outsider* with at least some of his or her stepchildren. Although some issues remain, much has been resolved. Divisive arguments about stepfamily issues have become more of a sharing of ideas, which include difficult and diverging viewpoints, within the context of increased intimacy and safety. The stepparent role is more clearly defined, and there is often a firmer boundary around the stepparent–stepchild relationship so that communication can occur without interference from the parent. In the resolution stage, substantial new stepfamily middle ground has been built, and norms for the unique family system have evolved.

More recently, Papernow's work has focused on delineating a framework that she called *stepfamily architecture* (Papernow, 2010). Papernow found that this model provided a useful framework for sharing up-to-date "driving directions" that help people to meet each of the challenges. In her clinical work, Papernow approached stepfamily members on three different levels: psychoeducationally, interpersonally, and intrapsychically. Psychoeducation normalizes the stresses created by stepfamily architecture and offers information about what works and what does not. On the next level, the therapist attends to the family's interpersonal skills, which according to certain theorists (e.g., John Gottman) are critically important to the success of any relationship. One needs to learn how to bring up an issue "in a way that is positive and connected" (Patricia Papernow, personal communication, November 18, 2009). Papernow warned that when working with stepfamily members, it is important that therapists begin with the first two levels, filling in psychoeducational gaps and improving interpersonal skills, before moving to the third level, exploring intrapsychic wounds that may make stepfamily living especially difficult.

Stepfamily Therapy: A Subsystems-Based Model

The model proposed by this book, SfT, is designed to (a) use the existing research to support psychoeducation interventions; (b) propose an explicit and orderly subsystem methodology to reinforce the stepfamily one subsystem at a time; (c) create an environment that engages the couple and then enables all subsystems to increase their empathic understanding of the other; (d) determine miscommunication and directly correct the mistaken beliefs that have taken hold; (e) teach stepfamilies about their own systemic patterns so that blame is shifted from individuals to interactions; and finally (f) integrate the subsystems into a functioning, unified stepfamily.

The SfT model has, at its core, a 10-step approach to give clinicians a clear plan to feel confident that they will not become easily overwhelmed in their work with stepfamilies. The basic steps are presented in Exhibit 1.1 to offer the reader some information to clarify the clinical discussion that follows in Chapter 2; however, the comprehensive examination of the model is in Chapter 3.

This model is based on the idea that stepfamilies need to be reconstructed one subsystem at a time. In other words, the stepfamily will benefit from strengthening various subsystems so that the entire system, the stepfamily itself, is strong enough to withstand the push and pull of stepfamily challenges. Although the approach is primarily centered in the present, we certainly advocate being aware of historical areas of sensitivity to assist these families and couples to recognize why understanding the systemic function of their stepfamily reduces the tendency to blame. Sometimes this step is the one on which all the other progress depends.

EXHIBIT 1.1
Stepfamily Therapy Model

Diagnostic Steps
  1. Recognize the structure of the stepfamily (e.g., simple stepfather family, simple stepmother family, complex stepfamily in which both adults are stepparents). Use the initial telephone intake to look for systemic similarities within the context of the research literature.
  2. Determine the membership of the first session—usually the marital dyad—and further delineate the unique concerns of the stepfamily.
  3. Clarify the distinct subsystems in the stepfamily, and use this to provide a direction for clinical treatment.

Primary Clinical Interventions
  4. Consider the research findings that normalize the experience of the stepfamily, and introduce them in clinical practice (when appropriate and meaningful).
  5. Actively assess and assist in the recognition of empathy when present, and increase the empathic experience between stepfamily members and subsystems.
  6. Identify and challenge unhelpful beliefs and specific miscommunication circulating in the stepfamily—the role of labels.
  7. Support the naturally connected subsystem (parent and child), and confirm that parent and child are capable of expressing mutual concern.
  8. Teach the stepfamily about its own systemic functioning.

Stepfamily Integration
  9. Assist in coparental work between any and all involved parental figures, including the binuclear family.
  10. Increase communication between all stepfamily members available, and move toward integrating the various subsystems into a functioning and satisfied stepfamily.

Some members of stepfamilies often have little idea why their family does not seem to function in a manner more reminiscent of the first-marriage family in which they grew up. When therapy is done well, the therapist identifies the primary systemic conundrums and informs the family of the likely effect of these invisible tensions.

There are numerous teaching moments in stepfamily therapy, and it is in these areas that knowledge of the available research is very useful. Research is not perfect; clearly there are always variables that are unique to a particular stepfamily, but research offers a great deal of information that can be used to normalize this new and often foreign family form. Of course, care is always taken when teaching clients in therapy because the area taught must match the stepfamily. Unlike a teacher who has a clear curriculum, the therapist looks for moments when the family is open to learning about what other stepfamilies in similar situations experience and do.

It becomes vital for stepfamily members to see the bigger picture. All people benefit from understanding how one system is impacted by another system. Of course, systemic understanding is useful in all family therapy, but stepfamilies have a unique need to understand this phenomenon because the tendency to blame one person often becomes too great.

The final stage of stepfamily therapy is moving into conjoint sessions that have multiple subsystems together, similar to typical family therapy. This process may still unleash strong feelings and genuine conflict, but the stepfamily is now capable of handling greater pressure without a sense that it is too unstable to weather a storm. We believe that some security exists within various subsystems that allows this progress to occur.

CONCLUSION

The field of stepfamily studies represents an intersection of research, clinical practice, and advocacy. As the research on divorced families naturally evolved into looking at stepfamilies, clinicians were starting to recognize that the stepfamily population presented challenges that were unexpected and did not respond adequately to traditional family therapy. At the same time, stepfamilies were emerging from being a hidden population to one beginning to request that their unique concerns be addressed and understood.

One can surmise that as the advocacy regarding living in a stepfamily began to rise, the shame once felt by these families began to fade. As stepfamilies recognized themselves to be a unique family form, the research community affirmed these anecdotal observations by showing that in a range of areas the stepfamily is not identical to the first-marriage family.

The SAA was unique among the organizations that responded to the call for stepfamily advocacy. Out of the collaboration of the Vishers and Pasley began a dialogue that resulted in a formidable movement. This movement helped to solidify the field of stepfamily studies and address the therapeutic needs of stepfamilies. The SfT model presented in this book is indebted to the significant contributions of research and previous clinical perspectives.

2

WHY ARE SOME
STEPFAMILIES VULNERABLE?

For many, stepfamilies are a healthy and vibrant family structure. However, slightly more than half of remarriages end in divorce, and this is somewhat higher than divorce in first marriages (Bramlett & Mosher, 2002; Raley & Bumpass, 2003). Though in this book we discuss certain problems that are often seen in stepfamilies, we clearly know that many members of this group have satisfying, fulfilling family lives. However, it would be naïve to discuss stepfamilies without acknowledging the trials with which many of them struggle.

A variety of factors make a stepfamily more or less vulnerable to having conflicts and difficulties. The primary factors include (a) the mental health of each individual, (b) the structure of the stepfamily, and (c) the interactional dynamics of the stepfamily. Although the mental health of individual family members and the interactional sequences are part of all families, these factors play particularly strong roles in stepfamilies.

One cannot entirely separate the functioning of individuals from their interpersonal context, but some people simply are better able to adjust to the challenges of living in a stepfamily. Others are particularly vulnerable to insecurity, fear, or anger-based frustration as they attempt to adjust to the newly formed family. The question of why some individuals are better able to accommodate to change has been extensively considered by psychiatrists and psychologists for more than 100 years, and no universally accepted explanation has been found. Thus, the model proposed in this book recognizes that some individuals are interpersonally impaired to the extent that a systemically based model, even one clearly comfortable with treating subsystems, may not address a profoundly needy individual. Fortunately, the majority of stepfamilies can benefit from a treatment model that, although valuing the individual, is attuned to the structure and interpersonal issues often presented by stepfamilies requesting services.

The term *blended* is conspicuously absent from this book because, as Engle (M. Engle, personal communication, October 16, 2002) clearly articulated, "stepfamilies do not blend." Blending, as a cooking term, refers to a process whereby the two products being blended become a unique product, with no way of determining the individual characteristics any longer. For example, the milkshake cannot be separated after blending to determine what part is milk and what part is ice cream. A stepfamily does not become an entirely new family with no memory of past attachments. It is an extended family, with all the advantages and stressors that growth implies.

It is, therefore, our premise that although the integrated stepfamily can have a sense of completeness, it will always be a collective of subsystems. We contend that this collective is capable of being as fully viable and positive as a biologically connected system can be. In fact, Mavis Hetherington (1988) found that stepfamilies and first-union families when assessed on multiple factors could not be distinguished from one another after 9 years.

The notion of viewing a stepfamily, or any family, as a collection of subsystems is not new (Minuchin & Fishman, 1981), but it is new in stepfamily therapy (SfT) to understand the stepfamily as a collection of subsystems that enter an "initial period of disequilibrium" (Hetherington & Clingempeel, 1992) following the creation of the stepfamily. Each subsystem is actually less viable following the remarriage. Although the couple, the first subsystem, may be in love, their relationship is impacted not only by the inevitable differences in how they view their roles and parenting obligations within the home but also by the sudden complicating emergence of additional extended family members (Hetherington, 1993). In addition, the biological parent and child(ren), the second subsystem, often experience a reduction in their bond, especially as reported by the child(ren) (Browning, 1987). The third subsystem, already weakly connected, is the relationship between the stepparent and stepchild(ren), especially if the children are preadolescent or adolescent versus those who are younger (Perry, 1995).

The couple generally enters recoupling not necessarily naïve about the possible difficulties experienced by many stepfamilies but rather lulled into a sense of safety from the dating period. In other words, dating behavior may be very different from married behavior, and though people may not be trying to fool anyone, the effects of context and structural change cannot be underestimated (Hetherington & Stanley-Hagan, 1995). For example, Mom's boy-friend Bill is not likely to examine the nuances of his girlfriend's parental behavior or a child's behavior with the same intensity or investment that he will use on assuming the role of stepfather. As Bill's reaction to his stepchild shifts after remarriage, he is perceived by the child to be different from he was just weeks earlier. This shift is then followed by a series of shifts in the wife's view of her husband, his view of her parenting, and the child's relationship with both stepparent and biological parent. In a reaction to the weakening and straining of relationships within different subsystems, a flawed belief often emerges that sets the developing stepfamily in a contraindicated direction.

The other two primary factors, the structure of the stepfamily and the interpersonal processes of the stepfamily, are separate but interconnected. Understanding the structure serves to define the immediate members of a stepfamily as well as to illuminate those additional people who are connected by familial bonds. The interpersonal process involves an articulation of all of the relational dynamics and patterns that commonly stress a stepfamily. The genogram is a vital tool to help clarify the structural factors and interpersonal dynamics of stepfamilies to a therapist. A full explanation of how genograms are used within this model and the specific symbols we use can be found in Chapter 3 of this book.

STRUCTURE OF STEPFAMILIES

Although some have described stepfamilies as "born of loss" (Visher & Visher, 1979), most scholars recognize that the greatest difficulty for these families is the multiple transitions that they need to go through (Hetherington & Kelly, 2002). Therefore, it stands to reason that this new family will face some specific problems in forming a coherent and lasting sense of security. Yet the longer the stepfamily survives, the more likely those members will perceive their family in ways that parallel how those in first-marriage families view their own family. The stepfamily will never become a first-marriage family; such a goal is useless and unrealistic. However, many of the nagging challenges that seem hardwired into some stepfamilies soften and often disappear over time (Hetherington & Jodl, 1994).

Despite the numerous potential variations within a stepfamily, a basic typology can be used to provide a shorthand method to begin a definition. The typology involves two primary categories, each with subcategories. The two primary categories or labels are *simple* and *complex* stepfamilies. The simple stepfamily is one in which only one of the two adults has a child. The complex stepfamily is one in which both adults have a child with someone other than their current mate.

The simple stepfamily has two dominate subcategories: the stepmother family or the stepfather family. Although there are some similarities between these two stepfamily types, in particular dealing with insider or outsider dynamics, clinically, there appear to be some significant differences. The stepmother family and the stepfather family differ seemingly as a result of the expectations of the paternal and maternal figures in society. Women are expected to be more nurturing. This is true even if no one appears to be demanding this nurturance (Ganong & Coleman, 1995b; Whitsett & Land, 1992). Fathers, on the other hand, are often seen as competent if they provide for the family and have some involvement in stepfamily activities (Robertson, 2008). Stepparents of both genders report feeling sabotaged or viewed as too controlling (Russell & Searcy, 1997), so these are both important areas for clinical exploration and potential interventions.

The complex stepfamily is formed when both adults bring a child or children with them into this new union. There are two primary subcategories within the complex stepfamily's general typology: the traditional complex stepfamily, which was just described, and the complex family in which a mutual child is born to the remarried couple, adding an additional layer onto the family.

Although the terms simple and complex sound as though they may be a reference to the relative difficulty of such a family, this is not the case. These are merely descriptive terms that allow clinicians and researchers to create a typology. Unfortunately, the challenges that face a stepfamily cannot be so easily defined.

COHABITATION

In this text, we have largely avoided any reference to the marital status of stepfamilies. We have done this to clarify that the treatment model outlined is meant to assist all stepfamilies. However, it would be inaccurate to suggest that unmarried couples and married couples are identical in all regards. Therefore, a discussion of cohabitation follows to increase the understanding of this population and to inform the clinician of some factors that need to be taken into account in the process of treatment.

Cohabitation has become more prevalent as a family form: from 3% of all married and cohabiting unions in 1980, to 5% in 1990, and to 7% in 1998. Among women, 41% in the age range of 15 to 41 years have cohabited (U.S. Census Bureau as reported by Skinner, Bahr, Crane, & Call, 2002, p. 74). The authors go on to say that "cohabiting couples with long-term plans might be similar to married couples in relationship quality and different from other cohabiting couples" (Skinner et al., 2002, p. 75). Although there is a somewhat pejorative cast to the research literature that follows, we do not intend by presenting this to devalue the fundamental nature of cohabitation. Many cohabitating couples have committed, monogamous, and meaningful partnerships in the United States and other parts of the world, and this brief overview is to lay the groundwork for addressing the subject of cohabiting stepfamilies.

Cohabitation is qualified by three descriptors: sexual intimacy, common residence, and the absence of marriage (Thornton & Young-DeMarco, 1996). One could expand the qualifiers to include sexual intimacy that implicitly bars sexual relations with others; sharing a residence as well as resources; and, in many cases, having children (S. L. Brown & Booth, 1996). As the social phenomenon of cohabitation has risen, it has been countered by a decrease in marriage and remarriage rates; this is not reflective of young people remaining single but rather of establishing lives together without marrying (Bumpass, Sweet, & Cherlin, 1991). In fact, unions are still being formed at the same rate; however, the percentage of marriages among these unions is decreasing (Bumpass et al., 1991).

Cohabitation begins with a state of singlehood and continues forward as an evolving process rather than as an event signifying the beginning, as in marriage (Thornton, Axinn, & Xie, 2007). Making the transition to living together can be preceded by living apart but being sexually active on a regular basis and/or coming together, for example, to share meals, sleep over, take trips, and more. Cohabitation itself can take many divergent and convoluted forms. Living together may endure for years or just months; couples can have or not have children; couples can reside together full time or part time; the cohabitation can eventually lead to marriage or not (Kiernan, 2004); if there is an inclination to marry in the future, a paucity of resources for the couple can lead to postponement (Cherlin, 2004). Jan Trost has categorized couples living apart together as "LAT couples," a concept that gathered some attention in Europe (Trost, 1997, p. 80). Some couples have remained together so long that they appear married; others seem single. Scholars see cohabitation as a "family status" that appears less stable when compared with marriage (Bumpass et al., 1991). Trost saw marriage and cohabitation as two "social institutions" that exist side by side (Trost, 1997). Because the goals and perceptions of the cohabiting couple differ, the boundaries between the different types of statuses are "fuzzy" (S. L. Brown & Booth, 1996). Kiernan (2004) stated that because cohabitation is so variable, it is difficult to formulate policy that addresses this societal phenomenon.

Cohabitation Versus Marriage

Cohabitation used to be known as trial marriage; couples would live together to see if they were compatible and could coexist in relative harmony prior to marriage (DeMaris & Rao, 1992). As cohabitation has become a more established status, couples may enter into it with a less sincere allegiance as an expedient thing to do at the time. The relaxed and gradual process (see Thornton et al., 2007) of entry into cohabitation may as easily terminate. If a cohabiting relationship is conflictual, it can be dissolved without legal hassles, third party interference, recrimination, and regrets. There would still be the associated pain involved with the conclusion of the relationship; indeed, divorce is second only to death as the most stressful event one can experience, according to the Social Readjustment Rating Scale (Holmes & Rahe, 1967). One has to expect somewhat the same response for cohabiting couples, although it has been suggested that when cohabiting unions end, it is even more painful because the dissolutions are less socially recognized (Bouchard, 2006). However, the expectations with which a couple enters into marriage at a well-attended "white wedding" are for lifelong commitment. Therefore, when the relationship breaks down, it follows that the sense of disappointment reverberates throughout the entire family system, not only within the couple. Kiernan (2004) stated that "the notion of marriage [is] increasingly being replaced by more flexible and contingent partnerships that have no formal commencement and that continue only as long as both partners derive satisfaction from the relationship," a concept earlier posited by Giddens (1992).

Bouchard (2006) noted that cohabiting couples are more likely to dissolve a relationship than a married couple, even if it is somewhat satisfying. Even though cohabitation has become the "modal path of entry into marriage" (S. L. Brown, 2000, p. 833), research has shown that levels of commitment are lower in cohabitation (Axinn & Thornton, 1992). DeMaris (2000) stated that there is less "investment" in cohabitors' unions when contrasted with marital unions. Cohabitors reported more fights and violence, less of a sense of fairness and happiness in their unions, and poorer relationship quality than their married counterparts (S. L. Brown & Booth, 1996). It is also significant to note that greater than half of all cohabiting unions end within five years, even if the couple marries (Bumpass & Lu, 2000). Less marital interaction and increased conflict and lack of stability were found in marriages of couples who had previously cohabited (Booth & Johnson, 1988). The more protracted the cohabitation, the more likely the marriage would be distinguished by poor marital quality and low spousal levels of commitment (Thomson & Colella, 1992). Research shows that cohabitation prior to marriage actually signals a higher likelihood of divorce (Booth & Johnson, 1988; DeMaris & Rao, 1992; Thomson & Colella, 1992).

In addition, researchers found that relationship length is negatively correlated with marriage plans. Apparently, cohabitors with intentions to marry do so rather promptly, and those without plans to marry maintain their cohabitation status. With the passage of time, there are more members of the latter group because the others have already married (Bumpass et al., 1991). However, if cohabitors have never been married before, they are more likely to get married (Bumpass et al., 1991). Researchers also found that if neither partner or only the female partner had marriage intentions, the likelihood of marriage was poorer than when both members of the cohabiting couple reported plans to marry. Relationship dissolution was more frequent when neither partner conveyed marriage plans because it was seen as evidence of lack of commitment to staying together (S. L. Brown, 2000). Also, women have been found to be more sensitive to the state of an intimate union, and if they feel it is largely a negative relationship, they are more inclined bring it to an end. Men, on the other hand, will stay in what they consider to be a poor relationship and not enhance their commitment to marriage (L. Thompson & Walker, 1989).

Changes in the economy and prevailing culture have led to a decline in marriage (Smock, 2004). Cohabitors may continue their unions to avoid economic difficulties but will not move toward the next level of commitment (Bumpass et al., 1991). Indeed, marriage rates are the lowest among the poorest socioeconomic groups in the United States, even though marriage commands a respect and is a family status to which they may aspire. Many cohabitors in such situations profess a desire to marry but only when they can afford it and be successful; they want their partners to be gainfully employed and to treat them nonabusively; they want to have a decent wedding that they pay for themselves and to move into a respectable home. Smock (2004) also recounted the connection between marriage and lasting marriage and financial security.

Other changes in the institution of marriage have led to an increase in cohabitation (and same-sex marriage). Because sexual activity and giving birth as well as needs for closeness can nowadays be fulfilled without the necessity of getting married, the power of the institution of marriage has been decreased. No longer are these activities exclusive to the state of matrimony. Andrew Cherlin (2004) called this the "deinstitutionalization of marriage" (p. 843).

Who Are the Cohabitors?

Experience and selection have been described as explanations for the more deficient end results of cohabitation (S. L. Brown & Booth, 1996). In the previous section, we discussed the effect of prior experience. In terms of selection, Skinner and colleagues (2002) suggested that certain people, because of "personal/social characteristics" in place before the relationship begins, choose to live together. Either they bring to their cohabitation experience more liberal ideas about divorce or within the cohabitation their attitudes are modified by having lived together. In either case, there is more of a likelihood of instability (Axinn & Thornton, 1992). Cohabitors can also be seen as more unconventional, with less commitment to intimacy in relationships (Thomson & Colella, 1992). Cohabitation is more likely to occur among poorly educated people, those on welfare, those with poor financial prospects (hence "poor marriage material"), and those with children (S. L. Brown & Booth, 1996). Cohabitors tend to have poorer communication and coping skills, which inhibit relationship quality (Thomson & Colella, 1992). A history of prior dissolution of relationships may be an indication that a person does not have the interpersonal skills to continue a close relationship (S. L. Brown & Booth, 1996).

The presence of children affected married couples and cohabitors who planned to marry in the same way; more arguments, more physicality, and raised voices were associated with children being present. Decreased interaction and contentment were also reported (S. L. Brown & Booth, 1996). One researcher compared unions with children and childless unions; relationships in which there were children were less likely to be disrupted. Wu (1995) found that it was not particular features of the children that were significant but their very presence that motivated each member to work harder to maintain the cohabiting union.

Implications for Therapy

Bumpass, Raley, and Sweet (1995) argued that if the cohabitating stepfamilies were not included when researching the stepfamily population, there would be too much room for error. The idea that people were not married did not negate the fact that the cohabiting family had a stepfamily structure (Cherlin, 2004). Cherlin called it an "additional layer of complexity" in stepfamilies (p. 849).

In applying the SfT model to a cohabiting stepfamily, the therapist must consider the factors of levels of commitment, instability, and the dissolution process.

Levels of Commitment

Moving through the 10 steps of the SfT model with a cohabiting stepfamily is very similar to working with married stepfamilies. However, the therapist needs to ascertain intentionality. Does the couple share the same level of commitment to each other or to the relationship? Does one member of the couple eschew marriage while the other visualizes the event in the future, or are they in complete agreement about maintaining the present situation? Are they aware of each other's feelings about this? How much is the couple willing to invest in the therapy process? What about the present situation is most upsetting or serious for the children? What are the stepfamily issues? The research does not describe the range and inclinations of all cohabiting relationships. Step 2 of the SfT model with the couple should supply many answers. In the process of clarifying the couple's expectations for the future and other issues involving the children, parents of the children, and former partners, the therapist will most likely quell much of the tension that brought them to therapy.

Instability

Cohabiting relationships have been found to be more volatile, conflicted, and unhappy, with poorer relationship quality than married relationships (S. L. Brown & Booth, 1996). Stepfamilies are already characterized by less cohesion, loyalty conflicts, role confusion, and less stability. When one works with a cohabiting stepfamily, the combination of these aspects coming from two different sources may place the stepfamily at an extreme disadvantage. The more ephemeral nature of cohabitation without the benefit of legitimization may put in question their tenacity in complying with the therapy process when it becomes more challenging. The therapist should provide the caveat to expect that it may get worse before it gets better, a clichéd but appropriate statement in this case. The presence of children often exacerbates any problems in the system, causing more conflict, shouting, and physicality. Ensuring that the couple dyad is committed to the relationship has to be accomplished prior to inviting in the other subsystems. If there have been multiple transitions for the children, the therapist may encounter more resistance and anger from them than expected, which may impede the process. A recalcitrant adolescent may already be drawing attention to the dysfunction of the cohabiting stepfamily.

Manning and Lamb (2003) found their results in agreement with prior research, which stated that children manage better in married households with two biological parents than in cohabiting stepfamilies. Children of cohabiting stepfamilies do as well as teens in single-mother families, except in delinquency and poor grades. This suggests that adolescents who live with their unmarried mothers do not gain when their mother's cohabiting partner is there. Of course, the relationship background of the mother is another variable to consider in terms of poor outcomes. Manning and Lamb conjectured that one should pay attention not only to the family configuration but also to the quality of the relationships in the family.

Dissolution Process

The therapist should be aware of the factors that contribute to the dissolution of a relationship and be able to discern if the couple is leaning toward that possibility. For example, if in the middle of a session the conversation gets heated and one of the couple dyad shouts out "I don't want to get married!" or "I never thought marriage made any sense" or "If you have that big a problem, you can be thankful we aren't married!" These volatile admissions about the institution of marriage can be an indicator of an entrenched negative attitude, which is a risk factor for dissolution. If the relationship does not work, it is expendable, simple as that. Financial stressors, the children's behavioral difficulties, volatile and ineffective communication, and the experience of prior cohabiting or marital dissolution are all issues that put the stepfamily at risk. The therapist moving through the 10 steps of SfT should constantly be vigilant about the concerns that set the cohabiting stepfamily apart from the general stepfamily population.

BINUCLEAR FAMILIES

After a divorce, all of the people related to the two divorced partners are part of a *binuclear family* (Ahrons, 1979). All of the people in this more inclusive family remain potentially very important to the functioning of the stepfamily. Anyone who has experience with an angry former spouse or a very supportive former in-law knows how much this wider circle influences life within the immediate stepfamily.

The former partner (the child's "other parent") is an individual of tremendous importance. Even in this person's absence, he or she casts a long shadow. Although many recognize that the other parent is part of their child's life, some state that they resent the idea that lives remain intertwined even after divorce (Ahrons, 1994; Whitton, Nicholson, & Markman, 2008). The binuclear family extends beyond the former spouse and grandparents. There is a cast of people who are part of one's family, and thus, relevant.

One potent example that highlights the impact of the binuclear family is the Berg and Solomon family. This binuclear family (see Figure 2.1) is chal-

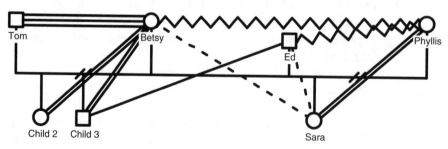

Figure 2.1. The Berg and Solomon family.

lenging to treat because of interpersonal dynamics that are left over from each person's first marriage.

Tom was originally married to Betsy, and Phyllis was originally married to Ed. The remarried couple in this scenario is now Betsy and Ed. Betsy and Ed have no children from their union; however, Betsy brings Bethany (10) and Ricky (8). Ed brings one child to the complex stepfamily, Sara (13). Betsy and Ed have been married for 4 years. (See Figure 3.1 for the genogram legend and Chapter 3, this volume, for a discussion on the use of genograms in therapy.)

This stepfamily is experiencing several difficulties. Ed cannot be sure if Sara will come for her visits distracted by a large amount of homework or if she will arrive in a position to be an involved member of the family. Betsy, on the other hand, still feels responsible for Tom, who has been diagnosed with major depression. For the sake of her children, of whom Tom is the father, Betsy frequently calls Tom just to check in and make sure that he has not hurt himself. One might hope that the conflict could be restricted to the original couple, but that is often not possible. Ed becomes furious at Betsy for calling Tom and keeping that relationship on the front burner, and Betsy argues with Ed that Phyllis (his former wife) purposely lets Sara avoid homework until it is time to visit her dad's house. Betsy feels that Phyllis is doing this to force Ed to take a more substantial parental role with Sara.

Untangling the various triangles of binuclear family members is often a difficult challenge. In the Berg and Solomon family, Ed and Betsy need to avoid permitting Tom and Phyllis to create a wedge between them, no matter how unintentional that wedge is. The clinician can assist the stepfamily by providing direction for treatment, but the efficacy of the treatment is improved by increasing the collaborative decision making between client and clinician (Higgs & Jones, 2000).

Therefore, options are presented to Betsy and Ed in ways that encourage them to assist the therapist in determining what clinical direction is most likely to succeed. Success in this situation would mean that Betsy and Ed are envisioning themselves as a team. This team might include one or both of the former spouses, or it might be a team in which neither Tom nor Phyllis is seen as an ally. Although it is often preferable to move the family toward a more collaborative unit, it may be impossible in situations in which someone does not have the capacity to pull together, even for the sake of the children.

The following questions offer various paths that treatment might follow:

1. Can Ed and Betsy be convinced that possibly involving the previous mates, in separate sessions, could be a useful clinical direction?
2. If yes, might a session with Ed, Betsy, and Phyllis be productive in working out a parental arrangement that satisfies everyone's needs? If no, the task of therapy might be to lower the tension

by acknowledging the impasse that is occurring when the former spouse is unwilling to change behavior.

3. Might Ed and Betsy meet with Tom under the agreement to discuss coparenting and form a *parenting alliance*? In addition, the session would aim to assist Tom in accepting some support from Ed. Ed would be offering this support because the previous session increased his empathy for Tom's depression.

These couple-based interventions are intended to serve as a method to decrease the frustrations that surface from the multitude of relationships within a complex recoupled home. It is important for the clinician to remain optimistic that some improved coordination can occur because the stepfamily members themselves are frequently reluctant to be hopeful. However, the clinician cannot hold on to unrealistic optimism when the other party has no interest in resolving the situation.

Overall, the benefit of understanding the structure of stepfamilies and the issues that often result within these structural constraints is that clinicians will be asking questions that comfort their clients; they will not fear that their clinicians are unable to comprehend the complexity of their lives. Often, simply knowing that a professional understands the circumstances of one's life provides hope to many stepfamilies.

INTERPERSONAL PROCESSES IN STEPFAMILIES

Why are interpersonal processes important? The following selected interpersonal scenarios are useful to explain common stepfamily dilemmas. Each scenario or issue is explicated to examine why the situation generally occurs. However, any effort to provide a clear reason for any interactional pattern is speculative, and proof is often not possible. The precise etiology of interpersonal processes has been debated for decades by systems theorists. This book does not depend on a central theory to examine why the interpersonal process occurs. However, each therapist can benefit from learning to rapidly determine the precise interpersonal processes for each stepfamily that comes for treatment.

Although the list of potential troubling stepfamily transactions is unlimited, the selections that follow represent six common issues that provide a template of potential clinical directions taken to understand and shift interpersonal interactions. The impasse that results from useless transactions is the enemy. The people who function to create these patterns deserve the respect and concern of the therapist, but the interpersonal transactions that are disabling the stepfamily must be dissected and often changed.

Rejection of a Stepparent

Stepchildren vary greatly on the extent to which they intend to embrace their new stepparent (Hetherington & Kelly, 2002). This determination is based on a variety of factors. Some stepchildren make this decision prior to meeting their stepparent; they may reject the concept of a stepparent, so when an actual person inhabits that role, there is no measure of acceptance. This response may be driven by loyalty to one parent or anger at the parent's recoupling, or it may reflect a denial of the marital dissolution entirely.

In many cases, the child is not eagerly anticipating the addition of a stepparent, but he or she has not prejudged the relationship. In this more common scenario, the rejection, if it occurs, is based on a relational factor. Sometimes, the child and the stepparent simply do not mesh well; they just do not find the relationship to be satisfying. Other reasons for a poor bond could stem from (a) a significant misunderstanding, (b) a reaction to a sense of loss with their parent because they view the new couple as too impenetrable, (c) the actual structural change that has occurred as a result of the presence of the stepparent, or (d) pressure from the noncustodial parent for the child to deny any growing affection or acceptance of the stepparent.

What should be understood is that many children, particularly latency-age and adolescent children, appear to be rejecting the stepparent when, in fact, they are often simply uninterested in forming a relationship with a new adult. Whether the stepparent is truly rejected or only feels rejected, the experience is still one of feeling invisible or actively disliked. In the following example we examine the reason for this reaction, the impasse that results, and the clinical reaction that can address the problem.

The Carlyle family (see Figure 2.2) provides an excellent example of stepparent rejection. Bill requested a divorce from Janice after 18 years of marriage. Janice, who has experienced depression for 9 years, claims that Bill's request to divorce came as a complete shock. Bill, on the other hand, states,

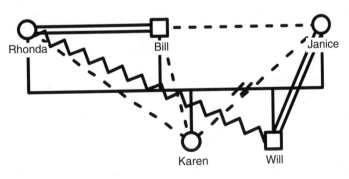

Figure 2.2. The Carlyle family.

"If she was surprised, then she has not been listening to me for years." Bill knew Rhonda because they work for the same company, but both claim that they never considered themselves to be a couple until 6 months after the separation. Bill goes so far as to insist, "You could not even call what we had an emotional affair; she was a casual friend, end of story."

Janice and Bill have two children together, Will and Karen. Janice has primary custody of the children. Because of Bill's work schedule (he travels a lot in the fall), his visitation is every other weekend and 2 months in the summer. The children are having a difficult time accepting that while staying with their father, they will have extended periods in which it will be necessary for them to interact with Rhonda.

Why have the children rejected Rhonda? The reasons for this rejection are threefold. The primary reason is that Janice, Will, and Karen each believe that Bill was having an affair prior to the split, although each one admits that there is no real evidence of such a relationship. The second reason is that Janice's depression causes the children to feel responsible for her, and they resent the person who "took Dad away." And finally, Rhonda openly states in the presence of the children that they are "undisciplined, a lot like their mom."

What is the resulting impasse as a result of these beliefs? Bill feels as though he needs to convince his children of Rhonda's innocence and must highlight Janice's intractable depression as the reason he left the marriage. Because of the clear message that both children reject her, Rhonda makes no effort to engage them in a positive manner when they are visiting.

The therapy recommended in this situation would be to determine the potential benefit of various subsystem meetings. Bill and Rhonda would be seen to hear the concerns each of them feels in regard to their marital relationship. If this session confirms for the clinician that the marriage can withstand some pressure, Rhonda would be asked if she would be tolerant of the clinician's efforts to strengthen the connection between Bill and his kids, especially Karen. Rhonda would be asked to accept that as Bill tangibly connects with his daughter, he would be offering her, Rhonda, additional time to strengthen their connection as well. Bill would be seen with Karen and Will, and the focus of that session would be the relationship between this father and his children. Attempts to comment on Rhonda would be discouraged for two reasons. The first is that it is common to shift the topic away from the importance of the immediate relationships, and the second is that Rhonda has the right not to be the focus if she is not there.

Following these sessions, the direction and goals for treatment would be more fluid. It would be useful to assess whether the children's anger at Rhonda is most strongly related to (a) their mother's mental state; (b) the interruption of their relationship with their dad, for which they blame their stepmother; or (c) the perception that an affair was the reason for the parents' divorce. The informed hypotheses that resulted from exploring these questions would dictate which subsystem might be seen to address the impasse and ongoing negative interactions.

Relationships Under a Constant Gaze

Any person who has understood academic material well and has frozen when called on in class can understand the idea that people act and react differently depending on the audience. The girl who is considered the funniest among her friends may be unable to make any quip when a guy she likes walks into the room.

One's own home is the setting in which most people feel it is possible to be themselves. However, the addition of a new family member changes communication because one's message is now aimed at additional people and is received by all people present. The Anderson and Green stepfather family is an excellent example of how communication can change with additional family members. Janet divorced her husband and lived as a single parent for 4 years before meeting and then moving in with Peter. She and Peter have now lived together for a little more than 1 year and consider their relationship permanent. If Janet's teenage daughter, Sandy, complains about a particular teacher to her mother and no one else is in the room, that complaint might be received as representing Sandy's frustration, and it might generate no discussion whatsoever. If, however, her stepfather Peter is in the room, this once innocuous comment generates a far greater reaction, as Peter has been adamant in the past about the importance of both education and showing respect.

This example (see Figure 2.3) shows how the complexity of communication can increase dramatically when the audience is larger and includes more authority figures. When Sandy made comments about this teacher in the past, Mom would joke, "Mr. Smith needs to start a stamp collection so he has something else to think about other than your grammar." Normally, this

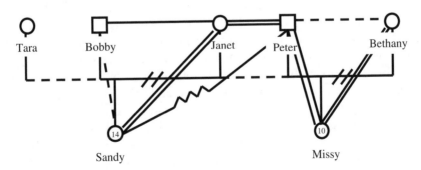

Figure 2.3. The Anderson and Green family.

would produce a small laugh from Sandy, who would return to her homework. Although Sandy might have remained annoyed with Mr. Smith, she would usually feel a bit calmer for having vented her frustration and having received some support from Mom. Now, however, with Peter listening to the conversation, Mom responds to Sandy's comments by saying, "Well, it is important for you to use *me* rather than *I* in that sentence." Mom has not changed her view of Mr. Smith; she still views him as too uptight; and she still wishes to be supportive to Sandy, but she is hesitant to make any comment that Peter will view as disparaging authority. Sandy, following this comment, becomes angry at Mom for, in her words, "losing your sense of humor and only caring what Peter thinks." Peter, hearing this comment, challenges Sandy for her problem with authority. Peter sees Janet, his live-in mate, as having responded correctly, and he is unaware that part of Sandy's frustration is directly related to losing Mom's support. Rather than helping to defuse the situation, Janet has inflamed it by supporting, in Sandy's view, Mr. Smith and Peter and leaving Sandy feeling ridiculed.

As complex as this brief example is, there is an additional dynamic that has not been addressed—Janet's annoyance that she feels unable to respond to her daughter in a manner that could have defused the tension. Because she is very reluctant to argue with Peter that sometimes a little innocent disrespect actually helps Sandy continue her work, she is stuck parenting less effectively because she has lost some of her connection to her daughter.

As the therapist begins to recognize the dilemma that flows from communication becoming more complex as a result of a new stepparent, an intervention can be offered that clarifies the shifting dynamics and the reasons behind these effects.

What makes the impasse especially frustrating in this example is that Janet does not wish to exclude Peter, and Peter actually means no harm. However, that is the nature of these sorts of situations; both parties can justify logically what they do, but the outcome is affected by a systemic phenomenon. The case may benefit if the majority of the interpersonal relations, at this stage, are dyadic. The systemic impasse is that Janet cannot be "real" when both Peter and Sandy are listening to her, particularly in regard to her mothering style. Therefore, by confirming with different subsystems the problematic pattern, a new respect for clear, nonaltered communication can occur.

The clinician might work with the following subsystems: (a) Janet and Peter, (b) Sandy alone, (c) Sandy and Janet, and (d) Sandy and Janet alone for the first 25 minutes and with Peter for the last half of the session.

The goals will be to (a) secure all relationships, (b) explain the inherent dilemma of the communication, (c) affirm the *best intent* of each person (this will need a "buy-in" by all members of the stepfamily), and (d) establish new patterns of interactions that encourage mutual sharing but acknowledge that dyadic communication (Sandy and Janet, Sandy and Peter, and Peter and Janet) will increase in the stepfamily.

Parental Guilt

Guilt is a powerful emotion that can cause people to act in a manner that they might see as less than rational (Tangney & Dearing, 2002). Reacting to guilt does not necessarily have anything to do with the correctness of the resulting behavior. In other words, one may feel guilty for yelling at one's child, and this guilt may motivate the person to buy the child candy. The purchase of the candy may be an unhelpful gesture because, in fact, the child had been misbehaving. Or the purchase of the candy may signal an apology or recognition that the child had not deserved to be reprimanded. An argument made by another adult about whether feeling guilty is merited is of no consequence. Guilt is a feeling and not entirely dependent on logic.

Therefore, when working with a stepfamily in which guilt is a factor in at least one person's actions, the legitimacy of the guilt is only partially relevant. This does not mean that the clinician does not attempt to confirm if the guilt can be understood by another, but rather the clinician cannot assume that if he or she assesses the guilt to be groundless, the related behaviors will cease. However, determining that someone is acting out of guilt is very relevant and needs to be understood to make clinical progress. Our experience is that simply to intervene to help someone change a behavior, especially if that behavior is born of guilt, will usually result in no change and a rejection of treatment by the stepfamily.

Adding to the complexity of guilt is that even if a clinician assists a client to recognize that his or her actions come by way of guilt, he or she may feel compelled to continue the behavior, even though it may infuriate his or her spouse and not necessarily help the person he or she feels guilty about. So unhelpful is guilt in interpersonal relations that the clinician needs to determine if it is a primary motivator, and if so, this must be addressed.

In the following clinical example, we examine a situation in which any reasonable person might feel guilt, but it still needs to be addressed and altered. The Attwood stepfamily came into treatment with the clear understanding that coparenting between the biological father and the stepmother is a chronic and intensifying problem. It is a problem both because the couple's relationship is in jeopardy and the parenting tactic is failing miserably.

Raymond Attwood was married to Sondra for 12 years (see Figure 2.4). Sondra and Raymond had been high school sweethearts who married shortly after graduation. They settled quickly into a lower-middle-class lifestyle with menial jobs, decent family relations, and a lot of partying. Although not technically addicts, they drank, smoked marijuana, splurged with cocaine, and used

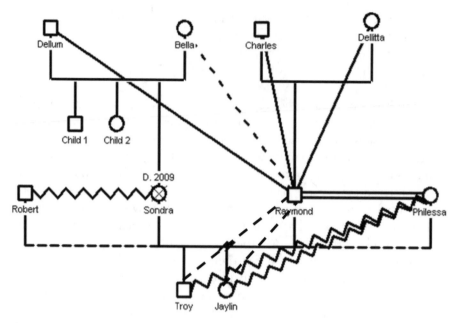

Figure 2.4. The Attwood family.

methamphetamines (speed) to make it through their work days. Although no one thought they were straight-laced, their level of substance use was well hidden. Even their parents thought they were *drinkers*. The couple attended church with their two sons on many Sundays and were nominally involved in traditional community activities.

Sondra and Raymond began to drift apart after 11 years of marriage, and they divorced in their 12th year. The couple found that as they settled down, they had little in common. Raymond had also decided to "clean up," and had started attending AA (Alcoholics Anonymous) meetings and the occasional NA (Narcotics Anonymous) meeting. Raymond achieved sobriety quickly, only relapsing once, and he became increasingly adamant that Sondra at least attend the family meetings. Sondra went to occasional meetings to support Raymond; however, she continued to insist that unlike him she was not addicted and could stop whenever she really needed to.

During the divorce process, Raymond and Sondra agreed that the boys would stay in the home with their mother and see their dad on alternate weekends and some Wednesdays. Together, the couple had also decided that they would not use their past (or present) drug use as a weapon in the divorce or the custody issues. They agreed that both of them had been abusing drugs and alcohol a great deal and that this information did not need to be public. Raymond kept observing Sondra when he picked up the boys to determine if her drug use was getting worse; however, he saw no evidence that things were changing in that area.

Sondra began dating a man named Robert, whom the boys nicknamed Robo because he looked like the actor from the movie *Robocop*, and he was very strict when staying over at the house. Raymond became even less involved with his sons when he began to date Phillessa. When he saw his sons, they complained about their mom and Robo arguing loudly. Although Raymond mentioned this to Sondra, he largely decided not "to make waves" with his ex-wife.

On a Thursday night, Raymond received a call from Deletta, his ex-mother-in-law, that Sondra had been killed by Robert during a fight. Raymond took custody of the boys and moved them into his house, where Phillessa had been residing for the past 2 months. As the stories began to come out, it became clear that the boys, especially Troy, had been very aware of the level of drug use and violence between Sondra and Robo, but he did not feel that his dad cared what went on in that house.

Raymond felt tremendous guilt for having been so cavalier about the conditions that his sons had lived in over the past year. He tried to make up for his mistakes by making the boys feel loved and secure. What he could not do was discipline his sons because even though he knew intellectually that they needed to have structure in the home, he felt unable to disappoint them in any way. He requested that Phillessa take over the discipline until he was able to be sure that they did not feel abandoned by him again. Although Phillessa saw this position as a setup, she also knew that Raymond was paralyzed by his previous inaction, and she did care about the boys' welfare. However, the boys, particularly Jaylin, resented Phillessa and ignored virtually any attempt she made at discipline. The more insistent that Phillessa became about Raymond getting involved, the more Raymond accused Phillessa of "not disciplining with love, but just being mean." Phillessa at first took his criticisms to heart and tried to really like the boys more, hoping it would translate into some mutual warmth and respect; however, the opposite occurred. The boys needed their father to be fully involved and, consequently, perceived Phillessa as an impediment to a real bond with their father. Although the boys did not request that their father become stricter with them, their behaviors clearly indicated that they were not going to give Phillessa the privilege of their respect.

This case clearly includes very complicated bereavement issues on top of the stepfamily concerns. The clinician's initial steps connected the boys to a child-based bereavement agency that provided both individual grief counseling and a support group with other children who had lost a parent to death. The clinician then concentrated on various subsystems of the binuclear family (see Figure 2.4).

The process of choosing various subsystems to work with clinically is fully elucidated in Chapter 3 of this book. However, this case example is longer than others in this chapter in order to clarify the importance of treating particular subsystems. The first subsystem to be seen would be Raymond and Phillessa. The initial referral clearly indicated that the couple was suffering, and they needed clinical intervention to (a) clarify to the therapist (and each other) their experience of the recent happenings in the home, (b) gain a perspective on their actions that would be presented by the therapist on the basis of both an understanding of related research and systems theory, and finally (c) explicitly support their union.

The next subsystem to be invited in therapy would be the two boys, Troy and Jaylin. The purpose of this meeting would be twofold. The first purpose would be to assess the welfare of the boys. Even though they were in treatment around the grieving, it would be very helpful to understand their view of their father. Was either boy blaming the father for the death of the mother? The second purpose would be to clearly give the message that they were an important subsystem in this family, and their opinions and needs were critical to the health of this stepfamily.

The next subsystem, although it was actually an individual session, to be seen would be Raymond by himself. Meeting with Raymond alone was designed for him to wrestle with his guilt, examine his bereavement issues, and determine whether he was prepared to truly return to his role as father. It was important that the meeting with his sons had just preceded his session so that the clinician could respond to Raymond's fears about his sons' welfare. This would be true if the clinician viewed the boys as having begun healing well or if the boys were still damaged by the recent past. The clinical work that followed was very dependent on Raymond's ability to forgive himself and his desire to be a fully functioning father with the range of emotions and stressors such a commitment implies. Adding to the complexity of Raymond's decision was his status as a recovering addict (a label he now recognized applied to himself). Those in recovery, especially in the early years (Schenker, 2009), are instructed to be selfish to the extent that they need to protect their sobriety at all costs. Some in recovery interpret this to mean that they pull away from family issues to prevent emotion from threatening their sobriety. In this situation, Raymond recognized that to delegate his parenting responsibility to Phillessa or even his parents would not serve the boys' real need, which was a responsible and involved parent. Although the clinician helped Raymond to reach this decision, he needed to commit to the task. When his commitment was absolute, the next subsystem could be engaged.

The fourth subsystem to be invited in to treatment was Raymond and both of his sons. The purpose of this session was to (a) allow the boys to feel safe to express what they need and how they feel and (b) reinforce that Raymond would be assuming full parenting responsibility but also that Phillessa was his partner and deserved cordial respect.

The fifth subsystem would be the stepfamily itself. Raymond, Phillessa, and both boys would be brought in together to clarify and reinforce new behaviors. In addition, the therapist would explicitly support the marriage, the parent–child bonds, and the mutual respect between Phillessa and the boys.

Although this example is intended to lay out the typical course of treatment, the therapist needs to be flexible to adjust to issues that might arise unexpectedly. For example, if most of Raymond's fear of using discipline comes from the opinion of his own mother and father, a subsystem session (maybe even with Phillessa) might examine his parents' concerns and determine if they remain as dogmatic in light of the effect of the actions.

The guilt experienced by Raymond cannot be washed away by trying to convince him that he has nothing to feel guilty about. Rather, guilt needs to be put into perspective and then new behaviors and cognitive constructs established to lessen the paralyzing power of guilt.

Loyalty Binds

Loyalty is interesting because of the complexity involved in understanding why it can result in stepfamily vulnerability. Loyalty, in general, is a positive trait. Certainly, one can be loyal to a person and be blinded by this loyalty, not seeing what is unhealthy about that individual. But most often, to be loyal means the person has a deep respect for the other and sees this alliance as a commitment to the bond between two people (Golish, 2003). True loyalty is given, not demanded by the other. In fact, if loyalty is demanded, and such an allegiance is not naturally occurring, often what will result is polite resentment or rebellion.

The twist that turns loyalty into a problematic interactional process in stepfamilies is the bind people feel when loyalty to one person causes rejection of another. Even though stepparents, for example, are not, in most cases, a replacement for a parent, the role similarity is confusing. To put this into perspective, we provide the example of the relationship of a student with three professors in college. A student might feel equally fond of these three teachers, and such a feeling causes no internal conflict because there is no unconscious rule that students need to be loyal to only one professor. Rather, students place professors in a category that permits multiple allegiances. Such is often not the case with a parent. When one's father moves out and 6 months later a stepfather moves into one's home, for many people, the loyalty toward the absent father causes a powerful reaction against the stepfather. In addition, many remarried parents strongly desire that their child or children wholeheartedly accept their new mate. As stated by Cigoli and Scabini (2006), "Pressuring children to accept a new partner (one of the ways in which parents reassure themselves that they have made the right decision) is a source of confusion and leads to conflicts in loyalty" (p. 120).

There are times when such loyalty is requested and other times when the desire to be loyal is strictly personal. In either situation the clinician will see an interactional process that is stressful to those involved, and they often report a moral correctness that accompanies this loyalty.

In the sections that follow, we discuss the loyalty experienced by three categories of people. An additional category, grandparents, is discussed in Chapter 7 of this book. The groups of particular interest at this time are (a) children in stepfamilies, (b) remarried residential parents, and (c) remarried nonresidential parents.

Children in Stepfamilies

Children in stepfamilies often acknowledge that loyalty binds are difficult to manage. They may feel loyal to their nonresidential parent. In the case of someone living with a difficult-to-like stepparent, this sense of loyalty only strengthens as examples of the stepparent's flaws multiply. This situation is best handled clinically by assisting the stepparent to become a positive presence in the stepfamily. Although this is not always easy, it is the primary direction that can assist the stepfamily to thrive. A more intriguing scenario exists when, for example, the father and stepfather are both caring and supportive of the child. The child's sense of loyalty to Dad may cause him or her to be rejecting of the stepfather's positive behaviors (Dunn, O'Connor, & Cheng, 2005). No person can be rejected repeatedly without beginning to either lash out or disengage. Therefore, in this situation, the clinician should consider having a session (or a phone call if the father lives in a distant location) with the nonresidential father. The goal of this discussion is to determine if this father is willing to relinquish the monopoly he holds on the child's loyalty. The clinician highlights that the father needs to be able to convey the idea to his child that loyalty is great but that a good relationship with a stepfather is not threatening.

These first two scenarios regarding the nonresidential parent assume that this nonresidential parent is not encouraging the loyalty explicitly as a means to support the child's rejection of the stepparent. In those situations in which the nonresidential parent actually does encourage the rejection of the stepparent and has no intention of accepting another's positive influence on the child, the clinician should take a different stance. Here the clinician works to increase the stepparent's empathy for the terrible bind that the child is in while simultaneously encouraging the stepparent to make fewer efforts to win the child over. In addition, the stepparent (and the residential parent) are informed that until the child sees that the request for devout loyalty is selfish on the part of the nonresidential parent, no amount of cajoling is likely to succeed. Unfortunately, it is often not until one is in young adulthood that the behavior of a selfish parent is recognized as such by the offspring.

Remarried Residential Parents

Remarried residential parents often describe feeling pulled apart by their spouse and child. These parents' position between these two people is almost unbearable at times because of the feeling that one can never satisfy both sets of interests. For example, in a stepfather family, the mother might feel that she wishes to affirm her daughter; she knows that her daughter has gone through a hard time with the divorce, and she really believes that her daughter is coping well. However, her husband points out various faults that the girl has (e.g., missed appointments, low test scores, a poor choice of a friend), and the mother is aware that these faults are real. A problem does not arise as long as the daughter is not with both of them together. With either one alone she can give her honest opinion; however, if asked to agree with either one of them while the other is listening, she feels caught and torn by her allegiance toward both. This position needs to be understood by all involved. Otherwise, Mom is perceived as lying, which she is not doing; she simply sees both perspectives and is trapped when her more expansive view is challenged.

Remarried Nonresidential Parents

Remarried nonresidential parents have two potential common loyalty binds. The first occurs when the parent is challenged by his new spouse for being too accommodating to his child (this is more common with fathers) when the child visits. When a father's child arrives for visitation, he or she may be given a royal welcome because Dad wants his child to enjoy the visit, and he feels that they have so little time together. The stepmother (the man's new wife) is aware that this child has a special place in the home, which is often intellectually understood, but if the child is given too much positive attention, the stepmother questions the father on why he goes so overboard. This situation is made even more confusing if there are other children in the home—either the man's stepchildren or a new mutual child—who recognize that they do not receive such lavish attention.

The intervention recommended in this situation is that a therapeutic relationship be formed. Although this is always the case, it is particularly true when some behavior may be challenged. In these cases, the systemic interactional pattern between the parent, stepparent, and child needs to be carefully understood. The clinician may feel a pull to affirm one person as the most aggrieved in this situation, but usually such a stance is a mistake. If the clinician moves to pass judgment that one person is right and the other is wrong, usually the clinician is missing some detail. Although the eventual intervention may very well challenge Dad to reduce the perception that his child can do no wrong, this is not recommended as a result of seeing Dad as too permissive. Rather, Dad, his wife, and the child or children have some concern that if left unacknowledged will result in the imbalance. Therefore, the underlying concern must be addressed. Is Dad concerned that his child feels unloved? Is the stepmother concerned for her own children and their sense of worth? Is the child worried that he or she was "divorced" along with Mom? Such concerns may be centered in one or all individuals involved, and the job of the clinician is to assess how the current interactional pattern appears to satisfy them, at least in the short run, and then find a way to acknowledge the concerns and shift the interactional cycle.

The second bind is less common but quite troubling when it does occur. A father might be in a very different place in his life when he has a child or children in a remarriage. At the time his children from his first marriage were born, he was busy with his career, was in a marriage that was starting to fail, and was possibly not that interested in the role of father. However, in the remarriage, he sees a second chance, has more money because his career is progressing, and is in a happier marriage. He therefore takes on parenting, or being a dad, with a passion and pleasure that did not exist the first time. Therefore, when his child from his first marriage visits, the difference in his expressed bond with the children from different mothers is strongly evident.

The clinical direction recommended in this situation may seem out of character with much of this book, but this situation may benefit from a more individually based clinical approach. In other words, the initial step is to assist this man to recognize his own reaction to his child from the first marriage. Yes, it is certainly possible that he is rejecting that child to start anew, but unless he wishes to actually abandon the child from the first marriage (which often creates another set of generational problems), he will not be able to avoid the conflicts that arise from treating someone as less equal. Therefore, he needs to recognize on his own (often with the assistance of a clinician) the origin of his desire to distance himself from his own child, even if it involves trying to reject the former spouse, and only then does the therapeutic approach shift back to being systemic in theory and practice. When the desire to repair the relationship exists, then meetings with the child alone, the father and child, and eventually the stepparent, occur.

Increased Volatility

Stepfamilies can benefit from a treatment focused on their particular needs and dynamics (Browning, 1994). All stepfamilies, not unlike families in general, have individual variation in the volatility they display, but the clinical population of stepfamilies often has exceptionally high emotional intensity. While emotional volatility may be evident in any family, the feeling of safety is lessened when there is less history between the members (Booth & Edwards, 1992). Therefore, a model of treatment for stepfamilies must address the issues that are most prevalent in these families and do so in a manner that increases the sense of safety during the clinical process.

A number of factors can result in stepfamilies having a high level of volatility. However, one very clear factor is that suddenly one is a member of a new family. Part of one's original family is gone, and a new person is in the role of a stepmother or stepfather. Certainly the person is crucial, but the role itself is an extremely powerful factor as well. In other words, although most stepmothers or stepfathers know that they are not trying to replace a parent, it is easy to understand why the term *parent*, regardless of the prefix, generates strong associations.

It may be that part of the stress experienced in a stepfamily can be attributed to the frustration between the unrealized potential of a close relationship and the actual relationships that are formed in some stepfamilies. If stepfamily members find their stepparent or stepchild to be annoying, a confusion or disequilibrium may result. Our years of clinical work have reinforced for us that most people enter into relationships with members of their stepfamily with ambivalence. Although few people are brimming with optimism about the deep familial bond that they are anticipating, most do not want to assume that this new relationship will be defined only by distance, anger, and frustration. Thus, it is common for people to gauge the relationship on a day-to-day basis. Even a few negative experiences can shift the relationship in an unsatisfying direction if differences are not resolved.

Over time, stepfamilies can become similar to first-union families. Hetherington (1988) found that when the researcher examined the descriptions of family made by undergraduate students, there was no significant difference between the description of first-union families and stepfamilies after 9 years. One can surmise that time together as a family provides a significant buffer against the misinterpretations and unmet expectations that are often experienced in the early years of the stepfamily. It is precisely because of the limited experience with one another that members of a new stepfamily explicitly need an empathic understanding of each other.

To treat stepfamilies, it is critical to foster an environment in which each person becomes truly aware of the experience of the other. The task of putting oneself in the shoes of another is not just a requirement for the therapist but for each family member as well.

When members of a first-marriage family look at the actions of other family members, these actions have a context. One usually knows about how the grandparents treated an adult member when he or she was a child. Parents view their children with the knowledge of their births, development, reaction to the divorce or death of the other parent, and a myriad of other factors. With this depth of context, it is infinitely easier to be less bothered by behavior that by all rights might be annoying to a newcomer. However, attempting to bring someone up to speed as to why someone might be acting in a particular manner often creates conflict. The person hearing the context often believes that he or she is being asked to overlook a behavior. Most people resent being asked to ignore their natural impulse because of new information. This occurs even when the speaker prefaces the statement with the comment, "I am not trying to justify why he yelled at you, but it is important for you to understand this about him." These explanations do not guarantee an increase in a true empathic feeling in most cases; instead, they often generate power struggles over the correct interpretation of irritating behavior.

The notion of a "correct" interpretation of a behavior is a costly error in family relations. The stepfamily is even more likely to be fertile ground for this useless debate. For such a discussion to be fruitful, those involved may either be wishing to expand their empathic understanding of the other or be willing to be converted. The term *converted* may sound inappropriate in this context, but in fact, this is exactly what it is. To convert is "to bring over from one belief to another" (Merriam-Webster, 1979).

PRIMARY INTERVENTION TO ADDRESS
STEPFAMILY VULNERABILITIES

Conversion, or changing one's view of another's intention, is the primary intervention to address stepfamily vulnerabilities. The parent of a child in a stepfamily is looking to alter the spouse's view of the child. When two people raise a child, whether that child is biologically conceived of their union or adopted at infancy, there is a depth of understanding that is often challenging to replicate. Parents seem to function with the idea that if the stepparent would only more fully understand in a more nuanced manner this child, then misperceptions would be reduced. The parent believes that the stepparent is focusing on the more negative aspects of the child and somehow missing the child's talents and goodness. The stepparent often feels that he or she is viewing the child through clear glass; the stepparent sees his or her perception as similar to the perspective that will be taken later by teachers, admissions officers, and future bosses. The stepparent is often proud of the ability to see the child as he or she will be viewed by the world. At the same time, the parent pleads or argues for a parental perspective, a more subjective, loving vantage, to be shared.

Because neither view represents a verifiable truth, each perspective is a belief, albeit a belief with ample evidence on each side. It is the recitation of this evidence that often causes each member of the couple to feel frustrated. One's belief about another rarely changes in small steps; rather, something occurs that makes one challenge the accuracy or usefulness of one's current belief.

Couples therefore either (a) fight and exist in the constant tension of an unresolved debate, (b) agree to disagree, or (c) have an individual or mutual conversion. Either one of the first two positions is commonly held by couples coming in for treatment. The overt fighting and constant tension are highly unpleasant and often a precursor to the relationship failing; agreeing to disagree is a stressful stance to maintain. Many couples reach the position of agreeing to disagree out of frustration, but usually an urge still exists to resolve the disagreement. Therefore, when either member of the couple again attempts to establish a point in an argument about the child (e.g., "I just think she is manipulating you"), that person is struggling with trying to settle the debate so that the tension in the home can be relieved. Murray Bowen correctly asserted that in highly emotional situations, it is a challenge to think clearly (Gottman, 1999; M. E, Kerr & Bowen, 1988).

In a state of genuine calmness, one can hold a dilemma in mind without a strong urge to resolve it. It is this capacity that leads to a healthy position for the couple, the position of *mutual conversion*. Mutual conversion, as we perceive it, consists of each member of the couple shifting one or more beliefs. For example, the stepfather may come to endorse the mother's belief that it is because her son (his stepson) is embarrassed about being a bad baseball player that he behaves in a manner that is easy to misinterpret as being obnoxious. And this same mother might agree with her husband that her son is being lazy about the household chores, rather than her original position, which endorsed that her son was just extremely forgetful. The result of such a shift is that both members of the couple soften their anger and are not so invested in disproving the other's view of the child.

As each member of the couple shifts a belief, a certain level of gratitude occurs because it is satisfying to have his or her opinion confirmed. However, the conversion of one's belief is a great challenge. People are, by nature, creatures who seek to support their beliefs and ignore evidence to the contrary. Even when the conversion does occur and one has truly shifted a belief, one may be reluctant to admit to this change out of a fear that other opinions will now be seen as less certain.

Although having each member of the couple shift his or her position regarding the child is most satisfying, it is not the only successful method to reduce interpersonal tension. In fact, on many occasions, only one member of the couple changes his or her view of the child's behavior. However, if one person really makes that shift in belief, that person moves from negative hypervigilance to acceptance. When this occurs, the second member of the couple will notice a reduction of interpersonal stress in the home, and usually that person will respond in a manner that signals that the couple is no longer disagreeing with each other.

It is important to recognize that even very effective coparents in a first-marriage family may not agree entirely about a child's motivation. Biological and long-time adoptive parents simply tend to have more charity in their view of their child. This does not make the slightly less charitable stepparent a beast. As long as the view of each member of the couple is largely in agreement, most couples can function as a team.

The problem for many stepfamilies, especially those stepfamilies that come in for treatment, is that this conversion, or change in belief, remains elusive. Both members of the couple can see the impasse that causes such stress in their relationship, but they hold on to their position because they believe that the correctness of their stance will eventually be endorsed by the other as well.

WHEN THE ARGUMENT CANNOT BE RESOLVED

There are two resulting postures that accompany the impasse that is experienced by couples who cannot interrupt the debate: disengagement or volatile emotional outbursts. Each of these postures results in relational difficulties and potentially serves as the basis for splitting the couple. As the work of John Gottman (1999) has demonstrated, couples that drift apart and become emotionally disengaged are as vulnerable as those that argue without reaching at least some level of mutual respect. Therefore, therapists who work clinically with these couples need to be aware of the serious consequences of these relational patterns.

Many couples move toward disengagement when confronted with a chronic disagreement. They may still be attracted to each other at a physical level, and they may enjoy each other's company in nonstressful situations, but they choose to avoid any discussion that revolves around coparenting. Although this stance may sound better than open arguments, it too has some significant problems. First and foremost, unless the child is about to move to another location, the conflict will not simply disappear. These disagreements can be compared with a computer on *sleep mode*, seemingly out of mind, but any issue, even a small one, can bring the disagreement back.

A second and possibly more toxic result, is that the stepparent so fully disengages on the topic of parenting that he or she loses all interest in any interaction with the stepchild. When one ceases to interact, it is not just the negative interactions that disappear but the positive ones as well. Without some positive interactions, it is impossible for a relationship to evolve; rather, such relationships just exist as casual and unrewarding acquaintances.

And finally, a couple that completely disengages from a coparental relationship can begin to slip into disengaging as partners and lovers. If the fear of having to address the "hidden" topic becomes too great, they drift apart. When two people drift apart, at least one member of the couple will find another to connect with and love.

The other common relational dynamic that emerges is that of constant bickering and biased observation. It is this style that is frequently presented in the clinical population. The level of disagreement is so great that frequently both members of the couple recognize that clinical intervention is necessary to avoid a split in the relationship.

Unfortunately for these couples, this situation does not result in the couple having a healthy argument and then some mutually satisfying accord. Rather, these fights involve a recitation of a series of examples to prove one parent's point about the child, and the mate follows by listing a different series of actions that this person believes proves his or her point. Arguing about a third person is quite different from arguing about each other. When a couple argues about an incident between them, they may accept a certain level of perceptual differentiation because it is common for people to recognize that an event might be perceived differently. For example, an argument about whether one of them was flirting at a party might finally be resolved by a partial apology and a recognition that it might have looked like flirting, but it wasn't intended to be flirting. The couple then accepts the possibility that they might both have acted in a manner that did not help the situation, and they feel a level of resolution. Because we have already established that these couples are not willing to accommodate the other's perception of the child in question, these arguments have no satisfying resolution. When there is no resolution or neutral position in which to retreat from an argument, these arguments often reach a blowup.

Emotional blowups will, if unresolved, become increasingly common and potentially damaging. When a behavior becomes more common, it does not follow that it becomes less toxic. In fact, the opposite is often true. As the blowups become more common, the members of the couple and the entire stepfamily begin to question whether any familial feeling can be achieved. This sense that the stepfamily is not moving toward greater stability is frightening to all involved, even to those who seemingly do not want the stepfamily to succeed.

The expectations for the structure that the stepfamily will have, including the roles of each member and their relationships with one another, are rarely clearly defined prior to remarriage. There is no model that serves to orient people toward adjusting their expectations. Invariably, the remarried couple holds out hope for a level of familial connectedness that will be, at minimum, self-reinforcing. For the adults, part of their optimism comes directly from the love they feel toward the other. It is not surprising therefore that this subsystem, the remarried couple, is initially the bedrock of familial stability in the new stepfamily. The other subsystem that is assumed to be unquestionably stable is that of the parent and his or her child(ren). However, parents often misjudge the strength of the connection with their own children after a remarriage.

Parents still love their children, and children continue to love their parents, but the addition of a new adult alters the dynamics such that children report perceiving their parents as less concerned following a remarriage (Thomson, Mosley, Hanson, & McLanahan, 2001). There is some evidence, however, that parents, following remarriage, may not perceive themselves as any less invested in their role as parents (Browning, 1987). Although it is difficult to determine if parents do become less invested in their children after remarriage, the perception of reduced parental attention can influence children to feel more wary of the effects of remarriage. One can speculate that children in first marriages are not looking at their other parent as competition. However, in a stepfamily, children become aware of their parent's shifting attention and the energy that is reasonably focused on a new marital relationship.

Given that the coparenting issues are so predictive of marital problems in the remarried couple, a clinician must focus on this issue in treating stepfamilies. Parents and new stepparents often enter in to the stepfamily with confidence that they will be able to coparent as a team that views the child from the same perspective. A common problem occurs when one spouse judges the child's behavior from a far more negative perspective than does the other spouse. Coparenting in that situation becomes virtually impossible.

The clinician can best serve a stepfamily by assisting one or both members of the couple to shift their views of the child's motivation. People are generally less troubled by another's actions than they are by the perceived intention behind an action. For example, although it is annoying when a child leaves a dirty dish in the family room, the assigned intention of that behavior influences the emotion one feels in response. One person imagines that the child simply forgot to grab the dish, and the other perceives this to be a clear statement that the child does not feel any investment in this new house, and by extension, the stepfamily.

It is around the area of perception of intentionality that many remarried people find themselves arguing. These couples often agree about the behavior—they both realize that the child was wrong to leave the dish—but the bond that forms on the basis of the agreement is dwarfed by the disagreement that emerges as a result of the wide disparity of opinion as to the child's intention; the difference of whether the child was forgetful or disobedient becomes the issue. The parent and stepparent may agree completely on parenting practices regarding the behavior exhibited; however, if they differ strongly on the perceived motivation of the child, the resulting consequence will seem unfair to one person. Therefore, the clinician is wasting time addressing the behavior as if it exists in a vacuum. It is necessary to give attention to assisting the couple to establish clear and fair rules, but such an intervention by itself only fuels the feeling in the stepfamily that the clinician does not understand the unique needs of remarried couples who are coparenting. To clearly demonstrate to the couple that the clinician understands the unique challenges of stepfamily coparenting, a specific directive can be helpful. The coparental team is supported in recognizing that it is normal for two people to view a child with whom they each have a very different history from distinct perspectives.

A RATIONALE FOR THE STEPFAMILY THERAPY MODEL

The SfT model presupposes that it is always preferable to understand a stepfamily from multiple perspectives. The clinician will view the stepfamily as a collection of subsystems. Recognizing different perspectives for each person will permit the clinician a fuller understanding. The clinician holds the privilege for the family. In other words, the clinician must be clear that he or she will listen to all perspectives and find a way to help each person have a deeper understanding of areas of agreement and areas of disagreement. The explicit model of SfT that we recommend is the focus of Chapter 3.

The clinical approach recommended for disengaged stepfamilies and explosive stepfamilies is the same in regard to the steps taken. The primary differences will involve the level of control taken by the clinician. The explosive or emotionally volatile stepfamily will need significant containment to reduce the numbers of blowups at home and certainly in session.

The disengaged stepfamily will be given a wider range of clinical experience to initiate an authentic connection between stepfamily members, and the rationale behind who to see in therapy and in what order is relegated to a secondary status. In SfT, these decisions, made in consultation with the remarried couple, take on primary importance. If the goal is first and foremost to stop the dissolution of the stepfamily, the early appointments will serve to reinforce any subsystem that is relatively intact and to gain individual perspectives, with the explicit agenda of sharing those perspectives with other stepfamily members to establish the legitimacy of various opinions and to challenge misperceptions that are eroding the stepfamily.

If the stability of the stepfamily is less tenuous, the protective agenda can be shifted to one in which sessions may resemble more traditional family therapy. Although a clinician may be aware of the needs of various subsystems that constitute the stepfamily, the clinician also encourages the strengths inherent in uniting stable subsystems. If the clinician has misjudged the stability of the stepfamily and perceives a session to be unhelpfully volatile, steps to restabilize the stepfamily must be taken. Fortunately, the remarried couple is often very astute in recognizing if they are looking at treatment as a last-ditch effort to save the stepfamily or if they are looking at treatment as a way to improve a flawed but stable stepfamily.

Through consideration of the perspective of each subsystem in the stepfamily, a fuller, more nuanced understanding of systemic patterns emerges. As these patterns are brought explicitly into awareness, the level of blame placed on any one person is automatically lessened. This lessening of blame is then accompanied with an increase in empathy, followed by a direct appeal to alter unhelpful interactional patterns. Following this sequence, the stepfamily becomes open to learning about themselves, both through psychoeducation and an understanding of their own patterns. Ideally, the positive feelings that exist in these stepfamilies are given a chance to emerge as the unhelpful cycles are understood and replaced.

WHERE THE STEPFAMILY THERAPY MODEL FALLS ON THE EVIDENCE-BASED PRACTICE SPECTRUM

There are various reasons why the creators of any therapeutic model need to establish where it falls on the spectrum of evidence-based practice. The first reason is that clients have the right to know that the authors of a model have been focused on the well-being of those who may receive the treatment. Although the time and the research necessary to prove a model's effectiveness create a system in which many models in their early stages are still forming the evidence needed to make a claim of being evidence based, the process of building a support base for the treatment being put forth is an important component of consumer protection.

Another reason that it is important to examine the level in which a model meets the criteria as an evidence-based practice is that the American Psychological Association (APA) has taken a central position on the issue through its guidelines and criteria established within the APA and through various divisions. The Presidential Task Force of Evidence-Based Practice in psychology recommended the following policy statement, which was accepted by the APA. The policy statement reads: "Evidence-based practice in psychology (EBPP) is the integration of the best available research with clinical expertise in the context of patient characteristics, culture, values, and preferences" (APA, 2005, p. 1).

Although the value of this movement to affirm the efficacy of practice models seems both self-evident and appropriate, there remains a tension in the field regarding the method by which the clinical community and the research community function together to reach consensus. This tension between practitioners and the researchers who critique the relative effectiveness of different approaches to treatment has been well documented (Goodheart, 2006; Norcross, 2001; Sternberg, 2006).

Interestingly, few people discuss the very positive relationship that many practitioners feel with the researchers who produce studies to assist in clarifying the factors that make any population more understandable. In other words, the research findings that have provided the clinical community with a more nuanced and fuller understanding of stepfamilies are welcomed and used regularly. However, even in this area, which represents a positive interaction between research and practice, both sides still find some fault with the other. Clinicians complain that researchers often form their questions so narrowly that the information provided is so tentatively worded that it is not sufficiently useful when applied to real people. Researchers, on the other hand, worry that clinicians will find one subsection of the overall findings and use only the part that matches their preconceived idea about a client or clinical situation. The fear is that in the desire to provide useful psychoeducation, practitioners will avoid the aspects of research that are either difficult to convey back to a client or do not match with the clinician's predetermined worldview.

In considering the status of the model presented in this book, we judge the SfT model to be potentially beneficial. Although we believe this model is exceptionally helpful to both clinicians and the stepfamilies being served, the level of evidence needed to support such a claim does not, at this time, exist. The status of potentially beneficial has been determined using three levels of evidence. The first level is that of clinical operations: (a) case studies and (b) investigations of clinical responses when the proposed interventions were implemented with created families (Browning, Collins, & Nelson, 2004). The second level is the structure of the model itself. SfT has 10 defined steps that allow the therapy to be largely replicated by others wishing to follow the same approach. Finally, a third level consists of the use of the extant research literature as the foundation of all psychoeducational interventions and all conceptual formulations of the stepfamily in treatment.

Two comprehensive case studies have been conducted using the SfT model. The case studies used a 5-point systematic evaluation process that recommends that goals be specified, processes and procedures be defined, measures be selected, assessments occur regularly, and the data be evaluated (Kazdin, 2006). Although all the steps were followed, the measure used was a process measure, rather than a strict goal-based measure. The results of these studies cannot be reported in a manner that establishes clinical efficacy; however, changes in the model were determined as a result of the systematic evaluation, and the interpersonal relationships were seen to improve in the short-term following both studies in which a formal evaluation process was used.

The evidence provided by the created family protocol is more speculative. Six stepfamilies were created by Scott Browning, using volunteers and graduate students. These created stepfamilies were then put through a course of treatment following the SfT model. Because these were not real stepfamilies, no suggestion could be considered in regard to the efficacy of therapy; however, the process did allow Scott Browning and Elise Artelt to assess the intervention for directionality. In other words, did the created stepfamily react to the intervention in a manner that was predicable? After the process, five of the six created stepfamilies reported that the subsystems approach increased the sense of security. Even though the stepfamily was artificial, the sense of security versus insecurity was still apparent to those in role.

Because the SfT model is based on 10 clearly articulated steps, it is a model that provides the clinician with a framework. Although the steps are not intended to be completely static, when one proceeds from the first to last step, a coherent and replicable system is produced.

Finally, the therapy is informed by the extant research literature. The incorporation of the research on stepfamilies is used to (a) provide accurate psychoeducation, (b) alert the clinician to potential problem areas in these families, and (c) offer the clinician an appreciation of the typical experiences of stepfamily members so that these clients do not feel responsible for teaching clinicians about all aspects of stepfamily life. Therefore, the clinician can concentrate on those clinical issues truly relevant to the stepfamily with whom he or she is working rather than use the template of the first-marriage family in an unhelpful way.

It is our intention to continue to work toward a more substantial evidence base to support the efficacy of SfT. Certainly, anyone choosing to implement this model in a controlled manner is welcome to do so and to share the outcome of these efforts.

3

STEPFAMILY THERAPY: THE 10 STEPS

Stepfamily therapy (SfT) is a theoretically sound and practical approach to treating stepfamilies. SfT concentrates on assisting stepfamilies by using a specific subsystem approach. SfT includes the establishment of clinical concern and the creation of a solid working alliance in which the stepfamily dynamics are consistently assessed and used as a point of reference for treatment.

CLINICAL APPROACH TO TREATING STEPFAMILIES

The 10-point approach of SfT is intended to serve as a guide to treatment. The order of some of the steps may, on occasion, vary, but the primary stages of diagnosis, treatment, and integration are a useful benchmark. Each of the points is further elucidated in this chapter. Therapists enter this work with an established theoretical foundation and an armamentarium of clinical

---

This chapter expands on ideas that first appeared in "Treating Stepfamilies: A Subsystems Based Approach" by S. W. Browning and J. H. Bray. In M. Stanton and J. H. Bray (Eds.), *The Wiley-Blackwell Handbook of Family Psychology* (pp. 487–498), 2009, West Sussex, England: Blackwell.

skills. This approach is not vying to replace the fundamental understanding one brings from years of training and practice but rather is serving as a framework to keep the clinician grounded during the sometimes overwhelming work of providing a stepfamily with therapy.

This clinical approach identifies the stepfamily as unique. The structural dynamics and accompanying emotional reactions make necessary a revised language and adjusted norms, based on research, that serve to comfort members of stepfamilies. The suggested clinical stance is explicitly based on perceiving the stepfamily as a collective of subsystems. It is important to recognize that an individual can also constitute a subsystem. There are specific benchmarks and topics that serve as an overarching framework for this therapy. The 10 steps are followed as a guideline, with the explicit agenda that each subsystem is considered important for treatment. When the various subsystems are predominately stable, there is no longer a constant emphasis on step issues. Only then does the treatment shift to a concentration on more generic issues of family life, influenced but not dominated by stepfamily dynamics.

Diagnostic Steps

1. Recognize the structure of the stepfamily (e.g., simple stepfather family, simple stepmother family, complex stepfamily in which both adults are stepparents). Use the initial telephone intake to look for systemic similarities within the context of the research literature.
2. Determine the membership of the first session—usually the marital dyad—and further delineate the unique concerns of the stepfamily.
3. Clarify the distinct subsystems in the stepfamily, and use this information to provide a direction for clinical treatment.

Primary Clinical Interventions

4. Consider the research findings that normalize the experience of the stepfamily, and introduce them in clinical practice (as appropriate and meaningful).
5. Actively assess and assist in the recognition of empathy when present, and increase the empathic experience between stepfamily members and subsystems.
6. Identify and challenge unhelpful beliefs and specific miscommunication circulating in the stepfamily—the role of labels.

7. Support the naturally connected subsystem (parent and child), and confirm that parent and child are capable of expressing mutual concern.
8. Teach the stepfamily about its own systemic functioning.

Stepfamily Integration

9. Assist in coparental work between any and all involved parental figures, including the binuclear family.
10. Increase communication among all stepfamily members available, and move toward integrating the various subsystems into a functioning and satisfied stepfamily.

Steps 1 through 3 should be completed before Steps 4 through 10. Typically Step 1 takes place during the telephone intake. Steps 2 and 3 can usually be completed during the first session. However, a second session may be necessary to complete these steps. Steps 4 through 8 are ongoing processes. These items are used consistently throughout therapy as appropriate and not necessarily in the order that they are listed (e.g., in Chapter 4, Steps 7 and 8 have been reversed to demonstrate this). Steps 9 and 10 can only be completed after there is an understanding of the family dynamic and a relationship between the therapist and the family members has been established. Throughout the course of therapy, as new concerns are explored, Steps 3 through 10 are used as needed.

APPLYING THE 10 STEPS OF STEPFAMILY THERAPY

In the sections that follow, we discuss each of the 10 steps of SfT.

Step 1

Recognize the structure of the stepfamily (e.g., simple stepfather family, simple stepmother family, complex stepfamily in which both adults are stepparents). Use the initial telephone intake to look for systemic similarities within the context of the research literature.

Stepfamilies, although individually unique, share certain dynamic truisms with other stepfamilies that are structurally alike. For example, the experiences of a stepfather family will usually have distinct similarities with other matched stepfather families. Research cannot tell a therapist what areas will be problematic in each stepfamily, but a comprehensive understanding of research findings may assist him or her in addressing potential areas of concern. Stepfamilies are often worried that the therapist, especially a therapist who has not resided in a stepfamily, may not understand their needs. This perception is exacerbated by the fact that many of these families are themselves having a difficult time understanding the powerful feelings, some of which are quite negative, that have arisen since the remarriage. SfT encourages the therapist to consider the stepfamily in light of the research gathered over the last 30 years.

Some of the challenges facing stepfamilies are confusing at a primal level. For example, although the sense of feeling included is not necessarily guaranteed in the biologically connected family, often the stepparent or, on occasion the child reports not feeling included in a new stepfamily, and this represents a fundamental emotional issue. Members of stepfamilies frequently mention feeling as though they are outsiders (Banker & Gaertner, 1998; Coleman, Ganong, & Fine, 2000); thus, the clinician must both confirm the prevalence of such feelings and begin the process of reducing the effect of the perception. Part of that process is to assist stepfamily members in recognizing that there is an interpersonal stepfamily process that can be expected. A person who marries into a cohesive family system cannot help but perceive him- or herself to be in an outsider position—something that is more a function of the stepfamily context than it is of individual personalities. The clinician needs to make the family aware of the systemic nature of the stepfamily and how it is likely to be affected by these dynamics.

Another example of expectable dynamics involves a mother in a stepfather family feeling pulled between her new husband and her children; this client may be relieved to know that this is a common problem in this particular family form. Although biologically connected to her children and in love with her husband, she is being asked to endorse two different worldviews, and the pressure she feels to give her support can be intense. She may experience some solace from the clinician's informed awareness of her difficult and very frustrating position.

A basic premise of SfT is that no one would seek out such an unfulfilling role intentionally. It is the structure of the system, by way of an interpersonal stepfamily process, that is more powerful than the basic personality structure of the individual family members. The SfT therapist must help the family understand that these common and predictable interpersonal processes are originating, at least in part, from the structure of the system.

When we focus on Step 4, we discuss how the research findings, when respectfully presented, serve as a clinical intervention. However, in Step 1, the clinician is increasing his or her own understanding of the stepfamily. The clinician delineates a number of baseline concepts that may explain many of the stepfamily's experiences. The primary purpose is to alert the clinician to a myriad of factors that may be affecting the formation of the stepfamily.

Unlike a hypothesis, which one attempts to confirm or disconfirm, a baseline concept deepens plausible explanations without attempting to prove anything. It is this process that is central to diagnosing a stepfamily. Information presented by the family forms the primary baseline concept, but the inferences based on research of structurally similar stepfamilies form a series of secondary baseline concepts. Using this approach, the clinician is attempting to explicate a systemic explanation that summarizes the pattern and the rationale for those patterns, in the presenting stepfamily.

For example, a stepfather family, the Phillipses, calls to request therapy because of Tim's (age 15) poor grades and a conflicted relationship with Ben (the stepfather). Although the primary concern involves assessing the variety of issues that may result in poor grades, the secondary concern involves determining the nature of the conflict between Tim and Ben. Stepfather and stepson do not exist in a vacuum, so certainly Karen (Tim's mother, Ben's wife) has a role regarding the relationship between Tim and Ben, but it is helpful for the clinician to have information about likely difficulties often experienced between stepfathers and stepsons. This information is not to substitute for a thorough intake interview or to be considered a "truth," but it serves as a baseline concept that widens the clinician's perspective. Examining a relationship without an idea of why seemingly atypical behavior may be normative tends to cause clinicians to shift their opinions in a direction of greater pathology, rather than acceptance. A perspective that originates from an understanding of the relevant research material comforts the stepfamily because they are less likely to be misunderstood than would be the case if they were seeking therapy from a clinician unfamiliar with stepfamilies.

Step 2

Determine the membership of the first session—usually the marital dyad—and further delineate the unique concerns of the stepfamily.

In keeping with this approach, the most frequent subsystem invited into the initial session is the remarried couple. This is not a pro forma decision, however; this subsystem appears to be the best clinical foundation for further progress, especially under the following conditions: (a) The members of the couple do not see eye to eye in how they describe the behavior and/or discipline of the stepchild, and (b) an initial session with the remarried couple and any stepchildren and children would predictably involve a blowup between either the stepparent and stepchild or the remarried couple.

The justification for seeing the remarried couple first is simple. Faulty communications, anger, and confusion are often the result of misperceptions. The new stepfamily is usually experiencing intense emotions (Rhoden

& Pasley, 2000) that become more complicated in the therapist's office if additional people are added to the interview.

When a mother is in an initial session with her new husband and her two biological children, she will be editing her comments in order not to displease anyone, and in so doing she will not be sharing her true thoughts and feelings; or she may tailor her comments depending on which family member she believes is stronger or most vulnerable. It is not that people want to lie in session; it is that they may be so aware of the possibility this family could break apart that they reserve some critical information rather than disclose potentially hurtful material. Therefore, the couple by themselves, although still potentially vulnerable, is often better able to explain their concerns without the children being present.

In other words, if the therapist asks a question of the mother and remarried wife, she will need to examine the potential effect of her response on her husband and child if both are present. Her response will be shaped by her feeling of being torn between expressing maternal love and romantic love. This example highlights one difference between the stepfamily and the first-union family. Generally, in a first-union family, of all the potential conflicts that may make such work difficult, annoyance directed toward a woman for loving both her husband and child is not a common problem.

It might seem that the emphasis on seeing the couple first is a rejection of systemic thinking in regard to the stepfamily, but this is not so. SfT is clearly systemic, but the therapist needs to be aware of the primitive emotions that are generated both within and among subsystems in a recently formed stepfamily. As Murray Bowen (1978) understood, most psychological healing occurs in a dyadic form, but this does not lessen the importance of understanding the dynamics of the entire system. In much the same way, SfT progresses by addressing the issues of all primary subsystems in the stepfamily, eventually helping the entire stepfamily become secure.

The remarried couple also presents with a parenting dynamic that is often quite distinct from the first-union couple. Typically, in first-union families with children, couples who cannot agree on parenting issues are experiencing marital difficulties as well. However, a remarried couple in disagreement about some aspect of a child's behavior or attitude is usually still romantically in love, but stressed about coparenting. Many stepparents enter into such a relationship with a great willingness to assist in the parenting and welfare of the children to whom they now serve as an additional parent. The stepparent is often the "unsung hero" (Rhoden & Pasley, 2000), providing financial stability, emotional support, and structure to the stepfamily.

The shift from boyfriend or girlfriend to stepfather or stepmother is a dramatic one that frequently has some negative connotations attached. This often unexpected relationship change has little to do with the psychological health of the adults or children in a stepfamily. It is too common to be written off as a symptom of an unwell or immature person. Most people are surprised by the transformations that have followed a remarriage. One factor that may cause couples to be underprepared for the shift that occurs in remarriage is the distinct difference between dating and familial commitment. Clinically, we have noted that many couples in treatment comment that before remarrying they were confident that the warnings about remarriage were overblown. This reaction is often due to the fact that things were going so smoothly during the dating period. The message here is that if everything seems fine while dating, it is hard to imagine why various relationships might change radically after remarrying. However, the changes are quite profound when the level of commitment and co-parental responsibility increases.

In the newly formed stepfamily, the remarried couple alters its reality the day after the marriage (or unofficial commitment). Bill has gone from boyfriend to husband and stepfather. This is more than just a change in title. Bill has now, at some level, become a parental figure linked to the welfare of the child from that day forward unless the new marriage dissolves. Prior to the marriage, he was a boyfriend who could, if he wished, believe that his fate and the fate of his girlfriend's child were not connected.

The emotional turmoil that accompanies the transition from dating to stepfamily is often underestimated. Therapists should understand that this is not a couple that avoided the evidence; rather, they had very little knowledge of stepfamily literature and really felt fine while dating. If the couple begins to reprimand themselves because they should have known, the therapist can assure them that at least some of the changes are due to the systemic shift that has occurred, not hidden personality traits that were ignored.

The interaction between a stepparent and stepchild is the most likely cause of stepfamily distress (A. C. Brown, Green, & Druckman, 1990). Therefore, an initial session with an entire stepfamily may quickly highlight this antipathy. The level of tension is additionally increased by the biological parent's investment in viewing the relationship between the child and stepparent as a positive and healthy one, and any evidence to the contrary is disheartening. This leads the biological mother, for example, to show less empathy for either position than, in fact, she feels. Therefore, rather than moving toward greater clarity, an initial session with all present may solidify misperceptions.

A stepfamily should not be placed in a circumstance that may increase its vulnerability. Harsh words may have been stated at an earlier time in the home, but those same statements reiterated in front of a therapist can be particularly humiliating. The stepfamily may see the therapist as unable to control the emotional temperature of the room. If this is the case, at least one stepfamily member may retreat from the process, usually fearing that the increased chaos will lead to dissolution of the stepfamily. It is potentially damaging to the outcome of a stepfamily case to have the stepfather, for example, leave treatment because of an insult spoken by an adolescent stepchild, yet that reaction is not uncommon.

Admittedly, the first-union family may also react by leaving treatment as a result of a session in which there is a blowup between members. However, our experience suggests that the tenuous bond in conflicted stepfamilies makes such increased tension too threatening. Whereas the members of the first-union family return to treatment after a difficult and conflict-filled session, many stepfamilies retreat to a position of perceived stability rather than push the system too far.

In those rare cases in which the stepparent–stepchild subsystem is the least contentious and the adult couple is not in conflict, seeing everyone involved, as one might with a first-union family, is perfectly appropriate. For example, on occasion, the stepfamily comes to treatment with a mellow and supportive stepparent and an agitated biological parent. As long as the two adults are not conflicted, just different from one another, this type of stepfamily proceeds in treatment much like a first-union family.

To determine if the case presenting to the therapist will be one in which the selection of the people involved in the initial session is important, certain questions can be asked in the pretherapy phone call that will clarify if the therapist should be flexible or an authority regarding those invited in to the initial session. We recommend that while listening to the caller's request and situation, the therapist create an interactional genogram (McGoldrick & Carter, 2001). This genogram will address the following issues:

1. Who are all the players?
2. What is the status (remarried, divorced but living together) of this family?
3. What is the interpersonal relationship for every dyad?
4. Are there predicable blowups between any dyad?

The genogram, first used by family therapists, is one tool that remains just as useful, if not more so, in treating stepfamilies. Simply stated, the stepfamily involves many people, in most cases, and to keep track of the various subsystems, a map is necessary. The genogram is a map of the stepfamily and the extended binuclear family. In addition to clarifying who is involved, the genogram makes it possible to track the quality of the interactional relationships. Although there are many systems that can be used (Gerson, McGoldrick, & Petry, 2008), there is general uniformity on the symbols to delineate gender, death, marriage, separation, and so forth. However, the systems for expressing the interactional relationships tend to vary; the legend shown in Figure 3.1 is the system we used. The genogram is always useful as a method of keeping

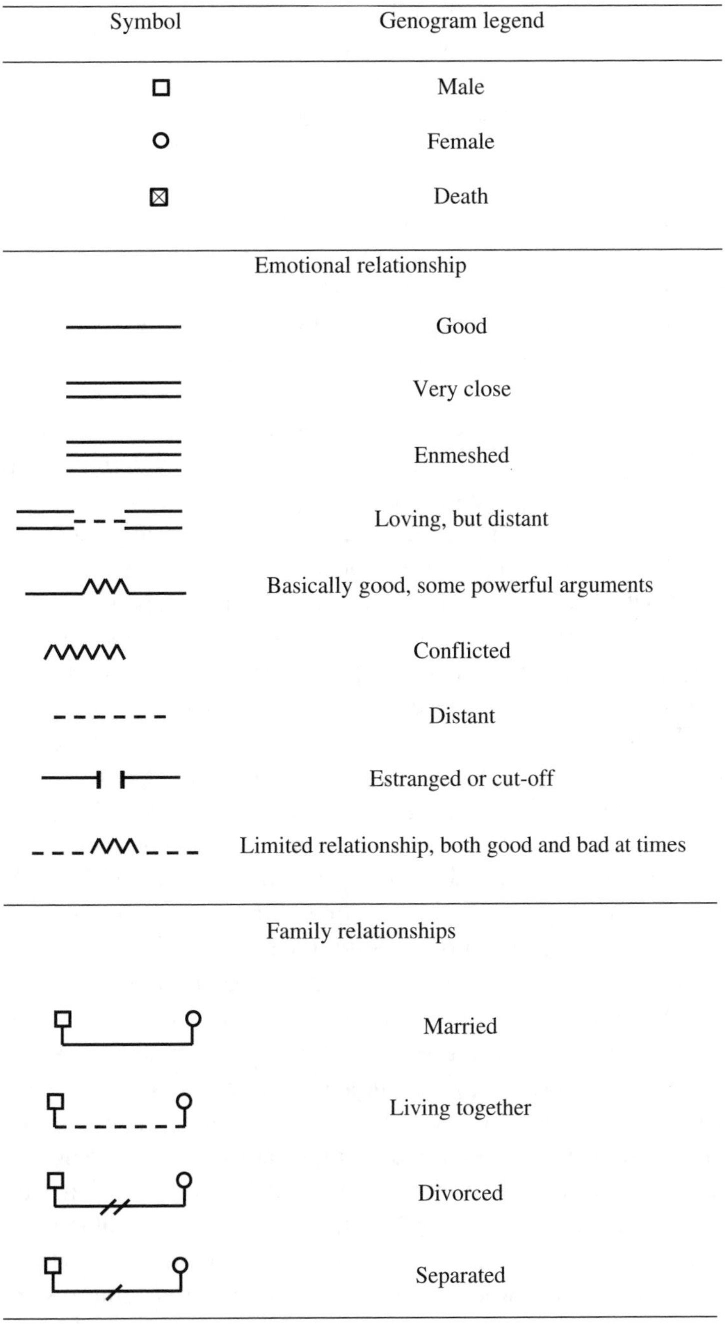

Symbol	Genogram legend
□	Male
○	Female
⊠	Death

	Emotional relationship
———————	Good
═══════	Very close
≡≡≡≡≡≡	Enmeshed
══- - -══	Loving, but distant
___∿∿___	Basically good, some powerful arguments
∿∿∿∿	Conflicted
- - - - - -	Distant
—⊣ ⊢—	Estranged or cut-off
_ _ _∿∿_ _ _	Limited relationship, both good and bad at times

	Family relationships
□_____○	Married
□_ _ _ _ _○	Living together
□___//___○	Divorced
□___/___○	Separated

Figure 3.1. Genogram legend.

track of the complexity of families, and certainly stepfamilies; it is also a map of projected treatment goals and potential subsystems to be seen in treatment. The clinician can see where two stepfamily members are cut off and potentially make clinical efforts to alter that relationship. Thus, a clinician can use a genogram as a visual method of planning treatment directions and possible interventions.

The genogram will continue to be expanded once treatment has begun in order to clarify the order in which different subsystems should be seen. In other words, the clinician will use the genogram in the decision-making process to determine the order of separate subsystems meetings. Although a complete three-generational genogram is ideal, at a minimum, the therapist should draw a genogram to highlight those directly involved with all members of the primary stepfamily.

The symbols described in the legend in Figure 3.1 are drawn between all members of the genogram. There may be some people for whom no relationship exists. For example, a stepfather may have no relationship whatsoever with his stepchildren's paternal grandparent. However, for most of the people listed on a genogram, some relationship does exist, and the therapist should gather enough data to complete the genogram with the symbols to have a clear picture of the interpersonal dynamics throughout the stepfamily. This process serves the purpose of giving the therapist a rationale for inviting in particular members of the stepfamily or overarching binuclear family.

There is no automatic second subsystem to see following this approach. The therapist is looking for the subsystem that seems most secure, one in which the interpersonal symbols suggest little disagreements and arguments. It may seem to be a waste of time to see those subsystems that appear, at least in the genogram, as most secure, but in fact, it can be very useful for the entire stepfamily. Again, the therapist's intention is to bolster stepfamily functioning one subsystem at a time so that the most conflicted subsystems do not weaken those subsystems that are continuing to maintain overall stability.

The clinical interview then moves into fact-finding, with an emphasis on the genogram and each person's perception of what is concerning him or her about the stepfamily. The couple will often describe a particular behavior of a child. The view of this child will often be quite distinct from one person to the other. It will be enormously important for the therapist to assess each person's empathic capacity while gathering information. Without the ability to see clearly the view held by the other, it is extremely difficult, especially in a stepfamily, to believe that one's own view is appreciated. This miscommunication insidiously weakens the foundation of the remarried couple. The therapist must listen closely to each member of the couple describe examples of interactions that each has had with the child or children living at home. The therapist is carefully determining if the stepparent thinks about the child's well-being as well as a desired change in behavior. If there is evidence of some true concern being felt by the stepparent toward the stepchild, the clinical task is easier than if no apparent concern exists.

If real caring exists between the stepparent and stepchild but is hidden by the strain in their relationship, the task at hand moves more toward stabilizing the remarried couple. Although this tactic may sound as if SfT is advocating avoiding the stepparent–stepchild relationship, that is not the case. The therapist will return to the more troubled subsystem after stabilizing other subsystems in the stepfamily.

The therapist avoids offering any teaching about stepfamilies early in the session except when the client poses questions that have a clear answer. The therapist is, however, alert for those experiences in the stepfamily that generate baseline concepts that match particular research findings.

As with couples therapy, or marital therapy in general (Gurman, 1991), the commitment made by the therapist is to remain as neutral as possible to discern the systemic pattern between the members of the couple. Neutrality, as intended in this context, has little to do with a therapist clearing his or her thoughts of likes, attractions, respect, and perceived correctness. Rather, neutrality is based on a commitment the therapist makes to hold natural feelings and biases in check by accepting, absolutely for the time being, the systemic nature of the couple. The therapist must begin by believing that each member of the couple acts, in large part, because of the actions of the other. This recommendation may sound naïve, but it is precisely that kind of openness that encourages the couple to feel an authentic bond with the therapist. There is little question that in time the individual psychological histories of both members will usually be examined to continue to understand their reactions to each other and other stepfamily members, but those details follow a comprehensive systemic understanding of the couple.

If the initial session left the couple feeling that the therapist is concerned and knowledgeable about stepfamilies, the couple will look to the therapist to clarify how treatment will continue. The SfT therapist must be able to quickly conceptualize, with reasonable accuracy, the clinical benefits of inviting in various subsystems to treatment. The selection of those invited to one of the following sessions is intended to both continue to assist the therapist in understanding the concerns and beliefs of everyone in the stepfamily and to strengthen the stepfamily, one subsystem at a time. The therapist lays out a small menu of possibilities of who might be invited to the next session and what clinical agenda would be the focus of each of these subsystems. It is important for the therapist to speculate with the clients about the potential advantages of various subsystems to avoid a likely blowup and to increase the partnership between the stepfamily and the therapist.

In determining the unique concerns of a stepfamily, the therapist looks explicitly for each member of the couple to clearly discuss the aspect of life that is difficult. Rather than attempt to comfort either member of the couple early on, the goal is to get a better idea of what each sees as happening and how each reacts to the other family members. In addition to the specific interactions that are reported, the therapist is also assessing how each client experiences the concern he or she reports. Does the concern seem to come from a misinterpretation, a deep hurt, or an openly fought disagreement?

After basic introductions, the therapist should ask if the couple understands why they were requested to come into treatment without the children. If questions remain, the explanation should be clear and brief. The therapist assures the couple that the emphasis on seeing them first is not due to a belief that a marital problem exists. Rather, it is because the couple represents the subsystem most likely to motivate the stepfamily to benefit from the SfT process. In that way, the couple subsystem might be seen as the "first among equals."

Step 3

Clarify the distinct subsystems in the stepfamily, and use this to provide a direction for clinical treatment.

To stem feelings of incipient chaos, often the remarried couple will mistakenly try to get the whole stepfamily to bond by spending more time together. The couple hopes that a feeling of connection will replace the current sense of confusion and frustration. The truth is that what results is quite the opposite. The stepfamily is a sum of the subsystems, and the pull to assure stability by trying to form a more cohesive whole as a first step is destined to produce only greater instability. In SfT, the therapist concentrates on reinforcing all subsystems that constitute the stepfamily. It is when the subsystems can withstand some additional pressure that the work toward integrating the stepfamily as a whole begins.

Unfortunately, many stepfamilies attempt to integrate and become a complete new family too quickly. The drive behind this effort is simple to understand: Both the parent and stepparent would like to affirm the cohesion of the stepfamily for everyone's sake. Living as a collection of subsystems is unfamiliar to those who have previously lived in either a first-union family or a divorced home. But until the natural process of building a relationship with new people and stabilizing all subsystems occurs, the stepfamily cannot be an integrated whole. Trying to force integration often only ends up pushing people apart (Bray & Kelly, 1998).

A parent and child will almost always be closer than a child and stepparent, certainly for the first 10 years of their relationship. Often, however, the parent, stepparent, or both greatly desire that members of this new stepfamily spend time together to get to know each other and grow in fondness toward each other. Interestingly, when a child reacts negatively to the pressure to be close to a stepparent, the reaction is perceived as a rejection of the stepparent (which it may be). However, the reaction is also commonly due to the child's fear that his or her connection to the biological parent will be jeopardized (Papernow, 1993). The great irony is that the parent is frequently frustrated by the child's anger at the stepparent and does not see his or her own role in the tension. As pressure continues to build between the stepparent and the child, the biological parent is caught in the middle, often feeling unable to offer any solution to the growing disharmony. According to SfT, stabilizing the different subsystems will alleviate tension so that the impasse can be broken.

There are times when parent and stepparent agree that they both would like a child or the children to meet the therapist alone. Often, this request is made because both partners feel that a child may have a diagnosable disorder, and they want a professional opinion. Or the couple may feel that the children are reacting strongly to the new stepfamily or the effect of divorce, and they would like the therapist to help the children with that problem.

If the therapist hears examples of the child's statements or behaviors that are cause for worry about the child's psychological welfare, then such a session will usually involve that child. The question that the therapist raises is, "Should there be others in the session with the child?" In SfT, the answer to that question is usually yes. It is likely that the therapist will spend some part of the next session with the child alone; however, the potential array of adults who could also be involved should be considered. The most common arrangement is for the custodial parent to bring in the child, be available in the beginning, and then spend some part of that session in the waiting room. However, if the stepparent believes that such a situation will simply provide a forum for the stepparent to be "bashed," the therapist needs to respond. The initial response may be to invite the stepparent to that session, but such a move may not be useful to treatment. The therapist does not want to force the custodial parent to either join the bashing or appear insensitive to the child's feelings.

Therefore, the therapist can clarify with the couple that the session with the child is, in essence, a diagnostic interview. The custodial parent will be involved only so far as to share observations and assist in the assessment. If the topic does segue into stepparent bashing, the parent will be excused so as not to be inducted into that conversation in front of the therapist. What the parent does in his or her own home regarding a child's anger at a stepparent is separate from what a therapist, even unintentionally, sanctions.

In understanding treatment as involving subsystems, one must not pollute any subsystem by encouraging a coalition to become strengthened by the weakening of another coalition in the stepfamily. It is the therapist's job to monitor. Clients do not need therapists to overemphasize the negative intent of someone hoping to push others apart. When a child asks a mother to see the negative traits of a stepparent, it usually comes first from a desire to feel closer to the mother and second to be heard. Even on those occasions when the child really does want the parent and stepparent to grow apart, the therapist does not allow that process to gain strength in the therapy. An individual session may be needed to allow the child to vent his or her frustration and be guided to address those feelings, even if those feelings are very negative about the remarriage. The SfT therapist should attempt to understand the exact nature of the disappointment that the child feels about the remarriage but do so without advocating divorce.

The list of potential subsystems is extensive; there are six subsystems that are typically considered when planning ongoing therapy: (a) the remarried couple, (b) the custodial parent and child, (c) the sibling subsystem, (d) the stepparent–stepchild subsystem, (e) the entire stepfamily, and (f) some members of the binuclear family. Although the couple is the most frequent subsystem to be invited into treatment for the initial session, the other five subsystems listed here are suggestions of who might be invited in as therapy progresses. The order presented is the most common sequence, but there can be great variability depending on the case. Some cases may never involve the binuclear family, or there may only be one sibling, so a sibling subsystem is not applicable. However, by examining the six common subsystems, the therapist is pushed to consider the different advantages of seeing various collections of people. Clearly, subsystems can include many people who have not been noted in these six scenarios. For example, it may become appropriate to invite grandparents and other relatives into treatment; however, it is best to start close to home until the requirements of the actual stepfamily are apparent. In addition, each individual needs to be considered a potential subsystem and may need to be seen alone to provide critical information or become more trusting in the direction of therapy.

In keeping with the goal of maintaining openness between the clients and therapist, the question of whom to invite into therapy and when to involve them is one that is usually discussed; any possible variation is worth considering. The question that the therapist must answer is, "What subsystem would most benefit from being seen together?" Secondarily, the ramification of meeting with any subsystem must be assessed as to how the overall stepfamily is affected. It is at this point in treatment that the genogram can be particularly useful.

Step 4

> Consider the research findings that normalize the experience of the stepfamily, and introduce them in clinical practice (when appropriate and meaningful).

By studying the research base, clinicians can increase the likelihood that the stepfamily will be assisted in understanding their reality in light of the experience of many other structurally similar stepfamilies. This is not to suggest that the therapist take a shortcut approach to interviewing a family but rather that the therapist be guided by an educated clarity in selecting those issues that may need to be understood. Each stepfamily member has an area of particular concern and may wonder why miscommunication or injured feelings continue to occur. Therefore, although the role of therapist as an expert has been challenged since the era of social construction (Anderson, Goolishian, & Windermand, 1986; White & Epston, 1990), SfT supports the importance of bringing not only respectful clinical awareness of the particular family dynamic but also a specific research-based understanding of the typical experiences of those living in each form of a stepfamily. For instance, if research strongly suggests that a remarried woman will frequently hold personal expectations of her role as a stepmother that are different from the expectations held by her husband, such information, if applicable, should be shared with the couple. This is not to say that the findings need to be conferred with the label of *truth*, but clients have the right to hear that some issues are more likely to come up than others.

Published research findings are most useful. The accumulation of these well-documented pieces of information helps the members of stepfamilies place themselves on some spectrum of typical functioning. Clinically, this step is referred to as *normalization*, and such an intervention has been strongly supported in the outcome research on stepfamilies in therapy (Pasley, Rhoden, Visher, & Visher, 1996). However, normalization as a clinical intervention has long been misunderstood. Many clinicians move to a normalizing intervention before the couple has the chance to explain why their situation is not a good match with the research finding cited. Such a clinical error often makes the clients feel slighted and therefore casts the therapeutic relationship in doubt. The true purpose of the intervention is not to somehow validate that a particular family is "normal." Rather, the therapist is aiding the stepfamily in understanding the fact that many aspects of stepfamily life have been studied, and commonalities across families have been identified. In other words, social scientists determined measurable descriptors that became the focus of research. The criteria chosen to assess a stepfamily's functioning help a clinician to avoid exhibiting bias in focusing an interview with a stepfamily. For example, explaining how research suggests that discipline is often an area of conflict in stepfamilies (Visher & Visher, 1996) allows the stepfamily experiencing this to see themselves within the broader context of stepfamily life. Consequently, remarried couples are less likely to blame each other. This understanding does not necessarily make the issues around discipline disappear, but it tends to make the problem less personalized and therefore less charged.

Just as Susan Johnson makes terrific use of the research by John Gottman (2001) and his associates in supporting her emotionally focused couples therapy (S. M. Johnson & Greenberg, 1985) by looking for some of the insidious patterns that lessen a couple's chance for success, SfT also uses research findings as support for clinical interventions. Most interventions can be supported in light of a research finding on the issue in question. When referring to research findings, the therapist must be very careful to clarify that the unique stepfamily concerns are being understood and validated. Although normalizing a stepfamily situation is helpful, the potential trap in this intervention is to overreach and thereby exhibit to the couple that the therapist does not yet understand their exact circumstances. Therefore, the purpose of the emphasis on clearly delineating the experience of the particular family in therapy is both to join them and gain their trust and, almost more important, to carefully assess when this stepfamily's experience matches the findings of the research.

Imagine a stepfather who says regarding his stepson, "There is no point trying to reason with him, he just hates me." It may be helpful to respond by discussing a research finding that might comfort or soften the view of the stepfather. If most variables (e.g., ages, culture, family structure) match, the therapist can intervene in such a way that opens the family member to see their situation differently. For example, the therapist might say,

> A study by Coleman, Ganong, and Fine in 2000 investigated stepfathers' perceptions of how well liked they were compared with an actual rating of being liked by their stepsons. This study found that stepfathers believed that their stepsons liked them less than was reported by the stepsons.

Presenting such a finding does not demand that the client change a perception; it does not even recommend it. Instead, it accomplishes two things: It introduces the idea that the stepfather may be reading the moods and the behavior of the stepson incorrectly, and it helps the stepfather to understand that his feelings are shared by other stepfathers, as demonstrated by the relevant research findings.

To avoid the trap of attempting to build a relationship with the couple by citing ways in which their experience is to be expected, clients are better served when a therapist sets a high standard for comparing a stepfamily's situation with those of others cited in the research literature. Even if the description presented by the couple seems to be a good match with a normalizing intervention, it is important to keep such intervention to a minimum in the first session. When the parallel is so close that it appears to be a useful teaching moment, it is advisable always to use qualifying language that encourages the clients to question or clarify the comparison made by the clinician. If a therapist accepts that the use of social science research can be a helpful tool in treating families, particularly stepfamilies, the question becomes not if but how to integrate research into clinical practice. What research will be useful to share with this remarried couple? Most research on stepfamilies in therapy looks at some aspect of stepfamily living which, when applied, reduces confounding extraneous variables.

Step 5

Actively assess and assist in the recognition of empathy when present, and increase the empathic experience between stepfamily members and subsystems.

When the therapist using SfT has gained a clear understanding of what each member of the couple is frustrated by and confirmed that point, the next likely intervention is two pronged: (a) establish if each member of the couple has an empathic understanding of the other's view and (b) put forward the idea that these two people will not view the child in question from the same perspective. If one or both members of this couple cannot summon even a rudimentary empathic understanding of the other's view, an empathy-based intervention will be less effective. This intervention is the nucleus of the early treatment with the couple and therefore must be approached only after some rapport has begun to build. It is likely that this intervention will occur in the first or second session with the remarried couple.

From an SfT perspective, it is this intervention, in particular, that mandates that the therapist see the couple first. It is almost impossible for the biological parent to show an empathic understanding of the spouse's view in front of the child in question. Such an exercise in the presence of the child early in the development of a stepfamily can feel like betrayal. Most parents are very aware of the balancing act they are forced into between the needs of the child and those of the new spouse.

The empathic intervention proceeds in steps. The first step is to determine the thoughts and feelings of each member of the couple with regard to a child in question. The therapist looks for clear evidence that the stepparent appears, at some level, interested in the welfare of the child. The stepparent does not need to be effusive in his or her concern; however, some indication that he or she wants the child to do well in the world is an important foundation. This is necessary to assess if this intervention is to be useful. Both members of the couple must be confident that the other cares for the welfare of the child, even though their approaches may be different. In a later part of the intervention, the therapist will need to clarify and corroborate this distinction. If the therapist hears no statement from the stepparent that can be honestly reframed as a desire for the child's well-being, this intervention is not recommended. If, however, as is most often the case, the stepparent does have an interest in the child's welfare, then the intervention is justified and often quite helpful.

Concern for the child does not need to come strictly from a position of unconditional love. It may be that the stepparent's commitment is primarily to ensure that this stepchild not be living in the home at age 22, but the desire for that child to succeed remains far more important than the current rationale for that stance. Too often, a person's worry is invalidated because the origin of the feeling is considered selfish. Clinically, it is far more important to support the concern and steer the questioning away from challenging its basis. Therapists must be willing to take a stand to support a client who cares about another family member without placing emphasis on the intention or origin of that concern. In other words, when Bill, the stepfather, says that he is, in fact, worried about the grades received by his stepchild, the therapist supports that position rather than endorsing the view stated by Sally, the mother, when she says, "He is just looking for her not to be any trouble at all." Sally will often look to the therapist at this point and say, "But shouldn't he just care about her?" The recommended response is,

> It is rare to have uncomplicated feelings. As a parent, your love for your child dominates your hopes for that child. Bill comes to his feelings having probably examined a number of angles. It is far more important at this time for you to accept that Bill does want Chelsea (Sally's daughter) to do well, rather than to focus on his motivation.

The second step of the empathic intervention is for the therapist to use professional judgment as to which member of the couple would be best able to empathically describe the experience of her or his spouse in relation to the child in question. If, for example, the therapist believes that Sally is more aware of Bill's experience of Chelsea, then Sally will be asked to speak as Bill to say why he is concerned about Chelsea's grades and behavior. The therapist listens closely to Sally's response. Any statements that are not empathic but are instead editorial or a statement of defense by Sally will be gently halted. The therapist coaches each member of the couple one at a time to make short empathic expressions of how the other feels. Once the first empathic response is offered, the therapist gets a simple confirmation from the other or, if the confirmation cannot be given, a correction to the other is allowed to help the original speaker to try again. When an empathic statement has been made and then confirmed by the other as accurate, the roles are switched. Therefore, in the example in which Sally says, "Bill feels that Chelsea could try harder and that she is not held to a very high standard," and Bill agrees that Sally has correctly understood his position, Bill is then asked to describe how Sally experiences Chelsea.

When both members of the couple have expressed the view of the other and have confirmed that view as being accurate or close to correct, the therapist completes the intervention. The therapist then asks each, one at a time, "Do you feel that there is anything your spouse could do or say that would cause you to abandon your perspective and embrace completely the view of the other?" Most often, each states that understanding what the other believes does not alter to any great degree his or her own belief. At this juncture, the therapist asks,

> Then why do you both spend so much energy trying to prove that your own view of Chelsea is the correct perspective? The two of you will never see Chelsea through the same lens. Bill, no matter how long you are her stepfather and no matter how deeply you grow to care about her, you will never have had the experiences of being with her when she was a baby and also seeing her suffer during the divorce. Sally, you see that Bill holds a less sentimental view of Chelsea. I am not judging sentiment as good or bad; it simply exists in established relationships, and Bill and Chelsea's relationship is only in early formation. Therefore, for you to try to picture Chelsea without the fuller contextual picture of the past 12 years is impossible. Neither view of her is the correct perspective. For lack of a better term, you see her through two different lenses.

When this intervention goes well, the tension in the therapy room drops. The couple realizes that they have become embroiled in a debate from which neither will emerge as the victor. The debate has become repetitive and oppressive because of how intractable each person's perspective has become. They are each staking out a position, which forces them to view the identified child in certain ways. This is not the kind of intervention that leads to the couple crying and embracing but instead assists people to see how they can become trapped by holding a narrow and fixed perspective.

Partners will often spend extraordinary energy pointing out evidence that confirms their own view of the child in question and dismissing the view held by the other. It is the job of the therapist to assist the couple in understanding if this process is taking place, to recognize it, and to attempt to empathize with the partner's position. This can, as Milton Erickson suggested, help people to see their situation differently, and once they see it differently, they cannot continue to do what they have been doing (Haley, 1973). Ideally, once one sees the systemic pattern of narrowly focusing on an issue, it opens the way to reaching a détente. Therefore, although this intervention begins by establishing an empathic understanding between the members of the couple, the eventual successful outcome involves reducing the desire to convince the other in an argument that cannot be won.

This first session should have given the therapist the chance to (a) begin an authentic relationship with each member of the couple, (b) determine through interviews with the couple the presence of the stepparent's concern for the stepchild, (c) create an empathic experience that alerts both members of the couple to an interpersonal process that is pulling them apart, and (d) determine the best possible subsystems to see in the next session. If these goals were not yet accomplished, a second session could certainly be used to complete this foundation of continuing treatment. If these tasks are still not completed by the end of the second session, one would speculate that (a) the couple is, in fact, in need of couples therapy for marital, not stepfamily, issues; (b) a different subsystem should be seen to try a different direction; or (c) the therapist has abandoned systemic thinking because the individual issues are too dominant to relegate to a secondary status. The other possibility that exists is that at least one member of the couple is unable to hear the perspective of the other because that one member's attachment bonds are weak and thus shifting away from that person's strongly held position causes him or her to feel unpleasantly vulnerable. In a situation such as this, the therapist could benefit from the work of Greenburg and Goldman (2008) in assisting the vulnerable member of the couple to be aware of the role that these emotions, particularly needs for closeness and validation, are playing in keeping that person in a self-protective mode. Finally, a narcissistic member of the couple will usually simply leave treatment rather than pursue this direction.

Once the couple is stabilized as a result of the empathic understanding of each other's position, the next session might be a great time to bring in a child or children to hear their perspective. Or the therapist could see those members of the stepfamily who are biologically connected if the therapist is concerned that the biological parent is losing a connection with his or her own child. As new concerns arise in therapy, the couple may again lose empathetic understanding of each other. If empathy cannot be restored within the session, it may be necessary to have sessions, or parts of sessions, with just the couple before continuing with the other subsystems.

Step 6

Identify and challenge unhelpful beliefs and specific miscommunication circulating in the family—the role of labels.

The SfT therapist will usually hear the issues clearly because clients come into treatment ready to explain their beliefs to a therapist. At times, the beliefs held by stepfamily members, especially unhelpful beliefs, can be difficult to discern, but nevertheless it is important to do so. Such beliefs can be particularly insidious in the functioning of a stepfamily because they can cause rigid interactions between members over time.

In first-union families, most people are cautious in assigning a negative attribute to a loved one. Certainly, as time goes on, if a family member consistently lets one down, the trust in that person erodes. However, there are many second, third, and fourth chances between members of first-union families. In the stepfamily, the steeper learning curve makes it more difficult for mistakes to be offset by successful or caring efforts. Therefore, it can be easy to slip into a belief that will profoundly affect how a family member acts and interacts with the others.

Because of the relative newness of the stepfamily, there are many ways for an inaccurate and unhelpful belief to take root and close down communication and different avenues to growth. Often an unhelpful belief is not totally inaccurate, but because it is drawn from a limited pool of expressed beliefs, or from stereotypes, it becomes more likely to be embraced.

To examine and understand the role of language and unhelpful beliefs in the stepfamily, one must identify three categories. The first category features those beliefs that have become culturally sanctioned truisms, although often inaccurate; the second category includes misinterpretations within the stepfamily; and the third includes labels and stereotypes.

Culturally Sanctioned Truisms

Culturally sanctioned truisms can be most insidious. An example of this is the assumption that a stepmother, although not expected to replace a child's mother, should love her stepchildren. Clearly, those stepmothers who do love their stepchildren have less criticism leveled at them. However, stepmothers do not always love their stepchildren. Still, a lack of love may not mean a lack of desire to assist in raising this child.

The great difficulty presented by this unhelpful belief is that someone may generate such an opinion with little or no exposure to the stepmother in question. Therefore, the stepmother may be aware that the expectation exists that she feel love for her stepchildren, and certainly many women are quick to place this expectation on themselves, regardless of how unrealistic it is. Feeling love for another is difficult to force. Love is interactional; there must be more positive interactions than negative ones to result in a loving relationship. Although many people may pretend that they feel love for another, when love is absent that absence is generally apparent.

Although the topic of a stepmother's love for her stepchild serves as a vivid example of an unhelpful belief, numerous other beliefs exist that need to be explored. Fathers may be accused of simply "mother shopping"; it may be assumed that children want their parents to reunite; and grandparents may be challenged because of the perception that they don't love all of their grandchildren, step and biological, equally. Unhelpful beliefs are particularly problematic because they affect both sides of an interaction. The child may not, in fact, be hoping his dad reunites with his mom, but if his behavior is interpreted in that manner, his true concerns may never be addressed. When the therapist comes across an unhelpful belief, the clinical response is to highlight it and then use both normalization and clarification.

The clinical thrust that emphasizes normalization will use research and popular literature to establish that although this stereotyped belief may often be accepted, studies do not show such a belief to be predictably present. In cases of stepmaternal love, one would acknowledge that many stepmothers feel guilty for not feeling love for their stepchildren, and many fathers want their children to experience love from the women they live with, regardless of whether it exists. Clarification involves determining with the couple, particularly the husband/father, why he is pressuring someone to feel what they do not feel. At this point a father will either discuss the weaknesses of the biological mother or his sadness at not being able to provide for his children a woman who loves them.

This can bring about a difficult point in treatment because the therapist neither wants to force the stepmother to pretend to love nor disregard the father's heartfelt sadness regarding this perceived deficit. In the interest of keeping the case moving forward, the SfT therapist advocates for what positive feelings can be expressed, supports the father's love for his children, and initiates recognition that the stepmother wants the best for these stepchildren, even if that desire is not based on love. Love comes out of a relationship. To build a relationship, time spent together is invaluable; however, pushing people together does not automatically increase a relational bond; the therapist may actually increase tension by doing this. Some stepmothers enter a stepfamily prepared to love a child, only to find that the child neither wishes for nor will accept love from her. Some stepmothers continue to love against all odds; for others, the child's rejection is simply too painful to ignore. In building the SfT approach, tremendous emphasis has been placed on the systemic factors that affect the stepfamily.

This systemic focus continues to be true even in working to address particular labels and stereotypes, but it would be naïve to suggest that individual dynamics are not ever a factor. Certainly there will be situations in which the individual dynamics of personality foster a proclivity to remain stuck in a pattern that is patently unhealthy. As Papernow (1993) discussed, some people carry a "bruise," which is aggravated by challenges in the new relationship. A stepmother may hold resentment toward the first wife; she may have been abused as a child; she may resent the love showered on the child while she feels slighted by her husband. On occasion, regardless of the best efforts of one's family and the therapeutic profession, some people remain stuck. In these cases, proceeding with couples therapy is necessary to provide comfort and support to the couple subsystem of the stepfamily.

Misinterpretations Within the Stepfamily

The second category of unhelpful beliefs transpires because of misinterpretation or miscommunication. The most frequent examples of misinterpretation are due to overhearing information that is intended to be private; miscommunication occurs because one person does not understand what the other person is saying or someone does not clarify a point when the implication is unclear. Examples of both misinterpretation and miscommunication follow to clarify how one can get trapped and what a SfT therapist can do in response.

In the first example, a stepchild overhears a phone conversation in which his stepmother says that she wishes that "this kid could spend every weekend with his mother." One reason for such a statement could be that the stepmother desires to be free of the child; another possibility might be that the stepmother is concerned that her stepchild feels abandoned by his mother. In most situations the child will overhear this comment and begin to solidify an unhelpful belief that may actually be wrong. Beliefs such as these may take hold very quickly, especially if overheard by a preadolescent or adolescent. One can misinterpret something overheard into a far more negative message than was the intent of the original communication. The result may be that while meeting with the child alone during the second session, the child states angrily, "Why should I care about being cooperative with her? Dad expects me to believe that she cares about me, right? I heard her the other day on the phone saying that I should be at my mom's every weekend." It is important for the therapist to mentally record these statements. Once the therapist has heard such a misinterpretation and the perceived motivation sounds too negative to be accurate, he or she looks for a counterbalancing statement. Is there a time when this stepmother did, in fact, behave kindly? If the adolescent affirms that yes, there was a time, then the therapist has a dichotomy and may intervene to shift the negative perception held by the offended party.

As the therapist begins to wrap up the time spent alone with the adolescent, he or she says, "I would like to make sure that you are OK with what I want to say to your dad." (This example consists of a stepmother family in which the second session was attended by the son and father only.) The therapist then presents a summary, which should emphasize primarily the positive aspects of what was discussed. The therapist then tells the adolescent that he intends to see the father and stepmother (the remarried couple subsystem) alone for the next session. "In that session, I would like your permission to let your stepmother know that you are getting some positive and some very negative messages from her." It is of course important to answer the child's questions. "No, I will not mention anything about your girlfriend," which is followed by, "I need you to believe me that I am just trying to help the two of you figure out what sort of relationship would work better. I do not intend to make you or your stepmother look bad." Surprisingly, most children (especially preadolescents and adolescents) want the therapist to figure out what would make living in the home easier, so they generally grant permission to the therapist to serve as an intermediary.

During the session in which the therapist is with the remarried couple again, and the time is right, the therapist lets the stepmother know that her stepson does appreciate her in some way, such as reporting that he said that he did "recognize that you were very nice the time he lost his keys and he knows that it was a real hassle for you to leave work and pick him up." On hearing this, the stepmother will usually be somewhat pleased and surprised that Tim even remembered that she did something nice for him. Although the therapist does not have to move too quickly, at some later point he or she will want to let the stepmother know that Tim accidentally overheard something that seems to be strongly influencing Tim's view of her. At that time, the overheard statement is repeated tentatively. Although the stepparent's initial response may be anger regarding the invasion of privacy, this is a time when the therapist does not let the topic get derailed. The therapist supports the stepparent but remains focused on clarifying the exact statement and what was actually intended.

In continuing this example, the stepmother says,

> Oh geez, I was talking to my sister and I was joking that Phil (her husband and Tim's father) is unwilling to be sexually alive when Tim is in the house because he gets paranoid about being heard, and I just was saying that I wish we could be alone every weekend. I didn't say that he "should" be at his mom's every weekend; I said that it would be good if he "could" be there.

Because she is a bit embarrassed, the stepmother may begin to become angry about her comment being overheard and misinterpreted. It is important for the therapist to shift the topic by saying, "Regardless of how he heard this, what do we do with this misinterpretation, which is really unhelpful to your relationship?"

In the situation in which the reason for such an error is a misinterpretation, it is still in the client's best interest to consider the possibility that an honest discussion of the misunderstanding can occur. Often the misinterpretation is innocent, and the explanation can be beneficial. Even in a situation such as the one in the example, if the child is at all mature, clarifying the real meaning is certainly preferable to creating an alternate version that invariably has a credibility flaw. Just because a situation is embarrassing does not mean that correcting it should not be considered. There is even some benefit of embarrassment in front of stepfamily members because such a discussion often enriches the process of humanizing everyone. However, if one determines that a direct discussion is out of the question, the therapist must assist the couple in determining how they can begin to correct the effect of the misinterpretation without addressing it directly. To that end it is recommended that the therapist assist the couple in clarifying what perception the child currently holds. For example, the child may feel that "she [the stepmother] doesn't want me around." The goal, therefore, is to begin creating an environment in which holding such a belief defies logic. One way to accomplish that is for the step-mother to actively begin making overtures that clearly suggest that the child's presence is welcomed. Even if the stepmother is disinclined to make this type of overture, the clinician needs to remind the couple subsystem that the child's unhelpful belief is likely influencing almost all interactions.

Phil and Kathy must talk together about how to correct the notion that Tim is unwanted in the home. The onus is not completely on Kathy; this is a family concern, and in keeping with the SfT approach, this point is made clearly.

> Phil and Kathy, this would be a perfect situation in which to throw blame at each other. Phil, you could certainly be annoyed that Kathy chatted with her sister about a topic that is both private and ripe for misinterpretation. And Kathy, you might be upset that Phil has a history that so clearly impacts your life together. However, I am going to ask you to not concen-trate on these issues. My concern is that to go into these issues will be tan-gential and has the possibility of derailing your relationship and possibly your stepfamily. This is the time that we need to figure out how to counter the hurt that probably occurred from the misunderstanding. It will take both of you to accomplish this, and if you choose to cast blame, you're sunk in my opinion.

This message will often result in greater teamwork, and although it may sound manipulative, the therapist does have the responsibility to work to address the greatest pain. Although Phil and Kathy may each have been hurt by the situation at hand, Tim's hurt is potentially the most insidious and damaging in the long run for this stepfamily. Therefore, the clinical intervention, in this case, is intended to assist the suprasystem, that is, the stepfamily, not simply one or another subsystem.

Labels and Stereotypes

The final component of addressing unhelpful beliefs is to be aware of the labels that unfairly lock people into stereotyped roles. The label can be attached to any member of the couple and, either overtly stated or covertly joked about, may have a most undesirable effect. Some common labels in stepfami-lies include *the worrier, the unappreciated provider, the permissive mother*, and *the drill sergeant*. These labels represent a tendency to assign others to a typology. The permissive mother or drill sergeant stepfather reduces the person to a caricature. Once one has found a way to narrow the complexity of the other through the use of labels, it becomes easier to justify the narrowing of one's own repertoire of behaviors. The stepfather views his wife as permissive, thus making his own forceful parenting style more necessary. This pattern becomes increasingly fixed in many stepfamilies.

Quick labeling of a stepfamily member weakens the likelihood of building a relationship. When someone becomes special in one's life, it feels important to understand that person's motivation and intent. In the absence of really knowing a new partner, the assignment of a label may occur spontaneously and can be difficult to shift without overwhelming evidence that it is inaccurate.

For example, in a stepfather family, the stepfather and husband may make the first impression on his spouse as a "nice and reasonable guy," only to have the label of *power-mad disciplinarian* assigned after a few months. The mother and wife in this stepfamily may have represented "an attractive woman and competent single mom." This perception becomes overshadowed by the assignment of a label such as *overly permissive mother*. Although the husband may still see his spouse as attractive, and she still believes that he can be nice, the new labels dominate in reference to how the couple views each other interacting with the children. As the therapist begins to further clarify the reason why each member of the couple has assigned a dominant style or typology to the other, clinical probes are useful in determining how intractable this label is.

Assessing why the couple has begun to label each other helps to determine if they are able and willing to see the other person as complex and not definable by a single dimension. First-married couples also have the same capacity to relegate their spouses to a single label, but such a tendency, if it occurs, is ordinarily not specifically attached to the person's parenting style; rather, it is a general assessment of the other formed over a long period. In terms of remarried couples, the usually rapid assignment of labels causes them to wonder, "Is this the same person I dated?" The job of the therapist is to assist each person, starting with the couple, to widen the lens each individual is using to view and judge the other.

Step 7

Support the naturally connected subsystem (parent and child), and confirm that parent and child are capable of expressing mutual concern.

The subsystems that have received the least attention in the clinical literature have been those that preceded the remarriage. Therefore, any parent–child relationship or sibling relationship will fall into this category. Although these original subsystems are usually formed through biological connections, long-term adoptions are also included in this category.

The original subsystem that usually needs some attention is the parent–child relationship. Even when it appears that this subsystem exists with little distress, the dynamics that place the parent between the child and the new spouse force many parents to pull away from the child simply to reduce the pressure of being stuck between two people whom the parent loves.

As a result of the higher level of distress usually evident in other subsystems throughout the stepfamily, the original subsystems are frequently overlooked because they are perceived as permanent and, therefore, more stable. Although they may, in fact, be more stable, they are not necessarily functioning well. Because they are identified less often as a subsystem in jeopardy, the members of these subsystems are generally seen either in individual sessions or with the whole family.

In fact, some therapists purposefully avoid inviting the original subsystem into a session because the stepparent feels nervous that any session that does not include him or her will devolve into a gripe session about that stepparent. It is not unusual for the stepparent to state, "All they are going to do is talk about me, and I am uncomfortable with that." It is the job of the therapist to be explicit in stating that any session with an original subsystem will focus on the relationship of those present in the room and not on the stepparent.

It is often useful to meet with the child prior to the parent–child meeting to determine if the child feels that he or she no longer has as close a relationship with the parent as the child desires. The knowledge that the child feels somewhat distant from his or her parent allows the therapist to clearly state that the parent–child relationship needs attention, thereby reinforcing that the purpose of the upcoming session is to work on supporting that relationship and not to interfere with other relationships in the stepfamily.

The parent is often surprised to hear that the child feels more distant since the remarriage. Again, this distance is better understood as the systemic result of adding a new romantic partner and the accompanying dynamics that follow such a change in the family; this distance should not be blamed on the stepparent. Not all parent–child dyads have the resilience to acclimate to the stepfamily without some fear that the distribution of love has somehow shifted. When brought together, the parent–child subsystem needs to clarify how the two are accommodating to the new family. How have the changes affected their ability to be together? How often do they have one-on-one time? It is critical that these questions do not open the conversation to complaints that the stepparent is siphoning off time; rather, the purpose of these questions is to clarify ways in which any unwanted distance can be corrected.

Certainly there will be occasions when the stepparent is fearful that he or she will be the focus, presumably negative, of an original subsystem meeting. Therefore, the therapist does need to be prepared to see the couple following such a meeting to reaffirm to the stepparent that the couple's relationship is still important. The married couple, of course, needs attention and time, but a weakening of the parent–child relationship can have an insidious effect on the stability of the entire stepfamily.

Step 8

Teach the family about its own systemic functioning.

Teaching people about systemic function does not relieve each person of responsibility for individual actions; rather, it elucidates for them how individuals affect and are affected by the system (or stepfamily). Although it has been made clear that the SfT therapist is not using a buckshot approach in teaching stepfamilies how their dynamics match with others in similar situations, the unexpected emotions that have been described previously are an extremely common occurrence, and explaining this is a safe and worthwhile intervention.

The therapist assists the couple in understanding the changes that increased commitment between them brings. Although this increased clarity about the shifts in the relationship may not lessen each person's frustration with the growing pains of the developing stepfamily, it does tend to help the couple see that the circumstances are more powerful than any one person. As one begins to see that his or her own willpower cannot, in and of itself, force the personal dynamics of each member of the stepfamily in a particular direction, the seeds of true systemic understanding are sown.

The therapist notes the patterns of behaviors that surround disagreements in the home. For example, although it may be reported that the arguments between the stepfather and stepson at the dining room table are a major family problem, the therapist examines the adjunctive behaviors that may appear only marginally related. Therefore, the therapist notes the mother's passive reluctance to notice her husband's growing frustration, the stepfather's comment to his wife that "he runs right over you," and stepson's eye-rolling while looking at his mother. The therapist brings these patterns out, but does so to highlight the patterns, not to accuse people of being "the problem."

These interventions to increase systemic understanding usually involve a specific description of the stepfamily's actions and how these actions can be understood as interrelated. In other words, the SfT therapist might say,

> Although Mom sees the logic in both her husband's comments as well as the comments of her son, she is unable to make either person feel supported because of her precarious position balanced between these two people, both of whom she deeply cares about and who want her loyalty.

The importance of interventions that highlight the systemic functions of a stepfamily is that frequently such an intervention propels each individual to expand his or her understanding of the situation beyond a personal perspective. Once behaviors are interlocked, the notion that one stepfamily member is guilty and the other is innocent becomes increasingly rare.

Step 9

Assist in coparental work between any and all involved parental figures, including the binuclear family.

Step 9 builds on some of the steps that have come earlier. It recognizes that the stepfamily is affected and influenced by extended family members, and it relies on an understanding of systems thinking to enable clinicians to help stepfamily members avoid negative coalitions and feuds. Although the issues of coparenting between those who were originally partnered will be the primary emphasis of this step, the inclusion of grandparents (including stepgrandparents) and other extended family members will also be considered.

Although many clinical issues that are presented by a stepfamily can be addressed without involving anyone from outside that immediate stepfamily, it is certainly important to expand one's vision as a clinician to include other family members in the resolution of a problem. The SfT therapist seeks out an opportunity to engage the binuclear family, especially when a lack of clear communication between the homes results in unnecessary agitation.

One concern frequently expressed by therapists considering whether to work with the binuclear family is anger, including anger demonstrated in the session. Therapists often fear that putting together adults who do not like each other will result in angry scenes that will be disturbing to the children. It is necessary for the therapist to respect the possibility but continue to advocate that a conjoint meeting is appropriate. Certainly, if there is reason to believe that a binuclear session needs to be only with adults because of a concern whether the adults can even speak in front of each other with civility, such a decision can be made. However, it is important to remember that children are privy to a great deal of disagreement and that seeing their parents able to converse, even with the occasional exchange of harsh words, is comforting (Ahrons, 2004).

The therapist must be in charge of the process. This means that he or she is responsible for not permitting the session to turn into a screaming match about some perceived injustice from years before. This responsibility is one that makes many therapists nervous about doing this type of work. However, it should be understood that in general, the adults are concerned about the needs of a child. Setting a clear agenda that addresses current issues will usually keep the specter of past hurts out of these meetings. The focus needs to be on understanding how this current family, albeit a loosely connected binuclear family, serves to continue certain problems in both homes.

The following example is a stepfamily that needs, in our opinion, both SfT and binuclear family perspectives to best treat them. The Wright family came into treatment looking to improve the relationship between the step-mother and her stepson. Although the first few months of treatment emphasized only their stepfamily unit (with the majority of session involving only the remarried couple), it became clear that the other parent (the resident mother) needed to be invited in order to reduce the miscommunication that was starting to negatively affect each home. Jennifer Smith, the first wife of Mr. Wright, felt concerned, on the basis of the boy's occasional comments, that her son might be being mistreated in the Wright home. However, by inviting Jennifer in to meet with her former husband and his current wife, it became clear that many of the son's stories were fabricated, and a pact between the three adults kept communication and binuclear living much more straightforward.

Miscommunication is not necessarily due to one person's trying to deceive the other; miscommunication can grow out of very basic mistakes. Therefore, it is important for the members of the binuclear family to understand that the therapy is not attempting to find a culprit but rather to determine mistakes in communication and ease the tension in both homes. In some cases, these meetings are the first chance for the nonconnected adults to understand each other's perspective.

Although it is not common for the primary issue to revolve around step-grandparents, they can be a major factor in creating a problem and resolving some concerns. Because the topic of stepgrandparents is the central focus of Chapter 7 of this book, we do not go into great detail on the topic here. However, in Step 9, the therapist considers whether inviting in a grandparent as part of a subsystem helps to address some impasse in which this person might be involved.

The SfT therapist needs to work diligently to remain balanced. Although there are rare occasions when the therapist will need to shift his or her support to one course of action, such an occurrence is generally unhelpful. For example, although a clinician may need to support a father's relationship with children from an earlier relationship, it is important to support the current couple to counterbalance treatment. Remaining largely balanced in treatment is not simply a technique but rather a way of thinking. As the clinician works with this larger binuclear family, he or she needs to remain aligned with the stepfamily, whose members are the primary client, but also to be aware of the larger system. To ignore any aspect of a family, in this case a binuclear family, may be shortsighted and lead the clinician to intervene in a manner that only offers limited help.

Step 10

> Increase communication among all stepfamily members available, and move toward integrating the various subsystem into a functioning and satisfied stepfamily.

The final step in SfT is the integration of the now more stable subsystems into a more coherent and satisfied whole stepfamily. It is best to set a dyadic meeting between a stepchild and his or her stepparent when some of the tension in the stepfamily has been reduced. A meeting between a stepparent and any and all stepchildren is often helpful just prior to the entire stepfamily session or sessions. These sessions are best used to establish a positive sense of the relationship. There is no point pushing the intensity of this session past the natural level of the relationship. Therefore, these sessions are largely dedicated to increasing the empathy for each other. In these sessions, the SfT therapist is very active in articulating some of the issues that are pressing between stepparent and stepchildren. It is not that the therapist is creating a false relationship but rather that the therapist is working to keep the flow between these people going so that they do not digress into disagreements. Certainly, if the people are unable to keep a session civil, even with the therapist working to keep it so, then the argument is clarified so that each member can follow standard rules of letting the other state his or her point to avoid choosing a winner.

Sometimes the stepparent–stepchild subsystem is not invited in together for a session. However, in most cases such a session is well worth the effort and is frequently perceived by those involved as useful, if not necessarily enjoyable.

At this stage of the stepfamily treatment, the therapist is first and foremost going to determine if any subsystem that has begun to make progress when being treated as a separate entity is unable to function well in the context of the entire stepfamily. In other words, is there a subsystem (e.g., stepparent and stepchild) that when seen together alone appeared stable but when thrust into the full stepfamily is destabilized by pressures and stressors? When this occurs, it is best to assess the distinct issues that emerge when the stepfamily is together. The reasons for this systemic push back may be as diverse as fear of abandonment misguided protection, or jealousy. It is the clinician's job to determine the source of the stress that exists only when the stepfamily is together and bring it into the awareness of the members. In so doing, the clinician is overtly informing the stepfamily that a relationship is suffering as a result of systemic pressures rather than from a unresolved issue between one particular dyad or subsystem.

For example, the Roberts stepfamily offers a perfect case in point (see Figures 3.2 and 3.3). This stepfamily was formed after the death of a spouse. The

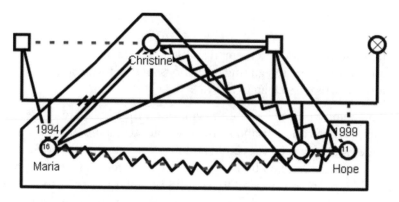

Figure 3.2. Relationships in Christine's presence.

genograms in Figures 3.2 and 3.3 show the stepfamily after 3 months of success-ful treatment. The two genograms are identical except for the relationship between Maria and Hope. The first genogram (Figure 3.2) explicates their relationship when they are interacting with the entire stepfamily; the second genogram (Figure 3.3) shows an increased level of tension between the two young women when interacting with only each other.

The conflict between Maria and Hope is only in evidence when they are with Christine. Hope keeps a distance from Christine, and Maria feels hurt on her mother's behalf; this hurt is contextually internalized by Maria. There-fore, when Maria is in the presence of both her mother, Christine, and her stepsister, Hope, she and Hope often fight. When Maria and Hope are with each other and no one else, they rarely fight. In a sense, the difficulty between the stepsisters has little to do with their one-to-one relationship but rather is directly related to Maria's defending her mother, even though Christine would not wish to have Maria sacrifice her relationship with Hope in this

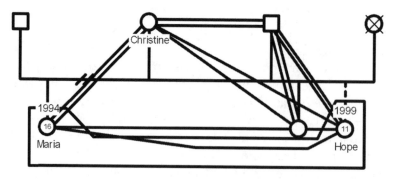

Figure 3.3. Relationships when Christine is not present.

way. In fact, Christine is totally unaware that Hope and Maria are more cordial at times.

One method of clinically addressing this larger system problem is to see Christine alone to determine if she does, in fact, accept Hope as distant but not overtly hostile. If this is the case, Christine really does not want Maria to be proving her love by rejecting Hope. The clinician brings in Maria with Christine; it may begin as a single session in which Maria is asked to wait until the clinician has had time to speak to Christine first. Christine needs to express gratitude to Maria for her support but also make clear that such support is coming at the cost of stepfamily cohesion. For Maria to comfortably interact with Hope in Christine's presence, Maria must be convinced that she will not weaken her bonds with her mother if she is nice to Hope. Following such an intervention, Maria and Hope may still experience some tension, but the emotional volatility will usually be lessened.

When there are no longer any subsystems that are "set off" by being with the entire stepfamily, an integrated session is recommended. Having entire families in therapy has always been important because having everyone in the room permits the therapist the clearest picture of those issues or relationships that seemed most conflict centered. In SfT, this view of the stepfamily was avoided early in treatment because of the stepfamily's vulnerability, but now resilience has increased as a result of the strengthening of selected subsystems.

In the integration sessions, the primary task is to proceed as one would with any family. The strengthening of the different subsystems now permits the therapist to use those family therapy interventions that are more commonly applied to first-union families. In this chapter, we have presented an approach for treatment of stepfamilies. Although the work with these families will always be somewhat different from that with first-union families, the unique needs of stepfamilies must be the focus of early treatment for them to feel understood and supported.

4

THE SIMPLE STEPFATHER FAMILY

In this chapter, we apply the stepfamily therapy (SfT) model to the Joneses, a prototypical stepfather family, which is the most common stepfamily configuration. We describe how the clinician moves through each of the 10 steps of SfT, demonstrating both in text and with the use of a genogram the family dynamics, concerns, and progress.

INTAKE INFORMATION

Stepfather: Tyrone (38)
Biological mother: Lashanda (40)
Lashanda's children: Leon (14) and Helen (12)
Biological father: Melvin (40)
Jobs: Lashanda is an office manager. Tyrone is a teacher. Melvin is an auto mechanic.
Race, religion: African American, Protestant

Lashanda makes the call. She reports that the family is in crisis. Leon will not do anything Tyrone says, and lately he has been shouting at her as well, although before they had a "really good relationship." Helen used to be lively and outgoing with a lot of friends; now she just goes to her room after school and stays in it. She comes down for meals and attends school, but her grades have fallen over the duration of the marriage. Tyrone complains that the "kids won't do anything around the house." Melvin is having trouble making the support payments, and Tyrone is complaining about the money situation in general. Lashanda thought the money situation would get easier and less complicated. Melvin does not see the kids regularly, but when he does, the kids tell Lashanda that he "badmouths" Lashanda and Tyrone. Lashanda is feeling caught in the middle and ready to "lose her mind, trying to please everybody and keep the lid on." She worries about Helen.

Tyrone and Lashanda knew each other for many years but became closer after the initial separation. Melvin suspected an affair, which had not occurred. When the divorce became final, Lashanda and Tyrone became intimate. They have been married for 5 months. Lashanda described her marriage with Melvin as "dead"; the couple had nothing to talk about and that situation had gone on for years. She says that the kids at first seemed to like Tyrone. He takes more of an interest in sharing activities and helping with schoolwork, but she admits that Melvin had been a steadfast and loyal father, if not that interested in disciplining or spending time alone with the kids, and he was always tired when he came home from work. The family is living in a different house since the marriage, which has resulted in a change in the school district.

The three sets of grandparents all have a different relationship with the new stepfamily. Lashanda's family lives in another state but stays in touch and is very supportive. Tyrone's parents live close by, are very excited about having grandchildren, and use every opportunity to get together. The children respond favorably to them. Melvin's parents also live in the area but remain somewhat distanced from the children since the divorce. Leon in particular was close to Melvin's father. As Lashanda speaks, the clinician generates an interactive genogram (see Figure 4.1) to visually depict family structure and dynamics. The therapist invites Lashanda and Tyrone for the initial session.

APPLYING THE 10 STEPS OF STEPFAMILY THERAPY

In the sections that follow, the clinician applies each of the 10 steps of SfT to the Jones family.

Step 1

Recognize the structure of the stepfamily (e.g., simple stepfather family, simple stepmother family, complex stepfamily in which both adults are stepparents). Use the initial telephone intake to look for systemic similarities within the context of the research literature.

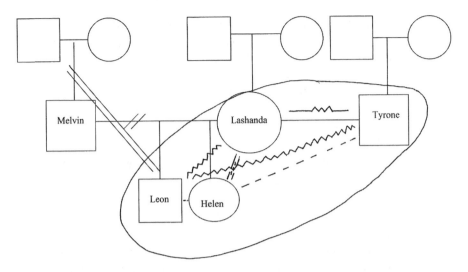

Figure 4.1. The Jones family.

The family presenting for therapy is a simple stepfather family, the most prevalent configuration of all stepfamilies, because in 85%–90% of all divorces in which children are involved, mothers are awarded primary custody (Stamps, 2002).

The clinician must be aware of the commonalities of the particular structure while discerning the unique concerns that bring the Jones family to treatment. The family is in the immersion stage (Papernow, 1993), one of the early stages when reality finally arrives. It is important that the clinician understand that the emerging conflict may be due to the stepparent voicing his or her concerns after a period of remaining relatively silent for the sake of family harmony.

The questions and critical issues listed in the paragraphs that follow are generated by objectively reviewing the initial information supplied by the family against a backdrop of research literature and prominent scholarly work on stepfamilies. From the telephone intake, the therapist hears the following complaints.

1. Leon will not do anything Tyrone says. Tyrone complains that the kids will not do anything around the house. Often in stepfamilies, there is an expectation on the part of the stepparent that this is an instant family, one in which there is an opportunity to belong, a role to occupy, and a particular function to perform (Visher & Visher, 1979). Tyrone may be attempting to rush into a position of disciplinarian before building a relationship

with the kids, which is a very common problem in stepfather families. In the stepfamily literature, continuing contention between the stepparent and the children can lead to problematic interactions between the biological parent and the children, which in turn leads to marital discord (Booth & Edwards, 1992). As an adolescent, Leon strives for separation and autonomy just when the stepfamily is attempting to draw together into a viable family unit. Loyalty issues are confounding factors in stepfamilies. Leon may be indirectly supporting and showing loyalty to Melvin by going "on strike" in the family home, particularly when Tyrone directs him to do something.

2. Melvin is having trouble making the support payments and does not see the kids regularly. In research studies, it has been found that most noncustodial fathers withdraw from regular visitation over time (Hetherington & Jodl, 1994; Seltzer, 1991); one of the reasons for this may be difficulty maintaining the support payment schedule (R. A. Thompson & Laible, 1999). There is evidence in stepfamily literature that children fare better when both parents are involved in a congenial coparenting relationship (Buchanan, Macaby, and Dornbusch, 1991).

3. Melvin badmouths Lashanda and Tyrone. One of the greatest obstacles to the positive adjustment of children of divorce, according to the research (Buchanan et al., 1991), is continuing conflict between the biological parents. For the benefit of the children, therapists should intervene to help the parents learn to control the expression of any residual anger they feel toward their ex-spouse, especially in front of the children.

4. Lashanda is feeling caught in the middle trying to please everybody. She is the most central member of the stepfather family, having biological connections to her two children and marital and postmarital connections to her spouses. The clinician knows that this is a common complaint of biological moms in stepfather families. Also, studies have shown that in the early months of remarriage, conflict and lower parental control characterize the relationship between mothers and their children (Bray & Berger, 1993; Hetherington & Jodl, 1994). Lashanda may have retreated from her usual more proactive parental stance as Tyrone asserted himself into his new role as stepfather.

With an informed overview of the research literature, the clinician can begin to listen for the common difficulties that many stepfamilies experience and move to normalize the family's experience as a function of stepfamily structure (Step 4). Lashanda and Tyrone may be relieved to find that the challenges that define their reality are shared by many new stepfamilies struggling to become a viable family unit.

Step 2

> Determine the membership of the first session—usually the marital dyad—and determine the unique concerns of the stepfamily.

When the clinician considers the membership of the first session, he or she can surmise that an initial session that included the whole stepfamily unit would not proceed smoothly (see Chapter 1, this volume). The level of conflict is already very high between the parental subsystem and Leon, who is actually shouting at both Tyrone and Lashanda at home. Within a clinical session, adolescent self-consciousness and embarrassment might intensify an already volatile situation and drive him right out of the room. The clinician needs to hear Lashanda's and Tyrone's disparate views of the issues, which are the children's responsibilities and the financial situation, to understand where the family is getting stuck, without worrying about Leon's reactions. More important, the therapist needs to begin to work with the couple to strengthen their relationship because of the lack of a shared history with the children from the beginning. The marital dyad routinely undergoes incalculable stressors and becomes destabilized. As reported by Visher and Visher (1996), "When they were asked what was the single most important factor in bringing stability to the family, adult respondents to the therapy research study overwhelmingly responded that it was improved bonding between the couple" (p. 10).

The therapist will cautiously interview each member of the marital dyad, listening for and highlighting common problem areas while using a format designed to reduce tension. Murray Bowen's model for interviewing couples, that is, one at a time with the other present, can be useful to ensure that each partner can hear the other's feelings from a nondefensive stance and to control the level of conflict during the interview process (M. E. Kerr & Bowen, 1988). The therapist will advise each partner to listen to the other with an earnest desire to understand (Weeks & Treat, 1992).

In the questioning process, the therapist listens with a focus on the implicit and salient points and clarifies the client position as he or she speaks so that the partners will comprehend each other's feelings. To demonstrate the therapist's processes, both internal and external, two narratives are presented.

> *Therapist:* I am going to speak with each one of you in turn about your concerns about the family. I want each of you to listen to what the other says so that you can hear the other's point of view and imagine how it feels. For the moment, I want

you to put aside your concerns and listen to your partner with an open mind and heart. What is your partner's experience? How is your partner feeling? Lashanda, I will begin with you. What is happening in your family that brings you to therapy?

Lashanda: I don't know where to begin. It seems that everything is messed up. Tyrone and I fight all the time—if it is not about money, then it is about Leon being disrespectful and sullen and not doing what he is supposed to. I don't blame Tyrone for getting angry. Leon is very sarcastic sometimes.

Therapist: So what you are saying is that you are fighting with Tyrone over two things, money and Leon.

Lashanda: When I was a single mom, I never had to ask Leon more than once or twice, and it would get done. Now so much time is wasted with arguing.

Therapist: So, Leon was more compliant when it was just the three of you.

Lashanda: Yes. I mean we would have our moments, but it seems like it is every day now. We also had a different system—a different schedule. Leon likes to have afternoon time to go play basketball with his friends, unwind, you know, not get right down to work when he gets home. I would let him go out for a couple of hours and then come in for dinner. Homework would be saved for later.

Therapist: And that seemed to work OK. What is different now?

Lashanda: Yes. Tyrone thinks Leon should come home and do his homework and get it over with before he goes out.

Therapist: [to both of them] Often in the beginning throes of a new stepfamily, it is helpful for the biological parent to assume the primary control of the children; the partner will support the parent when there and be responsible when the parent is gone. Tyrone would become a *parental monitor*. This usually takes the stress off the Tyrone-to-Leon conflict and might level off tension between the two of you, but we can talk more about that later.

Lashanda: Yes, that might help. Also with the three of us, it went fine, because then I would have alone time with Helen. Now I don't even know what's up with her. She retreats to her room. I mean she doesn't want to have anything to do with anybody. I am really worried about her.

Therapist: Now it seems like you have no time with her at all?

Lashanda: Not really—sometimes we go clothes shopping.

Therapist: So, Lashanda, your concerns are the arguing going on between you and Tyrone and between you and Leon as well as concerns about Helen isolating herself in her room and not spending time with friends or family.

Out of Lashanda's disclosures, the therapist is internally delineating the implicit and relevant points associated with stepfamily issues as well as the ancillary, more idiosyncratic concerns of the family and individual members. Against a backdrop of disquieting conflict, which needs to be addressed promptly, the individuals struggle with problems that are common in many stepfamilies. The conflict only serves to exacerbate the situation and can be somewhat mollified almost immediately by structural changes recommended by the therapist.

During the session, the therapist has already mentioned a shift in which Lashanda will become the predominant overseer of the children, and Tyrone will serve as parental monitor. Research findings strongly suggest that for the first 2½ years, the biological parent needs to be the family disciplinarian, with the stepparent serving in the important function of a parental monitor (Bray, 1988) of the children and a support to the spouse. It is a common pitfall for the stepfather to assume the role of disciplinarian prematurely, and this is particularly difficult when the children are preadolescent and adolescent (Bray & Kelly, 1998; Ganong & Coleman, 1994; Visher & Visher, 1988). The implementation of house rules generated by the family and upheld by Lashanda and Tyrone when Lashanda is absent will alleviate tension; these rules have to include that each family member is entitled to respect. Tyrone will be enforcing the house rules as opposed to making premature unilateral disciplinary decisions regarding the actions of Leon and Helen.

Taking into account and reaffirming the importance of the routines of the single-parent family will smooth the transitions for the children into stepfamily life. This was an interlude during which the family of three pulled together to manage the house and had a different routine; the relationship between Lashanda and her children was more collegial, as is the case in single-parent families (Arditti, 1999).

Lashanda has voiced a considerable amount of anxiety in understanding and trying to balance the needs of both Tyrone and Leon; the therapist can view this in a positive way as Lashanda's having a capacity for empathy, an important element for success in stepfamily therapy. By the very nature of being in the middle, Lashanda is between two adversaries and wanting to sustain relationships with each of them. When conflict breaks out, she may become defensive on one or the other's behalf, all the while not wishing to take sides; she is denied the luxury of demonstrating this freely to either

Tyrone or Leon. Each of them may not have a clear idea that she understands or even cares about how they feel.

Money is a stressor in many families. However, when a divorce occurs, there is an immediate conversion from one household to two, which necessitates two mortgages, two utility bills, and more. Melvin can support himself, but sending Lashanda child support each month may be difficult, especially when he manages his finances poorly. In the new step-family, Tyrone may be asked to assume more of the share of the expenses, which may be an explosive issue for him. After all, they are not "his children." This is a fairly concrete issue and needs to be addressed within both the couple subsystem and the biological parent subsystem to reach a satisfactory resolution.

Lashanda is concerned that Helen may be depressed. The clinician may need to have Lashanda take Helen for a psychological evaluation to determine if she is at risk. Although this is not a stepfamily issue per se, the new family configuration often resonates through the entire system, affecting each individual and vice versa. Helen has had multiple losses, her school, her neighborhood, and proximity to her friends. She may also feel that her needs are not as important to her mother, having to share Mom's attention with her new stepfather. Interrupting Helen's isolation and procuring treatment will not only keep her safe but assure Helen of her mother's concern and love.

The therapist then turns to Tyrone.

Therapist: Tyrone, I would like to hear from you about what you see as the problem and concerns for yourself and the family.

Tyrone: I am feeling really frustrated by all of this. I mean, I got along better with the kids and Lashanda before we were married.

Therapist: So you feel things have changed since you married and not necessarily for the better. You sound really upset about all the fighting.

Tyrone: Yes, I am. Everyday someone is in an argument with someone else. Usually it's just Leon and me; sometimes Lashanda joins in. And then there is all this tension.

Therapist: So this happens all the time. Is it usually over the same things?

Tyrone: Well, with Leon, he is just such a bright kid, and his grades are so mediocre. He could do so much better with a little self-discipline. I am a teacher, and I could help him with homework. Sometimes, before Lashanda and I were married, I would help him, and he would be happy and so would I. Now it just seems that I am a nag.

Therapist:	Because you have to continually repeat yourself?
Tyrone:	I just feel like that is the way I sound all the time. I am sure Leon feels that way as well. His expressions certainly say so.
Therapist:	So you hear yourself repeating yourself to Leon?
Tyrone:	And Lashanda.
Therapist:	And in the meantime, you really think highly of Leon and feel that he has potential and could do better with a little help. But it doesn't seem like he wants it, even though you want to give it to him.
Tyrone:	It's not only that. He is supposed to have chores, and Lashanda never enforces them—it seems that this is up to me. He is supposed to be in charge of his own laundry, but he puts a load in, and then when the machine is finished, the wet laundry just sits there. After a couple of days, it starts to smell, and well, you can see what a pain that is, tying up the machine and then the clothes just have to be rewashed anyway. And he always has to be reminded to take the garbage out.
Therapist:	So you feel like you need to make sure that he follows through with his chores.
Tyrone:	Yes. Somebody has to.
Therapist:	And this is when you start sounding like a nag to yourself and perhaps Lashanda and Leon.
Tyrone:	It just gets on my nerves that the situation in the house is so lax. I was living alone before, and I never had to deal with this stuff.
Therapist:	So you feel like it is quite an adjustment.
Tyrone:	Yes, I thought I would make such a contribution to the family on so many levels, and now I just feel like I am a thorn in everyone's side, even Helen's. I really worry that she spends so much time alone; she is really a sweet girl. Sometimes I try to talk to her, but it seems like she just gets annoyed with me.
Therapist:	It sounds like you really like Lashanda's kids and are feeling very frustrated that things are like this.
Tyrone:	. . . and left out. I feel like the three of them have this little club, and they have their inside jokes and little routines—and my relationship with Lashanda [looks at Lashanda]—we have fights or we hardly talk. We don't go out anymore. There is no laughter, just all this tension.

> *Therapist:* So you sound like you hardly recognize your relationship with Lashanda and are wondering what happened. I hear real sadness in your voice.

Common stumbling blocks to stepfamily life are expectations about the way things could or should be. Tyrone sees his role as a stepfather who could enhance the lives of this struggling family; helping Leon to get better grades and to follow through with his chores while maintaining order constitutes his self-defined agenda. Why would it not work? Tyrone doggedly pursues the life he imagined and, in quieter moments, like Lashanda, muses over his former calm and ordered life when things were simpler and wonders what happened.

Tyrone mentions in the session that before he was married the kids accepted him. In a stepfamily, one cannot underestimate the power of the marriage commitment and how that is viewed in preadolescent and adolescent eyes. What may have been a casual relationship has been formalized and becomes more of an impediment to returning to the way it was. Now Mom's boyfriend is a fixture in the house and not going away.

Papernow (1993) discussed the stepparent as an outsider when thrown together with the biological subsystem, which has accumulated middle ground together, described as "shared experience and values" (p.39). Tyrone describes "this little club" that Lashanda, Leon, and Helen have, of which he is not a member. The therapist notes that in terms of stepfamily development, this is an early and common feeling of stepparents.

Both partners are describing a deterioration of their relationship, with Tyrone distressed by the person he appears to have become. As the clinician processes Tyrone's feelings, he or she concludes that some of the interventions for Lashanda's distress can also be applied to and helpful for Tyrone's sense of despair. His concerns substantiate the need to formulate a set of house rules, which Tyrone will reinforce only when Lashanda is absent. Attaining respectful communication is a priority for him as well. As mentioned previously, Lashanda will be advised to assume the role of disciplinarian, but it will be made clear that Tyrone will implement the house rules as parental monitor when Lashanda is not there and be given due respect. Thus, Tyrone will move into a position of mentor and friend and out of the role of policeman and drill sergeant. These interventions are accompanied by validating acknowledgments of his interest and his sincere desire to be of help to the family while explaining that without a relationship, his attempts to control or even influence the children are fruitless.

The couple will benefit by meeting with the therapist for a second session. A therapeutic goal is to help Lashanda and Tyrone communicate from a more realistic, unified, and unrestricted perspective and increase their ability to deal with the challenges that arise before they become more intractable.

The clinician has heard from each member of the marital dyad that there is love, loyalty, and empathy—very positive ingredients in any family. He or she has also been witness to the couple's sadness, anger, and bewilderment, emotions that are predominant in family interaction. Having gathered information from the couple as to their unique reality, the clinician can intervene to provide relief in assuring them that their stepfamily is not alone. The dynamics and processes of stepfamily life often are more influential than the individual self-determination of the family members. Becoming sensitive to that probability establishes an informed awareness with which to better manage the problems that come up in the new stepfamily.

Step 3

Clarify the distinct subsystems in the stepfamily, and use this to provide a direction for clinical treatment.

The stepfamily is going through a period of *disequilibrium* (Hetherington & Clingempeel, 1992, p. 13) or the aforementioned immersion stage in which "the constant clashes between step and biological cultures can be disorienting and irritating" (Papernow, 1993, p. 84). Each subsystem is destabilized and needs to become stable as part of the process of moving toward integration. With the data gleaned from the initial phone interview and further amplified by the meeting with the couple, the clinician can delineate the various subsystems and anticipate the state of the relationships within them.

The identified and distinct subsystems in the family are as follows:

1. The marital dyad: Lashanda and Tyrone. It appears that as the family enters the therapy process, the marital dyad is conflictual and entrenched in patterns of communication that are negative and destructive, from which they see no escape.
2. The biological residential subsystem: Lashanda, Leon, and Helen. The biological unit seems less cohesive because of Leon's anger and Helen's isolating behavior. The closeness they shared with their mother as a single-parent family is interrupted by a sense of betrayal that she has married Tyrone and welcomed him, a seeming intrusion, into the family system. The marriage has also erased their hope of Melvin and Lashanda getting back together someday. This is quite common among children who have experienced divorce. Wallerstein and Kelly (1980) pointed out that the hope that parents will reunite, or *reunion fantasy*, persists well beyond the initial stages of divorce, frequently even after parental remarriage. In fact, 5 years after the divorce, over

half of the children queried would have preferred a return to the original family (Wallerstein & Kelly, 1980).

3. The sibling dyad: Leon and Helen. The sibling dyad appears to be emotionally distant and disconnected, with each individual exhibiting different attitudes and behaviors in response to the new stepfamily. Leon seems actively intolerant of Tyrone's proactive parenting stance and Lashanda's laissez-faire attitude about intervening in the arguments, whereas Helen's abject feelings of loss of her friends, home, and neighborhood seem to have led her to a position of retreat and isolation from the entire family system. Is she clinically depressed? The clinician may want to explore this possibility by using a simple screening tool. On the other hand, she may be using avoidance to set boundaries, regulate communication, or protect her privacy when she is feeling most vulnerable. Whatever the reason, Leon leaves the solitary Helen alone.

4. The parental coalition: Lashanda, Tyrone, and Melvin. The parenting coalition appears discordant as the family begins therapy, as a result of Melvin's bitterness and the conflict between Lashanda and Tyrone. It is reported that Melvin is creating tension and unrest, rather than being a positive support. The children may view him as someone about whom they need to worry. A clinician might consider a separate session with Melvin, whom Lashanda acknowledges historically as a nice guy, albeit an uninvolved husband and parent. To move him from a stance of blaming and anger to a position of strength and support, Melvin needs to understand what is helpful for the children in terms of their adjustment. Tyrone may be angry because of the extra and rather sudden financial responsibility.

5. The biological residential subsystem Melvin, Leon, and Helen. Melvin, in his seeming bitterness to strike out at the remarried couple, does not realize that he is confusing the children whom he genuinely loves. Their confusion may arise out of loyalty issues for each parent and a somewhat grudging recognition that Tyrone means well. The children have been subjected to Melvin's negativity about Lashanda and Tyrone and may see their father as lost and alone and feel that they have to take care of him.

6. The stepfather, Tyrone, and the stepchildren, Leon and Helen. This subsystem has undergone a transformation with the formalization of the relationship between Lashanda and Tyrone in marriage. From the perspective of the children, it seems that things have changed considerably. Now Tyrone does not say

goodnight and go home. He is there and actively trying to help Lashanda manage the house by getting involved in *their* chore schedule and schoolwork. Not only that, he takes her time and attention. What appeared to be a comforting and relaxed friendship between Mom and a boyfriend is now the obstacle to resuming the old life with Dad. Seeing this subsystem in treatment will come in the end stages of the therapy process.

7. The extended family. The clinician needs to explore the relationship between Melvin's parents and the family members since the divorce. How has it changed? What will be their role and involvement?

In evaluating the state of each subsystem, the therapist can formulate a plan that will move each of the family subsystems toward more stable functioning. The clinician will have in mind a brief rationale and a plan for therapy, which will include working with most, if not all, of the aforementioned subsystems; the family will then be informed of the plan. This also lays the groundwork for the next step.

Step 4

Consider the research findings that normalize the experience of this family, and introduce them in clinical practice (as appropriate and meaningful).

Psychoeducation can begin in the first session. As the therapist begins to glean from each member of the marital dyad what their unique stepfamily experience entails, he or she can begin to normalize their reality with careful and fitting use of research findings, scholarly stepfamily work and clinical experience. Appropriate respect for the stepfamily's personal situation should be given while ascertaining the commonalities that they share with other stepfather families. For example, Tyrone and Lashanda may appreciate learning that boundaries in single-parent homes are different, allowing for a more informal and relaxed relationship between mother and children (Arditti, 1999). Daughters may see the stepfather as a person with whom they have to compete for the "affection of their mother" and as "threats to the precocious power and autonomy" (Hetherington & Jodl, 1994, p. 70) that they have enjoyed in the former family structure. Tyrone may have a new understanding of Lashanda within the context of single-parent family functioning, and Tyrone will indeed recognize the fact that, on occasion, it was Leon who provided some comfort and stress relief to his mother after a difficult day because no mate was available. This would have naturally altered the traditional parent–child hierarchy.

In terms of the literature, researchers found that stepfathers are more likely to disagree with and challenge stepsons than stepdaughters (Ganong & Coleman, 1994), especially if they are adolescents (Hetherington, 1989). In fact, stepparents report less agreement and more conflict with stepchildren than do parents with their own children (Hetherington & Jodl, 1994). If Tyrone has expectations of stepping into the role of father, this information may produce a more realistic perspective.

When Lashanda says, "I feel like I am caught in the middle," the therapist may respond that this is a common complaint of biological mothers in stepfamilies. They are the center around which the family circulates, and they have a connection to each family member. Research has shown that in the early months of remarriage, mothers' relationships with their children are exemplified by low monitoring and conflict (Bray & Berger, 1993; Hetherington & Jodl, 1994). Lashanda may recognize her withdrawal from the parenting role as an alternative to voicing disapproval or objection and comprehend her position with more insight and depth. With appropriate use of normalization, there is immediate relief that the family members are being impacted by the very nature of typical stepfamily dynamics.

Step 5

Actively assess and assist in the recognition of empathy when present, and increase the empathic experience between stepfamily members and subsystems.

The couple subsystem is invited in for a second session to see how things are progressing. The therapist will also want to make certain that each member of the marital dyad recognizes not only that divergent points of view are impossible to avoid because of unshared family history, but also that the couple's acceptance of and empathy for these disparities are critical to the success of therapy.

The clinician has heard from the couple that Leon is directly in the center of most of the family disputes. There are also monetary concerns, Helen's isolation, Melvin's negativity, and household chores, but they seem less of a priority in terms of restoring peace and order to the struggling stepfamily. The clinician may choose to begin an empathic intervention on the basis of the disparate views of Leon held by each member of the marital couple.

The first steps are to clarify the concerns of each individual member regarding Leon and to highlight Tyrone's interest in assuring Leon's well-being. Although Tyrone reports that he wants to help and feels that Leon has the potential to be a better student, the therapist has determined through the interview process that Tyrone may be less able to empathically describe Lashanda's experience. Prior to the marriage, he was a single man who had never had the experience of living with someone, with the concomitant tasks of anticipating and accommodating the needs of that person. Now Tyrone must also consider adolescent and preadolescent needs, characterized by the constant fluctuation of moods and energy levels, peer pressure, and the importance of friends. Each day can be radically different from the day before.

Lashanda has shown an empathic concern for both Leon and Tyrone, so the therapist will start with her. The therapist needs to keep this intervention emotionally safe for it to be effective. After preliminary greetings, the session begins.

Therapist:	How has your week been going?
Lashanda:	Better. We tried that whole "monitor" thing. Leon didn't like it that I became more involved because he thinks that I have gone to "the other side," but it has at least cut down on the arguing between him and Tyrone. And now he is calming down a bit for me too.
Therapist:	Well, that is terrific. How about Helen?
Lashanda:	She has come down a couple times because we aren't shouting at each other as much, but she is not back to normal.
Tyrone:	I told Lashanda that Helen had asked me a question about a math problem this week, so that made me happy. We haven't done the house rules meeting yet.
Therapist:	You can schedule the meeting when it suits you. But I think that is great about Helen. I guess that made you feel like you were contributing. Right?
Tyrone:	Yes.
Therapist:	For now, we are going to move in a different direction. Lashanda and Tyrone, I am going to ask each of you in turn to step into the other's shoes and describe the other person's experience relative to Leon. Lashanda, I am going to start with you.
Lashanda:	[sarcastically] I think Tyrone would like a tight ship.
Therapist:	Lashanda, I hear sarcasm in your voice. Can you step away from your anger for the moment and tell me what you openly feel are Tyrone's feelings about Leon.
Lashanda:	[sigh] I think he likes Leon, but I think he gets more upset by the relaxed structure in the house as it applies to Leon . . . I mean . . . Leon not taking out the garbage unprompted, Leon not finishing the laundry, and Leon not doing a thorough job on his homework. It drives Tyrone crazy because he is so organized and methodical.

Therapist:	Tyrone, did Lashanda describe your feelings accurately?
Tyrone:	Sort of.
Therapist:	What part did she miss?
Tyrone:	Leon and I used to really get along before the marriage and now it seems that the communication is just off somehow. I mean, I think he needs to be held accountable for his chores, but I just open my mouth these days and he explodes. I feel very frustrated. I don't know how to fix it. I want to be a good stepfather and a part of the family. I love Lashanda, and I have grown to care deeply about the children.
Therapist:	Lashanda, can you try again to describe how Tyrone is feeling about Leon?
Lashanda:	Tyrone cares about him a lot, but he really feels frustrated. He feels like Leon should do his chores and homework, but when he tries to get him to do it, Leon gets angry. Tyrone has good intentions and feels confused as to what he should do with Leon. He wants to have a good relationship with him.
Therapist:	Tyrone, is that now pretty accurate?
Tyrone:	Yes, I think that is about it.

The clinician intervened to keep the atmosphere emotionally safe and controlled by catching Lashanda's sarcasm and reclarifying the nature of the exercise. After Tyrone spoke about his feelings, the clinician realized that Lashanda still did not have an adequate understanding of Tyrone's position and sought again to have her describe Tyrone's stance until he felt the representation was accurate. After he or she is assured that Lashanda understands Tyrone's feelings, the therapist turns to Tyrone to relate Lashanda's feelings about Leon.

Therapist:	Tyrone, I would like you to try to describe Lashanda's feelings about Leon.
Tyrone:	Lashanda loves her son. I think she feels bad about the divorce and tries to go easy on him so she won't upset him. She talks about how close they got when she was alone with the kids, so sometimes I think she feels that I am in the way and wishes I would just not make a fuss. She wishes that she was that close with Leon again. I think it pains her when he yells at her.
Therapist:	Lashanda?
Lashanda:	It's true . . . all of it. That is how I feel. But I love Tyrone, and I don't want him to feel like he is in the way. I know he means well.

Then the clinician moves into the next stage of the intervention.

Therapist:	So you both have described each other's feelings. Is there anything that could motivate you to let go of your view and adopt the other's position?
Lashanda:	[looks at Tyrone] No. I don't think I care as much about whether Leon does this or that. I just want him to be happy. I mean I already have a good relationship with him.
Tyrone:	I don't have the history with Leon that Lashanda has. I still think he should be pulling his weight around the house without being reminded. I don't see how it is even possible to change my perspective completely.
Therapist:	And you have pointed out a common problem in stepfamilies. Lashanda does have the time and history with Leon. She has built a relationship with him from the time he was born, so you cannot expect that you will step in and feel the same way about him having only known him a few years, right?
Tyrone:	Yes.
Therapist:	So both of you have your own points of view of Leon and the situation, and you feel that you could not change your feelings to match each other's idea of Leon.
Tyrone and Lashanda:	No.
Therapist:	The two of you may never have the same view of Leon. Because you both love each other, it must be distressing to not agree.
Lashanda:	It is.
Therapist:	Neither one of you is "correct." You will never be able to convince the other completely. In some years from now, your views may be more alike but probably never the same. So can you see that you both are spinning your wheels, caught in a position so fixed that you spend a lot of time and energy arguing, when your basic position can never be the same? Do you think that you can abandon your intent on being the one valid viewpoint and accept each other's right to have a different outlook?
Lashanda:	I can try.
Tyrone:	So can I.

Once the couple is able to see that they have been spending a lot of time arguing from a basic position that is naturally quite different and out of their individual control, and they can allow and accept this disparity in the other, they can begin to negotiate issues from an insightful new perspective. Leon needs both structure and nurture, a fact of which his mother is likely to be aware once she is not entrenched in a defensive stance. Tyrone may also recognize that he does not understand the pain of divorce but can allow that this experience is hurtful for Lashanda and the children and not be so driven or exacting in his expectations.

This intervention releases the couple from allegiance to a tight pattern of interaction that was based on misconceptions about the partner's feelings. At the same time, it may serve to generate an empathic process for the couple, one that can be used not only in future therapeutic sessions but also in daily interaction in the home. Once initiated, this process can add depth, meaning, and insight to the couple's dynamics, certainly useful and enriching features.

As the second session ends, the concerns of the family have been clarified, and two basic interventions used in the SfT therapeutic process have been introduced: normalization and an empathic exercise.

The therapist may also choose to assign interventions to be applied at home to reduce tension and alleviate distress in the family system. He or she may advise the couple to take certain steps on the basis of research and the writings of experienced stepfamily theorists. For example, the clinician already knows that shoring up the couple is of critical importance to the survival of the stepfamily (Visher & Visher, 1996). He or she may recommend that the couple enjoy a night out to reawaken the feelings of love implicit in their participation in the therapy process and their narrative.

The therapist will caution the couple that for the welfare of the children any arguments or discord should be conducted in private using empathic concern and healthy communication techniques (e.g., I statements, active listening).

Lashanda and Tyrone will present a more unified presence through these three at-home interventions—explore the unhelpful beliefs and use of labels, monitor the use of empathy in the couple dyad, and continue to work to strengthen their relationship—which will work to strengthen the boundary between the parental hierarchy and the children. In so doing, control and order can begin to quell the seeming chaos in the young stepfamily. The couple can feel a sense of hope and direction and can begin immediately to make changes that will improve the atmosphere. The clinician asks to see the couple again in the third session to process how the three in-home interventions have proceeded. In explaining the purpose of the subsystem work that will begin following the next session, the therapist will also need to affirm the importance of the parental coalition in working as a consolidated whole for the welfare and optimal adjustment of the children.

Step 6

Identify and challenge unhelpful beliefs and specific miscommunication circulating in stepfamily—the role of labels.

The therapist has isolated various issues and stressors that are destabilizing the family system. Through the context of the therapeutic process, he or she has drawn from the research to educate the family on various aspects of stepfamily life that apply to many stepfamilies. It is time to address the unique problems, idiosyncratic to the Jones family. In the SfT model, the therapist establishes a relationship with both Lashanda and Tyrone by listening carefully to their concerns from a nonjudgmental and neutral stance.

The clinician also knows that Tyrone seems well meaning and sound but may have had certain role expectations that are guiding his behavior ("I thought I would make such a contribution to the family"). For example, Tyrone had heard Lashanda complain about the lack of involvement and support from Melvin in her prior marriage. Tyrone had therefore determined that he would be a better husband and father. His zealous and self-directed behavior, which is quite resolute, originates from a genuine desire to do right, but its application in the young stepfamily is misconceived. In a two-parent biological family, Tyrone's parenting style would have been in place from the beginning, giving the children firm guidelines while being nurturing and encouraging, all within the parameters of an established relationship as their father. In a stepfamily, without the relationship in place, Tyrone's advice, admonitions, or guidance may seem annoying and burdensome. It is quite common for children at Leon's and Helen's ages to shriek, "You're not my father!" at a well-meaning and sometimes confused stepfather.

The therapist might ask Tyrone how he defines a contribution in terms of this stepfamily. Tyrone may respond that certainly at the very least he was saving Lashanda from economic hardship by adding his salary to the family resource pool, an immediate and quite tangible contribution. Prior to the remarriage, Lashanda had to be mother, wage earner, homemaker, troubleshooter, and more; Tyrone feels he is in a position to be a comfort and touchstone, a solid source of emotional support for her. The children's lives can be positively impacted by his willingness to help them become better students. He can provide them with nicer clothes; teach them how to study, be better organized, and use their time more efficiently; and so forth. As the therapist listens to Tyrone's clarification of what a contribution entails, he or she can not only appreciate and validate Tyrone's openhearted and earnest intentions but also recognize the need to examine with Tyrone his expectations for the role he was about to assume.

While preparing to enter this family, Tyrone may have seen himself as a rescuer of or a pillar of support for the beleaguered mother and her children. In keeping with this image, he may envision his role within the family system, including implementing his role and, without awareness, set an agenda for Lashanda and the children that may not be agreed on or even welcomed. A basically unilateral decision is reached not only about how he will contribute but also about the manner in which he expects the family members to respond. When they do not respond according to his expectations, he may feel bewildered and eventually become angry at the perceived slight.

One can even conjecture that Tyrone sees the marriage as some sort of starting point for launching the new role, whereas while in the position of boyfriend, he was more relaxed and less determined in his relational style. Having moved in, he is now driven by an inner dictate to be of benefit to the family. Thus, Leon and Helen are suddenly unwilling participants in a design (of someone else's choosing) for the "betterment" of their lives.

Once Tyrone makes the connection that his belief (I want to make a contribution) has become a forthright and goal-directed effort, it may be easier for him not only to recognize and own the behavior and its origins but also to relinquish his expectations. Tyrone may even begin to relax and enjoy a more paced and tempered entry into stepfamily life.

The clinician also needs to be listening for the use of global generalizations or labels used in the family system: the *permissive mother* (Lashanda), the *uptight stepfather* (Tyrone), the *rebel* (Leon). These categories promote family polarization and can be used to give the therapist a solid and well-defined understanding of how family members view each other. Dispelling these labels as overly simplistic and unhelpful within the family context becomes a clear goal for therapy. How does Tyrone's view of Leon as a rebel alter his ability to be alert to the nuances of his behavior? Can Tyrone see irritability in Leon as a possible function of illness, stress, or school pressure if Tyrone persists in viewing Leon as a rebel, a one-dimensional black-and-white image? Can Lashanda see in Tyrone's exhortations to Leon to study for his test a genuinely concerned and involved adult as opposed to a drill sergeant? Labels detract from the potential for family harmony in any family system, but in stepfamilies, without the biological connection and shared family history, they are particularly insidious and destructive. Labels, although at first seeming to help clarify relationships, can serve to keep family members stuck in counterproductive and unfair interactions.

Step 7

Teach the stepfamily about its own systemic functioning.

In the next session, the couple presents with a more optimistic outlook. The last several weeks have gone better than anticipated. There has been even less conflict between Tyrone and Leon because Lashanda has taken over the role of disciplinarian. Tyrone and Lashanda had one argument and a slight disagreement, both of which were over the same tired topics (Leon and his chores) and were resolved behind closed doors. The rest of the time they felt more at ease and hopeful, even if Leon remained somewhat sullen and unsociable. There were no shouting voices, and this change drew Helen from her room on many evenings before dinner.

Often in stepfamilies in therapy, extricating the stepfather from the role of primary disciplinarian will yield such positive results; however, at other times, the stepfather may have real difficulty surrendering the more active parental stance. Sometimes, the mother, who as a single parent felt overwhelmed with economic and temporal demands, welcomes the respite and abdicates control. When asked to resume a position of leadership, she may resist in subtle ways. This intervention then does not flow as smoothly or as quickly. At this point, the clinician needs to slow down the therapeutic process and take a closer look at the motivations, emotional readiness, individual mental health, and/or residual issues of each member of the marital dyad. However, even if more sessions may be required to accomplish this intervention, it is imperative that the couple be able to place the needs of the children and the stepfamily as a whole firmly in the forefront.

The clinician continues with Lashanda and Tyrone, who have experienced a more congenial rapport. The clinician uses this opportunity to process the various interventions in a manner that will feature the family systemic functioning and thus explicate how a change in one member's behavior reverberates through the entire system. For example, the clinician can ask Tyrone what he noticed when Lashanda assumed the more directive role in the family. Tyrone may report that Leon was recalcitrant as usual but less volatile and not as argumentative with his mother. Tyrone also may point out that when Leon had been struggling with an algebra problem, Tyrone had made a deliberate point of staying out of the situation, even though it had been very difficult. Later in the week, Leon had, with a respectful reluctance, asked Tyrone for help. Tyrone noticed that when he stayed back, Leon came to him. He watched Lashanda become less agitated and apprehensive as she parented Leon. Indeed, she seemed to become more definitive and proactive throughout the week.

Lashanda had become aware that as Tyrone avoided confronting Leon regarding the issues of chores and homework, she found herself more upset with Leon's petulance and peevish ways. She noticed that when she did not have to defend Leon, she could regard his behavior more objectively and actually get a better perspective on Tyrone's earlier responses. Without the constant tension, she realized that she was beginning to relax and smile more and was drawing closer to Tyrone.

The couple reported that one evening Helen had come downstairs before dinner and sat down in the family room to watch television. She had even been somewhat conversational. The therapist asked Lashanda why she thought this had happened. Lashanda felt that Helen came down because the noise level in the house had been minimized. Helen had always hated the sound of quarreling, even as a small child.

As the clinician increases the family's awareness of how changes in one individual's behavior influence and modify the family as a systemic whole, he or she prepares them to optimally manage their respective roles in the new stepfamily. Learning about their stepfamily's unique style and interactive patterns allows them to make choices from an informed position.

After thoroughly processing the week's events and confirming the new behaviors, the clinician discusses the idea of a family meeting run by Lashanda, with everyone present, to establish a chore schedule for Leon and Helen. The children will be involved in setting time and frequency for the chores and consequences if they are not done in a timely fashion. The entire family will generate house rules with guidelines for behavior, which will probably include respect for each member. Lashanda, feeling newly empowered, affirms that she can do this. Tyrone acknowledges and accepts his role as a supportive husband. Leon and Helen are expected to take on responsibility in the new family system, as adolescents and preadolescents do. The individual members are setting a course of action with routines and rules for conduct and, in doing so, with this new synergy, are leaving their history as a single-parent family and a single person and shaping a different experience together as a stepfamily.

The following week, the clinician asks to see the biologically connected subsystem, Lashanda, Leon, and Helen.

Step 8

> Support the naturally connected subsystem (parent and child), and confirm that parent and child are capable of expressing mutual concern.

It is of vital importance that the biologically connected subsystem be supported and confirmed. The children had adjusted to the painful process of divorce and settled into a single-parent family. Now they have to accommodate a new family member, not chosen by them, as well as adapt to a new family configuration, one in which Dad is absent and Mom's attentions are directed toward someone besides them. One can be sure that there are extant issues of loss and loyalty, which should be addressed. Left unspoken and unresolved, these issues could prevent a smooth transition by transforming into a variety of behavioral and emotional complaints, that is, passive-aggressive anger, substance abuse, isolation, and depression. The relationship between the members of the biological subsystem needs to be examined to be certain that there is empathy and concern for each other and, more important, that they are aware of these feelings in each other.

The clinician begins the fourth session with Lashanda, Leon, and Helen. For the past weeks, Lashanda has assumed a more directive stance with the children. This may have created a shift in the family process, moving Tyrone and Lashanda closer and forming a more defined boundary around the marital dyad. However, Leon and Helen may perceive this as a polarization of sorts—marital dyad versus sibling subsystem—leading to feelings of abandonment. The clinician needs to fortify the biological subsystem, the former single-parent family, and help the members recognize the profound and enduring bonds that exist between them. The clinician welcomes the family into the session, noticing that Lashanda sits alone and Leon and Helen move to the other side of the room. He encourages Lashanda to move to a seat in between Leon and Helen, a move designed to promote more of a sense of togetherness. The therapist asks about the week's events and the family provides an update.

Therapist: How has your week been going?

Lashanda: It continues to improve. There is an eerie calm, almost like time standing still. The children seem detached and in their own worlds. Sometimes a day passes and there have only been minor squabbles. Compared with a month ago, it is almost unbelievable that we are all getting along so well.

Therapist: So things are looking up. Leon or Helen, how would you describe the atmosphere in the house?

Leon: It's OK.

Therapist: Just OK? How could it be better?

Leon: I can't—I don't have any control over anything. It is not my house.

Therapist: Helen? Do you feel the same as Leon? That you have nothing to say about how things are?

Helen: I don't really care.

Therapist: Helen, is it that you don't care or you don't feel you can do anything to change the situation.

Helen: I am just annoyed with the situation.

Therapist: Tell me more about feeling annoyed.

Helen: I thought I would be happy if they could stop yelling at each other, but now Mom and Tyrone spend more time together and even go out without us once in a while, and I feel like she has gone on with her life and has everything perfect and doesn't care if I miss my friends.

Therapist: So you not only miss your friends, you miss your mom. Lashanda, how are you feeling about what Helen is saying?

Lashanda: I feel really sad. I am always there for her. I love my kids dearly. I do care that she hasn't made new friends.

Helen: I don't want new friends. I want the old ones.

Therapist: Lashanda, do you know which friends Helen is talking about?

Lashanda: Yes. She had a great group of girls she hung out with, and now we are on the other side of town, and it is difficult to get them together. She misses them.

Therapist: Do you understand how she is feeling?

Lashanda: Yes. I remember this one friend I had—we were inseparable— and then my dad got a new job and relocated. We wrote for a while but eventually lost touch. I still think about her to this day.

Therapist: Can you tell Helen that you understand what she is going through?

Lashanda: Oh, Helen, of course I understand how you feel. I didn't realize how badly you have missed them. I guess I was hoping that you would make new friends and settle in to your new home and neighborhood. There was so much else going on that I was distracted. I am sorry. Maybe we can get you together with them, have a sleepover or something. Would you like that, dear?

Helen: All six of them?

Lashanda: Sure.

As the therapist draws out Helen's feelings and guides Lashanda in the process of listening and empathizing, there is an inchoate rekindling of the closeness that existed between the members of the biological subsystem when they were a single-parent family. Plans are also made to address the issues that are troubling Helen in an individual session. (Helen may be more reluctant to talk than the example shows, given that she has been isolating herself and been somewhat depressed.)

The reality that Lashanda described—"There was so much else going on that I was distracted"—does not denote a lack of interest in her daughter's needs but does express her feelings of being overwhelmed. The therapist will direct the session so that the children will be able to reaffirm that

Lashanda loves and cares about each of them and has throughout the formidable changes that have reshaped the family configuration. Lashanda may need to meet with the clinician in an individual session. As an overtired, stressed parent, she may not be able to cope with all the divergent needs of the new stepfamily and will need the extra support. After processing Lashanda's feelings, the clinician can recommend a variety of actions that may relieve some of the stress and mitigate Lashanda's sense of being inundated, for example, time alone, advocating for herself, delegating more responsibility for chores to Leon and Helen, and more.

Processing Leon's anger is vital not only for allowing him expression of his feelings but also for removing Tyrone from the role of scapegoat. The clinician needs to help him comprehend that his anger represents many feelings and that it may be directed at other factors inherent in the many transitions, starting with the divorce.

Therapist:	Leon, I heard you say you don't have any control over anything that happens in the house, because it is not your house. Can you help me understand exactly what you mean by that?
Leon:	I mean that it is just another house that I happen to live in.
Therapist:	So it could be any house?
Leon:	Yeah—it doesn't matter. There are all these new rules, and we have to do homework at a certain time, and they bug us if it is not done and hang around and are just pains. I feel like I am in elementary school and don't belong there.
Therapist:	How would you like it to be?
Leon:	Oh, I am not sure Mom wants to hear the answer to that.
Therapist:	Mom?
Lashanda:	I want him to be honest. Go ahead, Leon.
Leon:	Well, first I wished Dad and Mom had never gotten divorced, but then I got used to that. Then Tyrone had to move in with us after I was comfortable with her and Helen alone.
Therapist:	What did you like about your life?
Leon:	Things were a lot more relaxed—sometimes Mom wouldn't come home on time, and she'd call and say, "Can you start dinner? Or are you hungry or do you want to eat out?" I mean there was no schedule to follow. Now Mr. Uptight has to have things a certain way, and we all have to follow right along.
Therapist:	It doesn't sound like you like Tyrone very much.

Leon: [pause] He was cool when they weren't married. He's kind of been better this past week. He's not a bad guy. I mean he's been leaving me alone, but I get tense just being around him at this point. I am sure he is going to nag about homework. When we were with Mom, she was usually too tired or had too much to do to check homework, but she never had to worry because I always used to do it back then.

Therapist: So when you were left on your own, you did it yourself?

Leon: Well, yeah, but not always. I got by.

Therapist: But now, because someone is nagging you, you don't want to do it. It doesn't sound like you don't like Tyrone because of who he is, but what he does. And that he is suddenly there all the time.

Leon: Yeah, it ticks me off; I am not a little kid anymore. I don't need someone telling me what to do. And we were managing just fine without him.

The therapist has isolated several reasons why Leon is angry. He is angry because Lashanda and Melvin got divorced and he had to adjust to a single-parent family, which he had managed to do. Subsequently, Lashanda and Tyrone began living together, and the new stepfamily moved into a new home. All the transitions appear to have left Leon reeling. Stepfamily research suggests that it is not necessarily the stepfamily issues that are at the root of children's unrest but the multiple transitions that occur and proceed through the remarriage (Hetherington & Jodl, 1994). Consequently, the child feels that he or she has no control over his life, and this alone would be an adequate reason for anger. Leon may feel all he can control is his homework. Although he does not seem to dislike Tyrone, he does see him in the outsider position in the house, intruding into their lives and interfering with the family routine. It is not necessarily a function of who Tyrone is as a person; rather, it is his new role as a stepfather. This is an important issue to tease out in therapy and may be illuminating for all concerned.

This dialogue not only allows unspoken feelings to be aired but also sets in motion a family process of more open communication and mutual concern among members of the biological unit. Several sessions may be required for members to feel that all the issues have been aired and their reconnection is vital and solid. In the meantime, Lashanda could be proactive in initiating one-on-one time with Leon and Helen or time with them both together, for example, taking them out to a ball game. Leon and Helen would have time with their mother like they used to and be reassured of her devotion, with the ancillary benefit of the biological subsystem's reconnecting.

Step 9

Assist in coparental work between any and all involved parental figures, including the binuclear family.

After feeling assured that the biological subsystem is stabilized and reconnected, the clinician may want to have the marital dyad in for a session to determine how things are progressing and to work out any problem areas. Tyrone may be feeling that after the biological subsystem sessions, he is in more of an outsider position, so the couple subsystem may need more attention. Also, issues that need attention are the couple's contention over Melvin's late support payments as well as the negative comments that Leon and Helen bring home from their bimonthly visits. The therapist needs to address the problems with Melvin, who, in his anger, is lashing out at Lashanda and Tyrone and, it is assumed, not realizing the effect this behavior is having on the children. Tyrone has already been informed of the necessity for the various subsystems coming to therapy and Melvin's eventual participation; however, considering and including Tyrone, by informing him as well as hearing his position, validates his importance within the family. After catching up with the progress of the various interventions in the home, the therapist turns to the issues at hand.

Therapist: Another thing I want to discuss with the two of you is actually an issue from the previous session. Tyrone, you were feeling upset with the support payments being late.

Tyrone: That's right, and I am still upset.

Therapist: Is this still a problem between the two of you?

Lashanda: Tyrone gets upset because Melvin is always late, usually a week, sometimes more, sometimes less. Melvin has always had a problem with money.

Tyrone: And now it has become our problem. My salary gets stretched to the point where we are really strapped. I guess it wasn't too brilliant buying a new house, but I wanted to get Lashanda out of that other place.

Therapist: So Melvin's late payments are often a problem.

Tyrone: And Lashanda doesn't seem to mind. We are different that way. It totally stresses me out, barely paying the bills at times.

Therapist: Lashanda, can you understand why Tyrone is upset?

Lashanda: Yes, I can. But what can I do? Melvin doesn't make that much, and then he doesn't manage money well. He at least never gets to the point where he misses a payment altogether. I mean—thank God for small favors.

Tyrone:	See? Lashanda doesn't care.
Lashanda:	Yes, I do, but again, what is the alternative?
Therapist:	Tyrone, what would you have happen?
Tyrone:	I don't know. Court would not really work, and it probably would just make it worse for both Melvin and us because of legal fees. I don't think he is doing it on purpose; it is just annoying every month.
Therapist:	So it is juggling the money that is so stressful.
Tyrone:	Right.
Therapist:	It seems like there is an impasse here, and Lashanda, you don't see any solution either?
Lashanda:	Not really. I can try to talk to him about it. [turning to Tyrone] Maybe we can restructure our bill payments to allow for this, like pay off the necessities with our salaries, so we don't have that stress, and leave the frivolous stuff for his support check. Something like that? All I know is it is not worth it for you and me to fight about it all the time when it is a given. I am much more upset with the stuff he says to the kids. That bothers you too, right?
Tyrone:	Yeah.
Therapist:	So Melvin is saying things to the kids?
Lashanda:	Yes, and it is really upsetting that he criticizes us, and the kids hear it and bring it home. I mean things are tough enough.
Therapist:	Which bothers the two of you more, the money or the comments?
Lashanda:	Definitely the comments.
Tyrone:	I guess if we have to pick, it is the comments for me. I mean the money stuff is really getting old, but maybe Lashanda and I can figure out a way around that, but the comments . . .
Therapist:	Do you remember how when we started working together I spoke of bringing in different subsystems in the family? Well, now may be a good time to have Lashanda and Melvin in session as the children's biological parent subsystem and sort this out. How would you feel about that, Tyrone?
Tyrone:	I guess that would be fine.

After stabilizing the marital dyad and troubleshooting a source of discord between them, the clinician will invite Lashanda and Melvin in for a session.

Melvin, who has been struggling with making support payments and therefore feeling very awkward about visitation and other issues, reluctantly agrees to come to the session with Lashanda. The clinician's goals are four-fold: (a) to educate Melvin about the nature of conflict between ex-spouses as negatively impinging on children's adjustment; (b) to hear Melvin's feelings about the support and possibly assuage his feelings of guilt; (c) to learn more about Melvin's anger; and (d) to discuss with Melvin the possibility of joining in a parental coalition to make the parenting practices more consistent. Melvin needs to be assured that it is important for him to be involved in the children's lives.

The clinician will immediately set the tone for the session and hope to put Melvin at ease by emphasizing the importance of having all parental figures at least appearing to have a united front for the sake of the children if it is not possible to genuinely come to an understanding. This may be a good time to introduce research literature to corroborate the fact that parental conflict negatively impacts the children. This may reduce Melvin's discomfort that he would be criticized for his payment difficulties. Lashanda has described him as a benign figure, so it is probable that he will be concerned about the children.

The therapist wants to make sure that Melvin is comfortable and relaxed before the session begins. Taking note of the dialogue between Melvin and Lashanda will give a better understanding of overall communication and possible problem areas.

Therapist: Melvin, you probably realize that I am already acquainted with Lashanda, but I want you to know that my priority here is for all involved parental figures to have in mind what is best for the kids. For that reason, we have come together to see how we can make that happen. Do you have any questions?

Melvin: Oh, I want that too. I love my kids. I am sure that Lashanda doesn't agree with that because I am always late with the support, but I really try to get it all together in time, but well . . . it is just not there to send.

Therapist: Lashanda, can you tell Melvin if that is the way you are feeling?

Lashanda: No. I know Melvin loves the kids and wants what is best for them. I remember when we were married, there was always a problem with money; he would lend it to friends or spend it on unsuitable things, like when he bought that pogo stick for Leon when he was just 2 years old. I know he means well, but it seems like it has always been really hard for him to save it and contribute to the bills. So I know that he is trying.

Therapist:	So you know that Melvin means well and that for you it is all right that the payments are late.
Lashanda:	Well, it is still an issue in the sense that Tyrone has to pay for so much for the kids, and he is just not used to that, so sometimes he will complain. But that is not what upsets me, Melvin. What bothers me is that when you have had the kids for a weekend, they come home and they tell me stuff you have said about me and Tyrone that is nasty, and then they watch me for a reaction, as if I am supposed to say something nasty about you.
Melvin:	Well, it ticks me off that you moved on so easily. I mean we got separated and divorced so quickly. We had a decent marriage. Maybe there were no fireworks, but we were happy. The kids were doing well.
Lashanda:	The marriage was dead. We didn't talk; we didn't eat dinner together as a family; we didn't have sex anymore.
Melvin:	That is because I was always working late on the cars, then I would be tired—like that is my fault! I was doing it for you and the kids. You were still my family, and you were still my wife. We didn't fight, did we?

The clinician hears that Melvin has not fully accepted Lashanda's divorce and remarriage. It even sounds like they had two separate realities of the marriage experience. Lashanda appears to have successfully navigated through the stages of an emotional divorce—decision, announcement, and separation (Ahrons, 1994)—whereas Melvin has not; he appears shocked at Lashanda's discontented view of their time together. Having been content with his former life, Melvin reacts with anger and considers the reason for the divorce to be unfair. The clinician realizes the source of Melvin's anger but needs to help Melvin understand that his anger is only confusing and hurting the children.

Therapist:	Melvin, I hear you saying that you are genuinely surprised by Lashanda's feelings about the marriage. I mean, to me, it feels like you lived in two separate lives—Lashanda very discontented and you contented with everything the way it was.
Melvin:	I knew things weren't perfect. Hey, I even knew that they weren't the same since the marriage, but the kids were happy, and we had a nice little life.
Lashanda:	The kids could have used a little more attention from you, Melvin.
Melvin:	That is because I had to work such long hours at the shop. It's not like I did not want to be there. You could have told me you weren't happy. You just went along with everything.

Therapist:	Sometimes we make choices that seem to make sense at the time. We cannot go back to that time. You two have been divorced for 17 months, and Lashanda and Tyrone have been together for 5 months. Life has gone on. Right now, we are here to sort through ways we can make it better for the children. You both agree that you want to make it better for the children, right?
Lashanda:	Yes, of course.
Melvin:	Yes.
Therapist:	First of all, we need to establish some ground rules about communication around the kids.
Lashanda:	Amen. Stop saying things about Tyrone and me to the children when they are over at your house.
Melvin:	Same thing goes for you.
Lashanda:	I don't say anything bad about you.
Melvin:	Leon told me that you and Tyrone argue about the money I am supposed to send you.
Therapist:	So it seems like you both have complaints in this area. How about if we come to some agreement about this right now? Tyrone and Lashanda will stop arguing about Melvin's late support payments in front of the kids, and you, Melvin, will not talk about Lashanda and Tyrone when the kids are visiting. That will require effort on both of your parts, and Lashanda, you will have to share with Tyrone what we have discussed here today. If it looks like an argument is going to occur, you move behind closed doors or wait until later. Do you think this is doable?
Lashanda:	I am going to say yes. I think Tyrone will be all right with this.
Melvin:	I didn't realize it was affecting the kids. I think I can stop.

The clinician sees the session going into another dispute on old issues and brings the session forward into the present, moving the children's welfare to the top of the priority list. Sometimes, it will take more than one simple dialogue to exact cooperation from both parents. Long-time grudges are hard to dismantle and discard, especially for Melvin, it seems; so it may take more than one session to do this work. It is essential to quell conflict among the members of the parental hierarchy and to promote communication for the optimal adjustment of the children and toward the goal of eventually forming a parental coalition.

The therapist will also need to recommend that Melvin meet with a counselor to discuss issues of anger that have lingered after the divorce, for his own sake as well as for the children. Support payments have been set by the court and are often difficult to change, but it would be prudent to revisit that area of concern to fully comprehend the nature of the problem. Is the amount too much for Melvin to manage, or is he just a poor manager of money, or both? If he feels the pressure of producing the payment each month, this could also fuel anger. Melvin needs to be informed of and cautioned about the tendency for noncustodial fathers to drop regular visitation when they have difficulty meeting support. Also, Lashanda and Tyrone need to be cautioned not to interrupt the visitation schedule as punishment to Melvin, only to succeed in hurting the children.

It is significant that Lashanda, Tyrone, and Melvin are addressing issues of structure and rules, as opposed to parenting styles. Biological parents as well as stepparents must be free to be themselves in their interactions with the children. How they implement the rules may be somewhat different, but the children will recognize the consistency in application of the rules. For example, Tyrone may be concerned with the educational needs of the children, whereas Melvin may be more relaxed on such matters. However, if the rule is to do homework before they go outside, both parent and stepparent can enforce that effectively while maintaining their own parenting style.

After the biological parental subsystem is clearly united concerning the needs of the children, the therapist can then include Tyrone and Lashanda in a session with Melvin, which would comprise a parental hierarchy or coalition. It is vital that this step not be rushed and that all members be ready to meet and discuss matters with objectivity. If the session is scheduled prematurely, it can often erupt in discord. The clinician therefore has to determine the readiness of the parental subsystem. Often, the noncustodial parent and the stepparent may come in contact at various times, for example, dropping off the kids for visitation, at school events, and so forth. It is important that there be no verbal exchanges that are unpleasant, sarcastic, or coldly neutral or nonverbal communications such as long sighs or rolled eyes, which may confuse or upset the kids. Melvin and Tyrone do not have to be best friends, but it is imperative that they act as adults bearing the best interests of the children in mind.

Discord among the parental hierarchy is an invitation for trouble. Children, especially at Leon's and Helen's ages, need structure; they cannot be allowed to manipulate the newly formed binuclear system to their own ends. Clinically, one can begin to treat the besieged child moving between two fighting households by helping the parents to communicate better, only to find that the child has, covertly or overtly, been creating a lot of the tension. Whether it may be a reunion fantasy, a passive-aggressive anger, or simply a desire for attention, the children, out of a need to feel stability and emotional connection, may contrive to create disharmony. By helping to unify the parents and to encourage productive exchange of parenting structure, rules, and visitation protocol, the therapist can assure that the children will not feel the need to challenge the system using tactics of divide and conquer.

If the sessions with the parental hierarchy are productive, the inchoate parental coalition takes form. Eventually Lashanda, Tyrone, and Melvin can demonstrate to Leon and Helen that they have the best situation: three parents who have put aside differences and can at last work together.

Step 10

> Increase communication among all stepfamily members available, and move toward an integration of the various subsystems into a functioning and satisfied stepfamily.

At this point, the therapist has worked with the following subsystems: the marital dyad (Lashanda and Tyrone), the biological subsystem (Lashanda, Leon, and Helen), the biological parents (Lashanda and Melvin), the parental hierarchy (Lashanda, Tyrone, and Melvin), and perhaps Helen, individually. One can see how central the resident biological parent is to stabilizing the various subsystems. If all has proceeded in a positive fashion, the stepfamily has learned through both the therapeutic process and the psychoeducational use of stepfamily research what is useful to promote healthier functioning. The therapist can now reinforce the successful interventions and shift his or her attention to the entire binuclear family system, which includes the grandparents.

The one problem area in the grandparent subsystem is the exclusion of Melvin's parents from all the birthday and holiday celebrations at the house. Lashanda has regretted this because she, as well as Leon and Helen, were very close to her in-laws prior to her remarriage. The clinician surmises that Lashanda has retreated from her more involved relationship with them out of deference to Tyrone and his parents. In fact, this change in holiday rituals may be construed as an additional loss for the sibling subsystem but one that may not be able to be addressed or even remedied. Melvin's parents have been seeing the children every other weekend for a couple hours but would like to increase their contact with them. They feel that as a result of the circumstances they are no longer part of the family and therefore have no say. Such assumptions may have taken the place of communication; this affirms the importance of opening and sustaining dialogue. Not only are additional supportive family members important to the emotional health and adjustment of the children but also to the existing biological bond that will endure regardless of divorce, so it is vital to respect and preserve this relationship. Whether the grandparents have any rights when their children divorce and custody is awarded to the other parent is a growing concern. These issues are addressed in Chapter 7. The therapist makes a decision to address this issue not only for the sake of the grandparents but also as an additional support to the family system.

In this particular stepfamily, the therapist brings Lashanda and Tyrone into the session to process expanding the role of Melvin's parents in the lives of Leon and Helen. This amount of involvement can range from visiting the grandparents more often to having the grandparents participate in holiday celebrations with the stepfamily. The latter is not impossible. As long as all involved adults are clearly motivated by love for the children and what is best for them, the transition to open communication and the resultant behavior between the various family members and extended family will be fairly smooth. The relationship between members of the grandparental hierarchy can even be cordial in sharing holiday celebrations and special events in children's lives. Melvin's parents probably feel relieved to have more regular contact with Leon and Helen restored and grateful for the supportive adults surrounding their grandchildren.

To facilitate this situation, the clinician will invite the marital dyad into a session. In anticipating a potentially negative reaction from Tyrone, the clinician would want to process this addition to the stepfamily system without the children. Lashanda and Tyrone could reach a conclusion about how they want to define the boundaries for Melvin's parents and Leon and Helen.

Time between sessions can be extended once the therapist notices that stepfamily functioning has improved. If certain clinical issues, such as Lashanda's assuming the discipline, Helen's depression, and Leon's anger at Tyrone, continue to be active and problematic, every other session can be used to work on individual concerns, and/or outside referrals can be used. The stepfamily must be allowed to establish their own rituals, modes of functioning, and routines, which reflect their unique reality and with repetition become family tradition. Eventually, when the stepfamily becomes less volatile, the therapist can include Lashanda, Tyrone, Leon, and Helen in a session to process various aspects of family dynamics and functioning. In this manner, the long-term goal of integration can be realized. Having the entire stepfamily in a session, the clinician combines four separate subsystems, the marital dyad, the biological subsystem, the step subsystem and the sibling subsystem. Each member of the stepfamily recognizes the needs of and has allegiance to his or her various subsystems as part of a greater whole. In this manner, the likelihood of understanding and empathizing with each other's point of view and feelings is increased by each family member's position in more than one subsystem within this unique family configuration.

5

THE SIMPLE STEPMOTHER FAMILY

In this chapter, we apply the stepfamily therapy model to the Walkers, a prototypical stepmother family. On the basis of information obtained during the telephone intake, the clinician charts the genogram. The clinician then moves through each step of the model demonstrating both in text and graphically the family dynamics, concerns, and progress.

INTAKE INFORMATION

Biological father: John Walker (39)
Stepmother: Cindy Walker (29)
Status: Married 6 months, have known each other 14 months
Biological mother: Pauline, deceased in car accident 18 months ago
John and Pauline's children: three girls—Jennifer (11), Ashley (7, hurt in the accident and undergoing physical therapy for a back injury), and Heather (3)
Pauline's extended family: Joan, Pauline's mother; Sally and Jane, Pauline's sisters

Jobs: Both John and Cindy are lawyers.

Race, ethnicity, religion: White, European American; John is Protestant; Cindy is Jewish.

John makes the call to the therapist and reports feeling overwhelmed and exhausted. He says he recently married, and there are already a great many problems. As John describes, the couple met when Cindy came to work at John's law firm. Cindy worked for a different law firm and had shown great promise as a tax attorney. John's first wife, Pauline, had worked part time as a paralegal in John's office and had taken maternity leave when Jennifer was born. The couple then had decided that they could afford to have Pauline be a stay-at-home mom. They had enjoyed a good marriage and their children.

After Pauline died, John was overwhelmed with being a single father and relied heavily on Pauline's family to take Ashley to the doctor and physical therapy as well as to care for Heather. Jennifer has been acting out since the accident, and this has grown even worse since the remarriage. Ashley is going along with all the treatments and has been improving steadily, albeit at a slow pace. Heather has little memory of her mother and is fond of Cindy.

John feels the couple needs to attend therapy for, among other things, Cindy's resentment that he expects her to continue staying at home and managing the responsibilities of the home and children, including taking Ashley to therapy. At the beginning, Cindy felt like she could manage the three girls— that she could be a young, fun mom to them. Now, after a test run, she longs to go back to work because she finds the situation overwhelming. When she mentioned this to John, they argued. When the discussion starts to escalate, the couple just changes the subject to avoid a problem. (Cindy and John had not settled the logistics of whether Cindy was going to work prior to the marriage.)

John admits he does not want more children; he already has three, and he feels, as he approaches 40, too old to have more. Cindy wants at least one, maybe two, in the future, so this is another contentious area. Another area of discord involves Pauline's parents and siblings, who want to remain actively involved with the children, including seeing them on holidays and one weekend a month. Pauline and John had been very close with her family; even Mary, John's mother, had enjoyed family gatherings with the in-laws. In fact, there were many holiday rituals in which all three generations were present and participated. In Cindy's family, they have different holiday customs. Cindy celebrates Chanukah and, at the very least, would love to tell the story of the holiday and share the ritual of the lighting of the candles. John worries that the kids are fearful that their holiday festivities will change. Cindy's parents live 1 hour away and want to be involved.

During the call, the therapist has made an interactive genogram (see Figure 5.1; again, see Figure 3.1 for the legend). He or she invites the couple in for the first session.

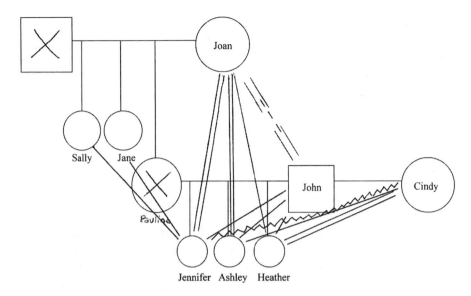

Figure 5.1. The Walker family.

APPLYING THE 10 STEPS OF STEPFAMILY THERAPY

In the sections that follow, the therapist applies each of the 10 steps of stepfamily therapy model to the Walker family.

Step 1

Recognize the structure of the stepfamily (e.g., simple stepfather family, simple stepmother family, complex stepfamily in which both adults are stepparents). Use the initial telephone intake to look for systemic similarities within the context of the research literature.

This family is a simple stepmother family formed by death as opposed to divorce. This presents different challenges for the forming family. Grieving is evident through the entire family system, including friends and family of the deceased mother. Even though loyalty issues are not played out on a weekly basis with visitation and overnights, they are present and can extend into the noncorporeal world, where the deceased can become idealized and an unchanging standard for comparison. Pauline's "ghostly presence" may remain an obstacle to Cindy's assimilation into the family.

In defining those obstacles to assimilation, the clinician will also want to remain aware of the many cultural stereotypes that exist about stepmothers, including even fairy tale myths in which stepmothers are portrayed as evil, vindictive, and cruel to their stepchildren. No wonder that as soon as the label *stepmother* is attached to a woman, she feels negativity and resistance to acceptance through societal expectations and opinion. Research has shown that even clinicians can be influenced by these prevalent unfavorable attitudes (Ganong & Coleman, 1997), so it is imperative that they monitor themselves to maintain an open and neutral stance in their work with stepfamilies.

In addition, Cindy may be feeling particularly isolated, vulnerable, and inferior because the stepfamily is now encountering an early stage of development defined by Patricia Papernow (1993) as the *immersion* stage, characterized by loss of initial fantasies and unrealistic expectations. The length of time the stepfamily has been together and the various dilemmas the family is encountering indicate this stage to the clinician.

After identifying the type of family, the clinician defines certain similarities to other stepmother families from the intake information.

1. Jennifer has been acting out; Ashley is going along with the treatments; Heather is fond of Cindy. One needs to pay close attention to the developmental levels and range of behaviors in the children; the different age responses to the new stepfamily are typical. The research notes that adjustment to the newly forming family is usually more favorable for younger children (Hetherington & Jodl, 1994). Also, the girls have been through two major transitions in less than 2 years. Often it is suggested in the literature that it is not the stepfamily situation that creates the problems but the stress inherent in the transitions (Hetherington & Stanley-Hagan, 1999a).

2. Cindy resents John's expectation that she continue to stay at home; she finds the situation overwhelming. It has been noted in the stepfamily literature that there can be increased opportunities for conflict and stress because stepmothers are expected to step into the role of a nurturing primary caretaker and be involved with their stepchildren on a more frequent basis than stepfathers (Bray & Berger, 1993; Hetherington & Stanley-Hagan, 1999a; Quick, McKenry, & Newman, 1994). This seems to occur in spite of how the stepmother may regard the role or how she may feel about the stepchildren. Research also says that stepfathers have better relationships with their stepchildren than do stepmothers (Ahrons & Wallisch, 1987; Fine, Voydanoff, & Donnelly, 1993; Hobart, 1987; Ihinger-Tallman, 1988), perhaps

because stepmothers find it more challenging to parent step-children than do stepfathers (Clingempeel, Brand, & Ievoli, 1984; MacDonald & DeMaris, 1996).

The stepfamily literature suggests that role ambiguity is a common problem for stepmothers (Ihinger-Tallman, 1988). In addition, husbands and wives often have divergent expectations of the woman's role, especially if the roles have not been discussed prior to the marriage (Visher & Visher, 1979). Differences between the couple regarding role expectations can be a powerful destabilizing force. Unlike first-married families, stepfamilies do not have a set of traditional norms regarding role performance (Cherlin, 1978; Cherlin & Furstenberg, 1994).

3. Another area of discord is Pauline's parents and siblings who want to remain actively involved. The extended family of a deceased parent can serve as a powerful constant in the children's lives as well as assist in adolescent adjustment and, by implication, family adjustments and relationships. However, these same relations may work at cross-purposes in the formation of the stepfamily if the presence of the new spouse is perceived negatively. The role of Pauline's family will have to be determined. The children's exposure to this extended family has indeed been interrupted and may be perceived as an added loss. Each family member's capacity for empathy is critical to achieving the best solution for the children, which may be the inclusion of Pauline's family in their lives.

Step 2

Determine the membership of the first session—usually the marital dyad—and further delineate the unique concerns of the stepfamily.

The clinician will invite the couple, Cindy and John, into the first session. The problems seem to be mainly within the marital dyad; this is not to minimize the significant impact of Jennifer's behavior on or her emotional adjustment to the new stepfamily. However, the therapist has surmised through John's report that the central issue stems from a lack of communication prior to the marriage regarding Cindy's role. This is a common problem in stepmother families and has led to role ambiguity and, hence, role confusion, which may occur on two levels. An interpersonal conflict may exist between John's expectation that Cindy would be a stay-at-home mom and Cindy's interest in furthering her career; this conflict is being aired and debated. However, Cindy may also be experiencing an intrapersonal struggle between what she sees as her moral responsibility to care for the children, coupled with a genuine concern for their welfare, and her enjoyment of and desire to further her career. She may have kept this confusion within her because she may see this as fodder for John's point of view in the arguments.

The couple is in a stressful conflict. The clinician needs to gather information about the nature of the problem(s) from each partner's perspective. The clinician also needs to determine from both John and Cindy their expectations of Cindy's role within the family and how much each of them understands about the function of a parental monitor. (The concept of parental monitor was discussed in Chapter 4, this volume.)

While inquiring systematically about the particular concerns that have brought the family for treatment, the therapist can ascertain the empathy present in each individual. Because the therapist has had a telephone intake with John, the therapist must provide a safe and balanced session so Cindy will feel comfortable. After introductions and some dialogue, the session begins.

Therapist: I am going to ask each of you in turn what is troubling you about the home situation. While I am doing that, I want the other to listen with a sincere attempt to understand the point of view being described. You each will get a chance to clarify what you feel are the problem areas. Who would like to begin?

Cindy: I really don't want to go first.

John: OK, I will. Well, I guess we should start at the beginning. My wife . . . my former wife passed away a year and a half ago. She died in a car accident. We had three little girls—9, 5, and 1 years of age.

Therapist: What was your former wife's name?

John: Pauline. The middle child, Ashley, was in the car with her and hurt her back. Of the three kids, Jennifer, the oldest, took it the worst. I have been having trouble ever since with her. So I became a single father and took care of my kids with the help of Pauline's family. Then Cindy came to the firm. She was such a ray of sunshine, so anxious to learn everything about tax work. But I really had my hands full at home. Thank God for Pauline's family. Her sister took Ashley to all her medical appointments, and Pauline's mother took care of Heather every day. She's the baby. After a while, Cindy and I were thrown together on cases. We really got along. After some months I was starting to enjoy life again. Cindy wasn't anything like Pauline, but she was exciting and fun

	and intellectually challenging. Then we decided to get married.
Therapist:	So it sounds like you and Cindy had a terrific relationship at first, with common interests and abilities.
John:	We did. Cindy and I went on our honeymoon. When we got back, she agreed to stay home and look after the kids.
Cindy:	No, I didn't. We never even discussed it.
Therapist:	OK, this sounds like it will be an important issue for us to attend to, so we will come back to that in a while. For now, Cindy, we are going to let John finish how he defines the problem areas, and then you will have the opportunity. Is that all right with you?
Cindy:	Yes, it's fine.
Therapist:	Please continue, John.
John:	After we got back, everything started to go sour. I would come home from work and Cindy would not be talking—just moving around kind of sullen. The house was a mess. The food wasn't ready. It was just chaos, and on top of that Jennifer was nowhere to be found, and Cindy didn't know where she was—they would have had a problem, and Jennifer would run out the door. Cindy would just let her go. I mean it was worse than when I was a single father.
Therapist:	So, John, you are frustrated by the chaos—the fact that the house is not clean and dinner is not ready when you come home. The kids are not in a routine, and Jennifer is missing so you are worried about her safety.
John:	Yes. I guess I have flipped out at Cindy a couple of times. Oh, and she keeps nagging me about going back to work.
Therapist:	Cindy has said repeatedly that she would like to return to her job?
John:	Yes, the firm really wants her back too. They said full time, part time. I told them maybe in 3 years when Heather is in school.

The therapist has been listening with a purposeful intent as John speaks about their stepfamily life and has been delineating various issues and feelings. In a stepfamily formed by death, the grieving process reverberates through the entire biological subsystem, exacerbating the already challenging process of stepfamily formation.

John may not have successfully completed the grieving process. He has been married to Cindy for 5 months and still refers to Pauline as his wife, albeit accidentally. The clinician needs to investigate this possibility. If John has not adequately grieved for Pauline, he cannot genuinely move forward with Cindy. This topic definitely needs to be explored.

John cannot help but notice Jennifer's tirades, moodiness, and avoidance. Jennifer may be having the most extreme reaction because she may hold the most vivid memories of her mother. One can never underestimate the significance of loyalty issues in stepfamily processes. The therapist may want to refer Jennifer for ongoing individual counseling. The longer her behaviors are allowed to continue unchecked, the more entrenched they become and the more damaging they could be to the fragile marital relationship. The consequential negativity that Jennifer's actions provoke in others may serve to perpetuate and stimulate further her maladaptive responses. The cycle needs to be interrupted. This discussion of Jennifer's extreme responses is not intended to minimize the reaction of Ashley, whose experience may be more internal. Her passively agreeable attitude needs careful scrutiny.

Pauline's relatives obviously rescued the single-father family from an impossible situation by lending support and covering the responsibilities at home at a painful and critical time. Their loss of Pauline can be assuaged by continuing contact with her family; conversely, their presence can yield tremendous support and comfort to the children. Additionally, John is very close to them emotionally as well. Is there a place for them after the remarriage?

It is important for the therapist to note that John initially was attracted to someone quite different from his former wife. He was aware that Cindy was career minded and ambitious when he married her, but he may have anticipated a change after the marriage to accommodate his expectations. After all, Pauline gave up her career and stayed at home. Why should he not presume that Cindy would do the same? These unilaterally formed expectations, based in part on the dynamics of his first marriage, may also account for his belief that the decision was made together.

To add to this dynamic, John values and respects Cindy; however, at work he may have assumed the role of mentor and consequently may expect the same power dimension at home. This possibility needs to be investigated. Also, is there an age difference that may imply a paternalistic cast to the relationship? Although these are not stepfamily issues per se, they contribute to the stepmother's inconsequential self-image. It will be important for the therapist to explore Cindy's feelings about staying at home and her involvement in the decision-making process.

The session continues.

Therapist: I think I have a clear picture of how you feel, John. Now I would like to hear where Cindy feels the problem areas are. Cindy?

Cindy: Well, what he just said. There is one of them. "I told them maybe in 3 years." Isn't that my decision? [glaring at John]

John: I think that is a rhetorical question. You know I believe in joint decisions.

Cindy: That is just it. There was no joint decision.

Therapist: Cindy and John, we are going to sort through how you make decisions as a married couple because I think that is an important part of communication. Cindy, you thought after a time you would go back to work, but you weren't thinking in terms of 3 years.

Cindy: No, I wasn't. I was thinking sooner. Now I am sure I meant sooner. I mean, John helped me with the initial settling in, and then I began to become really comfortable and proficient; I was told I was really surpassing the firm's expectations, almost on a daily basis. It felt good to be appreciated and respected.

John: Yes, they really liked her work. I felt very happy for her.

Therapist: So it sounds like professionally Cindy was really making strides. Cindy, I can hear the energy in your voice when you talk about it; it sounds like you really miss it. Is there anything else?

Cindy: Yes, since the honeymoon, I have felt so alone.

Therapist: Can you tell me how you have felt alone?

Cindy: We came back from our honeymoon. Everything seemed so different. John was so busy with work. I felt so much like I was plopped down in a family that I did not know and in which I had no place. I really don't know how to cook and have never had to clean for someone else and never as big a place, and I have never taken care of children. I am doing the best I can. And there are all these pictures around of the family with Pauline, everybody looking so happy, and everything in the house the way she left it. If I try to do anything differently, I hear that is not the way Mom did it or something like that. I mean I know that it must be difficult for John and the children. She was young and taken away from them so suddenly.

	But with me, John seems more remote now, almost like he didn't like me anymore. It has been very difficult and lonely.
Therapist:	It appears that you really understand and are respectful of the family's loss, Cindy, but you feel like John is slipping away from you?
Cindy:	Yes.
Therapist:	If I can sum up what you have been saying . . . your idea of what the marriage was to be and coping with its challenges do not match the current reality or what seems to be required of you. You feel this has something to do with John's becoming more distant.
Cindy:	Yes, I feel totally incompetent.
Therapist:	At work, you were getting praised for your accomplishments, and John shared in your success because he helped you early on. In the home, you feel you are at a loss.
Cindy:	Yes. I love John, and I want to be with him, but I am not sure I can do this. I don't miss my old life, just the work aspect. I am really good at being a lawyer. And I want some control over my life, some stimulation and confirmation of my worth as a person and someone who cares how I feel. I think John has lost respect for me.
John:	I care how you feel, Cindy. I really do. It is just the chaos; it is so upsetting . . . and I do respect you.
Cindy:	The chaos isn't me. It just seems like you have been so irritated with me. We are like strangers some days.
Therapist:	And when you feel like you two are strangers, the loneliness sets in.
Cindy:	Yes.
John:	I don't want you to feel lonely, Cindy. I am here for you.

The therapist recognizes Cindy's isolation and loneliness, which in stepfamily life often accompanies the outsider position of the new stepparent. The biological subsystem, although obviously in some turmoil, nevertheless retains its strong and cohesive bond to the subsequent exclusion of Cindy.

The family is accustomed to the daily routines that Pauline had instilled in the home. Pauline was a competent housekeeper and mother who maintained a sense of order. Cindy may be threatened by hearing about her predecessor's competence when she feels so inadequate. Having to accommodate to the day-to-day rituals and customs of the previous family is an unappreciated and daunting challenge. Also, Cindy, unlike Pauline, has not had the luxury of time to learn and grow in the role of wife and mother from the beginning

As was previously mentioned, Cindy was a promising young tax attorney. Not only does she miss the stimulation of work but also there are critical features of her self-image that are being denied. Cindy felt competent and valued in her work role. She apparently feels somewhat annoyed that John unilaterally made the decision about her taking a hiatus from her career. It is probable that in his enthusiasm to resume married life, he did not even realize that he had reached this conclusion on his own.

During the systematic inquiry into the particular problem areas of this new stepfamily, the therapist has been further informed of each member's concerns. With this overview of the family, he or she can prioritize issues and plan the course of the treatment.

Step 3

Clarify the distinct subsystems in the stepfamily, and use this information to provide a direction for clinical treatment.

The clinician delineates the subsystems in this stepfamily.

1. The marital dyad: Cindy and John. The couple is 10 years apart in age and a world apart in life experiences. John had been married 11 years and is a father to three children. He was settled and happy within a supportive extended family and accommodated to the needs of all three generations of his family. Cindy has been goal-directed in her educational pursuits and responsible for no one other than herself.

   There is empirical evidence (Crosbie-Burnett, 1984) and clinical support (Visher & Visher, 1988) that shows that problems between the stepparent and the stepchildren can negatively impinge on the marital relationship (Fine & Kurdek, 1995). It is possible that the discord that was described in the initial telephone intake is already having a negative impact on the marriage.

   John had a positive relationship with Pauline and may want to duplicate it in his relationship with Cindy; whereas clinicians have noticed that in stepfamilies formed from divorce, the spouse usually does not want to repeat his first experience in his second marriage. John, who realizes Cindy needs support but is afraid to alienate his daughters, has a similar problem to other biological parents who feel very anxious trying to please all members of the family at once (Papernow, 1993).

2. The sibling subsystem: Jennifer, Ashley, and Heather. The three girls are all mourning their mother; their behavioral and emotional responses to this loss are varied. As reported, their willingness to accept Cindy ranges from outright rejection (Jennifer) to quiet neutrality (Ashley) to affectionate acceptance (Heather). Heather's acceptance of Cindy is corroborated by the research, which suggests that a relationship between the stepparent and stepchild is more easily established when the child is younger (Hetherington & Jodl, 1994).

Jennifer may need individual attention and counseling to address her anger and aggression. Ashley needs to be evaluated for posttraumatic stress disorder because there may be residual trauma from the accident in which her mother died that has gone unnoticed because of her complacent nature. The clinician needs to ascertain how the children respond to each other and how connected they seem.

3. The biological subsystem: John, Jennifer, Ashley, and Heather. John may feel tremendous intrapersonal upheaval. Present circumstances may seem more exaggerated than even the chaos of being a single parent and rife with complications that challenge John each day. Evaluating John's various connections to his daughters and working to strengthen the biological bonds are therapist considerations regarding this subsystem.

4. The stepparent–stepchild subsystem: Cindy, Jennifer, Ashley, and Heather. This subsystem is somewhat contentious because of the ongoing conflict between Cindy and Jennifer, and for this reason, a session involving this subsystem is not advisable in the early stages of treatment. It is possible that this discord, which was described in the initial telephone intake, is already having a negative impact on the marriage. Bearing that in mind, the therapist can address the contention indirectly through work with the couple to strengthen their bond and move Cindy from such an intense outsider position. A session with the stepparent–stepchildren subsystem may be possible after the couple bond has been reinforced and Cindy has achieved more role stability in the family.

5. The extended family: Pauline's mother and siblings. Defining the role of the extended family in the future is an important objective. They can be seen as an invaluable source of support to the family or people refusing to acknowledge Cindy.

At some point, the therapist may want to open up communication between Cindy and this subsystem in a conjoint session;

however, this should come later in the therapy process. It is necessary to be sensitive to Cindy's needs and fears and, at the same time, to have respect for the significance of Pauline's family in the children's lives. Empathic understanding of each other's interests and concern for the adjustment of the children are factors that may enable this family to achieve accord. The extended family subsystem may also be instrumental in giving courage and comfort to the children as they grieve for their mother as well as in providing an additional source of child care and support for Cindy and John.

The subsystems and the issues involved have been reviewed. As the therapist begins to work with the family, he or she will attempt to use these appraisals to establish a rudimentary course for treatment. Normalization of the Walker family's difficulties and feelings compared with the researched stepmother family is valuable, but the integrity of the family's unique process must be clinically maintained and respected.

Step 4

Consider the research findings that normalize the experience of the stepfamily, and introduce them into clinical practice (when appropriate and meaningful).

During the session, the therapist becomes more acquainted with the specific problems from John's and Cindy's points of view. Psychoeducational treatment of these areas of difficulty will bring relief to the beleaguered couple and recognition that the problems may be a function of early stepfamily formation.

For example, Cindy may be relieved to know that stepmothers often experience more role ambiguity than stepfathers (Ihinger-Tallman, 1988). With no prior experience, Cindy would hardly understand the full scope of this role; she was competent in her professional career, but she also knew what was expected of her. She may feel sad for the kids' loss but angry when Jennifer ignores and disrespects her. She may want to care and minister to them but, at the same time, long for intellectual stimulation and positive feedback. Cindy's role confusion creates internal dissonance and manifests itself externally as anger, resentment, or disengagement, terms that describe her behavior in allowing Jennifer to run off alone. Normalizing Cindy's behavior as common to stepmothers may lessen the tension between the marital dyad immediately.

Stepparents often feel like outsiders when "plopped down" in a family that is biologically related and has well-established routines and rituals. As mentioned before, and in contrast to stepfathers, stepmothers often are expected to assume the role of primary caretaker. Naturally this position provides more opportunity for spending time with the children, although it is not necessarily quality time but time spent in a functional capacity, shuttling them to and from after-school activities, to and from friends' houses, and for Ashley's sake to numerous medical appointments.

Cindy's relationship with Heather is very close because younger children adapt quickly to the new stepparent (Hetherington, 1993). David Mills (1984) conjectured that the age of the child is equivalent to the years it would take for a stepparent to form a relationship with that child. The second factor is that Heather's memory of her mother is vague at best. It would then be almost predictable that Cindy would have less difficulty with Heather and the most with Jennifer. Cindy may find immense relief in knowing that her discomfort is natural and to be expected.

John feels overwhelmed and sometimes works late on weekdays and spends weekends catching up on errands and chores. If his involvement with the parenting and discipline at home is minimal, then the stepmother is inclined to have more negative behavior from the children (Fine & Kurdek, 1992, as quoted in Hetherington & Stanley-Hagan, 1999a, p. 151). John may often wish for less complicated days, unconsciously avoiding the complexity of the developing stepfamily. Goldner (1982) calls this "the retreat from complexity" (p. 205), stemming from a natural inclination to look upon the stepfamily using nuclear family norms. It may seem that everywhere he turns there is a problem, and he may mistakenly blame Cindy, possibly expecting her to slide into the role effortlessly and automatically and love it as well. Expectations of the husband are often disparate from those of the stepmother (Ganong & Coleman, 1997).

The extended family is an added complication, which can be viewed in a positive fashion as an added resource for the stepfamily or negatively as a constant reminder of the former spouse. As stated before, adjustment of children is more favorable if extended family supports are in place. This will also somewhat compensate for the loss of Pauline. Enlightening Cindy on the research findings may enable her, assuming she is well intentioned, to understand the importance of Pauline's family. The clinician will need to facilitate the relationship between Cindy and Pauline's family for the optimal benefit of the children but must balance the intervention so Cindy does not feel more isolated.

Citing the available research about other stepmother families normalizes the family's reality. Dispelling the myth of the wicked stepmother as well as the expectation that Cindy can easily assume the vacated role of the biological mother may release Cindy from a very constricted existence; she can then begin to define her role within her abilities and bring to her new position in this stepfamily her unique personality.

Step 5

Actively assess and assist in the recognition of empathy when present, and increase the empathic experience between stepfamily members and subsystems.

Cindy and John have already demonstrated a mutual respect and fondness for each other. Disagreements and challenges have been described and delineated in the first session, and the primary source of discord seems to be Cindy's role after the marriage. John expected her to be a full-time wife and mother; Cindy has discovered that not only is she not very good at this but also it is not what she wants. The couple has been arguing and becoming more polarized with each attempt to put forth their personal positions.

In the second session with the couple, the therapist will attempt to move them toward an empathic understanding of each other's viewpoints. Empathy and its communication are crucial to a stepfamily's success. While Cindy was talking about the loss of Pauline, the therapist noted that she had shown empathic concern for John and the family and has decided to begin this session with her.

Therapist:	Today I am going to ask each of you to speak from the other's point of view. In other words, I want you, Cindy, to be John for an instant and arrive home from work and describe how he must be feeling.
Cindy:	He's tired. He works hard at the office; he is one of the best lawyers there. He opens the door, and he sees toys on the floor and clothes around and goes into the kitchen. He greets me and Ashley and Heather. They are not always cleaned up and tidy. He doesn't like that. Then he wants to know where Jennifer is. I tell him I don't know, and he gets angry.
Therapist:	How does he feel when he hears she has run out in a snit and you don't know where she is?
Cindy:	Angry.
Therapist:	What is under the anger?
Cindy:	He is worried and scared. He doesn't want anything to happen to her, and she is acting so crazy lately that he is beside himself. He wants to keep her safe. He looks at me as the adult in charge and blames me. He thinks I should be more attentive to her. He wonders what I do all day. He has actually said that.
Therapist:	John, does that describe how you feel?

John: Well, I think she left out the part about me feeling over-whelmed. I just get home, and now I have to go chase Jennifer, and I feel like I have to clean up, clean the two kids. I just had a busy day. She is right about my blaming her.

Therapist: I can hear you're feeling overwhelmed and how it is going to anger. The point of this exercise is not to relive the moment and become angry. It is to see if you both can understand and feel what the other experiences. Cindy, is there anything else you want to add about what John might be feeling?

Cindy: That it must be awful to come home from working all day when everything is out of control, especially when he is tired. I would just want to sit down, be with me and the kids, and relax. Instead, he runs out the door calling for Jennifer.

The therapist has had to intervene to keep the session from escalating into a replay of the afternoon's events. When Cindy was describing John's experience, he could feel the frustration and exasperation welling up inside him. Cindy could feel that the exercise has led her into an unsafe place. By trying to understand how he feels, she has stirred up feelings that he may feel justified and entitled to have. The safety issue is important.

They continue.

Therapist: John, I wonder if you can be Cindy on a usual day when you return from work. Try to step into her mind and understand her reality.

John: It's difficult. OK, I guess she is hanging out and playing with Heather (because the toys are all over the place) when Jennifer and Ashley get home. She tries to be nice to Jennifer, and Jennifer sasses her and is nasty. Cindy starts dinner—maybe the kids are watching TV or something. She knows I am coming home soon. Jennifer bugs her while she is cooking, and Cindy raises her voice, and Jennifer leaves. She decides not to chase her, she says because of the other two kids and the meal.

Therapist: John, it sounds like you are having a hard time understanding Cindy's experience. I want you to put yourself in that kitchen and really try to feel what Cindy is going through.

John: OK. She knows I am going to be pissed off that Jennifer has left, and that makes her anxious. I think she is really preoccupied that Jennifer has left. Sometimes Cindy tells me she is scared that something might happen, but she doesn't know how to stop her. She has never cooked, so I guess she is worried about the meal. She has never taken care of kids, so I guess she would be a bit on edge, making sure they are all right. And then I am going to be home soon; she knows that I am going to fly off the handle because of the house or Jennifer or just because I am tired, and she braces herself. She wishes she wasn't in the position she is in. She feels sad. I am supposed to care and be a friend, and I am yelling. She can't turn to me, so I guess, as she said, she must feel alone.

As John goes through the process, he embarks on a sequential account of Cindy's afternoon and slowly begins to fathom Cindy's struggle. The therapist sums up the dialogues in an objective manner.

Therapist: It feels like the two of you have gotten a glimpse of what it feels like to be in the other person's shoes. It may be impossible to reach a resolution if you maintain the status quo. Something has to change. You both feel overwhelmed with the situation as it is.

John: I didn't really understand that Cindy was also feeling this way.

Therapist: It may be that we will have to brainstorm other possibilities to relieve the stress and have both of your needs met. John, what do you think would be helpful for Cindy?

John: Maybe we could get someone to come in and help with the house.

Therapist: Cindy, would that take care of your stress and unhappiness?

Cindy: Of course, part of it.

Therapist: You say "part of it"—what is missing?

Cindy: I want to go back to work part time . . . maybe 3 days a week. I would use what I earned to pay for someone to come in. I really need to work. I would be so much happier. I miss it.

Therapist: John, how are you feeling about Cindy's ideas?

John: I guess I knew what she was going to say.

Cindy: John, I need intellectual stimulation and challenge. I am not cut out to be a full-time mother and homemaker, at least at present. I didn't realize how not ready I was for this. We should have talked about it before we married, then you would have known. Sometimes I thought I could do it, but I didn't realize what it entailed. I have to hand it to Pauline.

John: She wasn't so great at the beginning either.

Therapist: That is a good point, John. In stepfamilies, the stepparent doesn't have the benefit of growing with the family—

knowing the kids from the beginning. Cindy has had to enter a family that was already established—ready-made with their own routines, with children of various ages in mourning for their mother. It is quite an adjustment.

John: I never looked at it that way.

Therapist: This is one of the problem areas, John. Each person naturally has different expectations when he or she enters into remarriage, and when the expectations don't play out the way you anticipate, it is hard to accept.

John: I had quite a different picture in mind, frankly.

Cindy: I really didn't have any picture—but it wasn't this one.

Therapist: So let's see where we were. John, you had the idea to bring someone into the house to help Cindy with cleaning and so forth. Cindy thought that would solve part of the problem for her, although going back to work 3 days a week was really what she wanted.

John: I suppose we could talk about the idea of her working and the logistics involved. I mean if the situation was such that it was less chaotic at home and Cindy was happier, then I guess we would both get what we needed.

By increasing the empathic experience of each member of the marital dyad, the therapist has moved the couple from polarized blaming and contention to a benign dialogue with a goal of compromise. Understanding and feeling the other's reality facilitates communication. It is no longer an argument of positions; it is a unified attempt to solve a problem.

Step 6

Identify and challenge unhelpful beliefs and specific miscommunication circulating in the stepfamily—the role of labels.

The therapist has been listening throughout the various dialogues for faulty beliefs or unrealistic or unhelpful expectations as well as instances in which clearly the couple cannot hear each other. Overlooking or defensively disregarding the other's feelings can provoke interpersonal conflict and should be attended to. It is important to identify the roadblocks in communication. Are there preconceived notions about the intent and motivations of the partner that sabotage effective connection? It is of particular importance in stepfamilies to optimize dialogue because of the plethora of disparate loyalties and inchoate relationships that are not of one's choosing.

In the initial interview, the therapist noted that John observed that Cindy's personality was very different from Pauline's, and he credits those exciting, intellectually challenging aspects of his then-young colleague for reawakening him from his grief and making his life enjoyable again. Yet John's expectations for Cindy's performance as a wife and stepmother seemed to be patterned on and closely resemble the reality he experienced and appreciated with Pauline. One can understand and even justify John's problematic presumption; however, without his becoming aware of its inherent unfairness and the uncomfortable position into which Cindy is placed, he cannot correct it.

Cindy may feel that John's unilateral decision about her employment appears to indicate a general lack of interest in her concerns, which may cause resentment and agitation. Often in stepfamilies, this type of issue becomes lost in more pressing priorities, such as children's needs and household routines. Clarifying John's response as a product of his experience of marriage to someone who enjoyed being a stay-at-home mom will be helpful in removing Cindy's mistaken perceptions that he does not care about her feelings. Seeing John as manipulating and controlling may be negative labels that detract from the real problem and prevent a solution.

There are multiple factors impinging on Cindy and the children and making their relationship vulnerable to dissension: the actual remarriage, Pauline's death and the children's various grief responses, Cindy's lack of comfort in her new role, and the absence of support from Pauline's family. All of these factors are rooted in loss. The remarriage represents a new, very different woman stepping into "Mom's place," which is confirmation that Mom is indeed gone. Cindy's lack of comfort in her new position and the fact that she supplanted the extended family as well as Jennifer's position as the oldest female member of the household may provoke hostility from the child that is based on circumstances rather than personality issues. Jennifer may assign negative intent to Cindy on the basis of erroneous notions of the situation. Cindy may interpret Jennifer's recalcitrant behavior as hostility toward her, rather than a call for help, and prefer the company of Ashley, who is quiet and compliant.

As a neutral observer of couple dynamics, the therapist can decipher and confront Cindy's and John's faulty belief systems; these reactive postures and perceptions obfuscate their actual feelings and needs, promote blame and fault-finding, and hinder effective problem solving and communication.

Step 7

Support the naturally connected subsystem (parent and child), and confirm that parent and child are capable of expressing mutual concern.

The biological family subsystem is fragmented and drifting. Since the marriage, the children have not spent much time with their dad. They have had to transition from their mother and father to a grieving dad and extended family to someone who is a virtual stranger intruding in their lives. They do not like it when Cindy tries to provide hands-on guidance or emotional support, and to make matters worse, she occupies Dad's time. In fact, she is a steady reminder that their mom is gone and Dad has moved on. The children may feel confused, angry, and resentful toward Dad.

Dad may also feel the disconnection as well as sense that his family is out of control. Cindy has been miserable and disorganized as a homemaker and can't seem to control his children. Jennifer is acting out and running off into the neighborhood; Ashley is unnaturally quiet. Heather seems oblivious to the very complicated and difficult situation. The need for this subsystem to be seen is apparent.

In the third session, the therapist welcomes the biological subsystem, which includes John, Jennifer, and Ashley, into the session. It has been determined that Heather is not only too young to benefit from the experience but also may produce too much of a distraction to the flow of the session. The goal is to reconnect the children to their father and reassure them that he loves them. That has not changed. The therapist notes that Ashley and John sit together and Jennifer moves to the other side of the room, away from everyone. After introductions and informal conversation, the therapist begins the session.

Therapist:	Jennifer, your views are very important to us, and we want to hear what you have to say. Would it be possible for you to move to the chair beside your dad?
Jennifer:	I guess so.
Therapist:	Thanks. I really appreciate it. There have been a lot of changes in your family in the past 2 years, haven't there, Jennifer?
Jennifer:	Yes, and not good either!
Therapist:	Well, we are going to talk a little about those changes today.
Jennifer:	[makes a face] Do we have to talk about Cindy?
Therapist:	No, but we may mention her from time to time because she is part of your life now. Jennifer and Ashley, can you tell me a little about what it is like for you these days?
Jennifer:	It sucks.
Ashley:	It's not that bad, Jennifer.

Jennifer:	Mom's dead.
Ashley:	[silence]
Therapist:	That was a very painful event for all of you, I am sure. We all feel an important loss intensely, but we don't always show it the same way. What else has changed for you, girls?
Jennifer:	Cindy's around.
Therapist:	OK, your dad has gotten remarried.
Jennifer:	Yeah!
Therapist:	So do you really dislike Cindy as a person or do you just feel like you don't want anyone coming into your home and telling you what to do?
Jennifer:	Well, I don't like anyone telling me what to do!
Therapist:	So if it was someone else, there still would be a problem.
Jennifer:	I guess.
Therapist:	Ashley, what else is different?
Ashley:	My grandma and aunt don't come over anymore. They used to come and help; Aunt Jane used to take me to PT.
Therapist:	That is something Cindy does now.
Ashley:	That's OK, I guess. I just miss them.
Therapist:	So that is a big change. Can you think of anything else?
Jennifer:	We never see Dad anymore!
John:	Jennifer, you are always gone when I get home. I have time to spend with you then.
Jennifer:	It is not the same, and besides, when I do get home, you and Cindy are arguing. It really is not fun.
John:	We are working on that.
Ashley:	We don't really spend much time with you, Dad. You work during the week, and on weekends, you and Cindy hang out. [turning to the therapist] Sometimes they take us shopping, but it's not the same as being with him doing something fun, like we used to, after Mom died.

Therapist:	So it sounds like you miss doing things with your dad. What would you like to see happen, girls?
Jennifer:	It would be fun if we could go out to Chucky Cheese; even Heather used to go.
John:	Yeah, we used to go there once every week or 10 days. I took them swimming at the free swim at the Y on Saturday mornings. That was fun. They have an indoor pool. I really enjoyed those times with the girls.
Therapist:	How would you feel about doing some of those things again together?
Jennifer and Ashley:	Great!
John:	I would like that. I really would, and I don't think Cindy would mind at all.
Therapist:	So perhaps you can set up an outing this weekend.
John:	I will. I have missed my time with the girls. I love them so much; we have been through a lot since Pauline died.

Clinicians would be lucky if all of their sessions proceeded to such a satisfactory conclusion, although this example is not entirely unusual. Most stepfamilies feel a push to spend time all together to support the idea that this new stepfamily is stable. The intervention that encourages the support of all subsystems is usually well received, particularly support of the biological subsystem and the couple.

Step 8

Teach the family about its own systemic functioning.

The family needs to understand how each individual is interwoven into the family's mode of functioning. Becoming aware of each family member's role in the total scheme and its interplay with others will, it is hoped, illuminate all family members' responsibility for change. Focusing on a solution, not remaining entrenched in vilification of the other, and affirming that they are all partially accountable for how the family functions will contradict the notion of their acting in a vacuum. They need to realize that their behavior is not without impact on others.

Jennifer's hostile, aggressive conduct alienates Cindy, who has no experience in child rearing. After experimenting with different responses and having no success, Cindy may settle into a complacent attitude; this in turn may infuriate John, who may see Cindy as uncaring and casually indifferent. It would be helpful for John to understand that Cindy has become frustrated trying to manage three kids, but this may not indicate a lack of caring for the girls. Likewise, Cindy's understanding of Jennifer's grief response would help her to see Jennifer in a less adversarial light. Clarifying the intentions of the family members also helps to delineate the cause and effect of each other's behaviors.

When John comes home at night, by his own admission he tries to spend some quality time with the children, but he may be distracted by the disorganization in the house. Cindy notices his negative response to chaos because she may already be chastising herself for the condition of the home as a result of inculcated societal expectations of a woman as a homemaker. The last feedback she may want to receive is an echo of what she is already feeling. This may escalate her reactivity to subtle communication cues. The children may notice and feel the tension and naturally ally themselves with their father, another confirmation to everyone that Cindy is an outsider who cannot be accepted by this family.

The two younger children do not manifest any obnoxious and alienating behavior, so they are given less notice in comparison with Jennifer. Jennifer may feel angry or jealous of this perceived preferential treatment to Ashley and Heather but not want a relationship with Cindy. This is a dilemma for Jennifer, which may add to her already oppositional behavior. On the other hand, Ashley's and Heather's needs are not highlighted and therefore may not be addressed. They receive positive or neutral attention from both Cindy and John but with little insight into the internal worlds of both children. Ashley may be struggling with enduring symptoms of posttraumatic stress disorder, and the family process diverts attention away from recognition of the problem.

Exploring, identifying, and clarifying the recursive cycle of family interactions may allow positive proactive choices to be made and the family system to function more smoothly. Once one understands that no single action is the cause of a problem, the cycle itself becomes the problem. Therefore, the therapist works to address the cycle.

Step 9

Assist in coparental work between any and all involved parental figures, including the binuclear family.

Coparental work includes the couple's arriving at agreement on house rules, discipline issues, family activities, and quality time for John to share with his children. In most cases, it would also include work with a third or fourth parent to promote cooperation and unity between the separate households in dealing with these issues. The children would not be getting mixed signals; rules and consequences would be more uniform so coparental work would decrease the opportunity to manipulate one parent against another.

In stepfamilies formed by the death of a spouse and subsequent remarriage, the parental coalition is composed of the remarried couple. Cindy was never married, so there are no ex-spouses. Ever present, however, are the members of Pauline's family, looming in the background as either a source of support or a cause of potential divisiveness. The optimal outcome is obviously the former, but ultimately this depends on Cindy's willingness to accept them as part of the family and the therapist's skill in providing a safe atmosphere for Cindy and the extended family to work toward this goal. In this way, Pauline's family could be included as part of the parental coalition because of the quasiparental relationships they have with each child, having provided child care and other forms of support after Pauline's death.

This part of the process may take many sessions to accomplish and advance the family toward a comfortable solution for all involved. Clearly, careful preparation is essential because if Cindy or the extended family cannot accept each other's presence, then a dialogue is impossible and the important collaboration on managing the children is unattainable.

The therapist would bring Cindy and John together again for the discussion of house rules and parenting practices. That would also be a time to reaffirm the necessity of presenting a united front to the children and taking conflictual discussions behind closed doors. The therapist would then want to process plans for Cindy's part-time work and the logistics involved in attending to child care, transportation needs, and medical appointments. What are the options? What do the afternoons look like when school is over? What happens when both Cindy and John are working and there is a sick child? Who needs to stay home? Who are the family supports? It is likely that the extended family will be brought up in the discussion as a possible option. In that they already have relationships with the children and an active interest in their wellbeing, the extended family members appear to be the perfect answer. Ideally, anything that would assuage the void created by Pauline's absence and the end of her family's brief but critically important involvement would also most likely promote more positive feelings between Cindy and the children.

The extended family has not yet been engaged in the therapeutic process because of other more exigent needs, those that involve the actual conflict and chaos in the house. Involving them is a delicate process. Cindy could easily be threatened by the presence of her predecessor's family, and, conversely, the extended family may feel proprietary toward the children, Pauline's house and possessions, and the old family rituals and traditions. This could be covertly promoted or overtly asserted and sabotage the stepfamily's adjustment. To this end, the process has to be slow and very respectful of Cindy's feelings and appreciative of the best interests of the children.

For the purposes of our narrative, we can proffer the assumption that Cindy, after a discussion with John in therapy, can entertain the idea of Pauline's extended family being involved as helpful supports. After all, Cindy is very eager to work as a lawyer again, and she may realize that the children need to spend more time with their mother's family. The therapist should not proceed until it is clear that Cindy is comfortable with the idea.

A session with John and the extended family is now scheduled to address the possibility of enlisting their help and support. Do they want to get involved and to what extent? One could conjecture that it would be difficult and painful to see someone else in Pauline's place; however, the rewards of continuing to have contact with the children would probably take priority. Structure and ground rules that would give adequate deference to Cindy's position and the couple relationship would have to be clarified. Once the extended family agreed to the necessary guidelines for respect and consideration of the new stepfamily, the process could continue.

The therapist would now schedule a session with Cindy, John, and the extended family to safely initiate communication among all parties concerned, emphasizing the importance of putting the needs of the children first and encouraging everyone to have an empathic regard for each other's perspective. John and Pauline's family have a prior history, which has been positive and is filled with happy memories and a shared tragic loss. Assuring Cindy's emotional safety by maintaining balance and providing a calm and centered approach to the issue at hand would be the therapist's most challenging responsibility in the session. It may be important that John and Cindy sit together, with the extended family next to Cindy. The desired effect is for Cindy to feel included and an integral part of the session, an imperative condition to assure the success of the stepfamily.

The therapist begins.

> *Therapist:* I have called you all together today to discuss the possibility of working out an arrangement that will benefit all involved, most importantly the children. I want that to be your focus as the session goes forward, always keeping in mind their welfare. They have been through a very difficult time, [turning to John and the extended family] as have you all, losing their mother. I am sure that goes without saying. [everyone nods] However, in stepfamilies, research overwhelmingly supports the

notion that conflict has a negative effect on the adjustment of the children. Again, to that end, I want you to put their needs first. Is everyone in agreement on this idea? [all nod] Any questions?

Group: No.

Joan (Pauline's mother): What is the arrangement?

Therapist: The arrangement entails child care after school and occasionally on weekends or during the day.

Joan: I am not sure I understand. I mean isn't Cindy doing that? We don't want to interfere, but we would like to see the kids once in a while.

Therapist: John and Cindy have talked about the possibility of Cindy's working part time at the law firm, and it has been decided that she will begin work in 2 weeks, 3 days a week, Monday, Wednesday, and Thursday. So there are times when Cindy will not be able to pick them up from school or take them to the doctor's or take them to soccer practice. They have told me that they are very fond of you, Joan, and also Aunt Sally and Aunt Ruth.

Sally: So if I understand you, you actually want us to help Cindy stay out of the house and avoid taking care of the kids.

Cindy: I like the children. It is not that I want to avoid them. It is more that I really miss the challenges of work. I am only out of law school 4 years, and I really want to keep working for now. I think I will be a better wife and stepmother if I have work. It will be more balanced for me, but I want to make sure we have good plans for the children.

Therapist: And that is where we want to keep the focus centered on what is best for the children. So the plans have already been set in motion for Cindy to work, and other alternatives to cover caring for the children have been looked into, but I think you would be helping the children more by their being with family members who love them. And you would receive the payment

| | for your time and expenses. If the schedules don't work for you, then we will look into other options, although I am sure Cindy will have some flexibility working part time. But for the sake of the children, you had to be considered as the first possible option for child care. |

Sally: I am not saying that I wouldn't want to pick the kids up from school or take Ashley to her PT appointments. I really like spending time with them. But I wouldn't want to take them to their home; I would rather bring them to my house or to Mother's. They could be picked up from there.

Therapist: Would that be OK with you? [looking at Cindy and John]

John: Yes, that is fine. Cindy or I could pick them up there.

Jane: I'm in, too—I used to take them every Wednesday, after Pauline died, because we would go to the mall. Heather would be with my mom. We would walk around and then all go have something to eat. But if we do get food, I don't want to hear that Cindy called it junk food!

Cindy: Have I ever called it junk food? I ate it all the time in law school. No, when you are caring for the children, you are in charge, Jane. I really appreciate what you are both doing for the children.

John: I agree! Thank you so much.

A concrete schedule with contingency plans in the event of illness or school activities could then be made. The therapist makes clear from the beginning and affirms during the session that by focusing on the children a solution can be reached, leaving personal feelings and the pain and reality of John's remarriage as secondary to the children's welfare. Not all new stepmoms would ignore the sarcasm of the two sisters, but the assumption is that Cindy is so eager to return to work and ease the conflict with John that she is very conciliatory. Also, for the purpose of the presentation of the model, it enables the clinician to move forward.

Following this agreement, a session could be held with John, Cindy, and the children to inform them of the upcoming plans for after school pickups and special situations, such as illness or appointments. Having John and

Cindy present the involvement of the extended family will demonstrate Cindy's flexibility and concern for the welfare of the children.

Therapist:	Jennifer, you don't look very happy today.
Jennifer:	I am not. I don't know why we had to come here today.
Therapist:	So your dad and Cindy didn't talk to you about it?
Jennifer:	They just told us that Cindy was going back to work, and they were going to tell us where we would go after school when she is working.
Cindy:	I am very excited to be going back to work again, but I wanted to make sure you all were happy with the arrangements.
Jennifer:	Yeah, sure . . . whatever.
John:	Have a little respect, Jennifer.
Cindy:	We have talked to your mother's family, and they have agreed to help out. What do you think of that?
Jennifer and Ashley:	That is great—all of them? Grandma and Aunt Sally and Aunt Jane?
Cindy:	Well, it will be different plans on each day. We have worked out a schedule, and we will see how that goes or if we need to change it to make it better.
Jennifer and Ashley:	When does it start?
Cindy:	Well, it was supposed to start when I went back to work, but we can maybe do a trial day to see how it goes. Would you like that?
Ashley:	Yeah, it's cool.
Jennifer:	Yeah, I've missed them.
John:	That doesn't mean that you can run off on them. You won't be at home, so you will need to do what they say and stick around. Can you do that?
Jennifer:	I suppose.

The parental coalition now includes John, Cindy, and the extended family members who are going to have direct contact with the children. Rules of behavior, consequences for actions, and timetables will all have to be worked out. Again, Cindy and John must maintain a unified presence with all involved. Without John's support, Cindy's position may be fragile and disempowered.

Step 10

> Increase communication among all stepfamily members available, and move toward integrating the various subsystems into a functioning and satisfied stepfamily.

To review, the therapist has now met with the following subsystems: the marital dyad (Cindy and John), the biological subsystem (John and the children), the extended family subsystem (Pauline's family with John and Cindy), and the stepmother family (a family holding four separate subsystems).

For integration to be successful, each person will have to focus his or her efforts on compromise and cooperation; this is difficult because of steadfast loyalties and traditions. The therapist uses psychoeducation to inform the family that conflict between ex-spouses is a very negative force impinging on the children (Papernow, 1993). Using the extended family as a representation of Pauline's former position, one could deduce that should there be arguing and discord between Cindy and the extended family, it would most likely produce the same consequence. Also, John would be placed in the middle and would be called on to support one side or the other, which would either put strain on the marriage or alienate the extended family. Thus, it is critical that the therapist proceed cautiously, affirming at each opportunity that the children's well-being is contingent on cooperation among the adults in the family. Cindy should be given emotional safety within the sessions because the plan depends on her ability to be objective and fair as well as conciliatory. The plan asks a lot of Cindy, and in many cases treatment does not work because of the usually threatening idea of having the ex-spouse's family involved in the daily or weekly routines.

If the needs of the children are adequately met in terms of care and support, there are still some problems to consider on an individual basis. Jennifer's recalcitrant behavior perhaps should be treated in therapy with another clinician. Because she is manifesting grief and loss in such an outer-directed manner, she could sabotage the entire scheme for family integration. The possibility of lingering posttraumatic stress disorder symptoms in Ashley should be attended to as well. Heather seems to have been accommodating to the new stepfamily better than anyone, but she should be monitored for the possible eventuality that she becomes symptomatic in any way.

Other complicating factors, such as addiction, family member clinical issues, or intense grief, for example, may preclude a propitious outcome. Often plans for a congenial and cooperative parental hierarchy can derail in such cases. The therapist should be aware of this and work around such a roadblock by formulating decisions by consensus. Excluding the family member from the sessions is extreme but may become the only alternative.

Family holidays, rituals, and traditions are a delicate subject. The therapist needs to approach this subject in the final meetings. Holidays are difficult under normal circumstances for many families. With the biological family, there is a history of holiday practices and traditions to which they are accustomed. A newly formed stepfamily has no shared memories of holiday celebration. The therapist could be helpful to them in devising their holiday plans by intercepting incipient problems. It is important that compromise around this subject include Cindy's needs, otherwise her position as an outsider in the family will be increased. For example, respect for Cindy's faith and practices could be shown by having Cindy explain the traditional holiday rituals and symbolism of the Jewish faith to John and the children. In addition, Cindy could support the family Christmas celebration. Perhaps, Cindy and the children could invite friends over for a sleepover and bake Christmas cookies to be wrapped up and given as presents to the teachers. The stepfamily thereby creates entirely different holiday rituals by assimilating the old and creating the new.

Cindy's parents, it has been mentioned, are eager to join the family system, which will be a source of comfort and support especially for Cindy but also for the family. Therapy can proceed until all family members are integrated into the family system.

6

THE COMPLEX STEPFAMILY

In this chapter, we apply the stepfamily therapy (SfT) model to the Coleman family, a prototypical complex stepfamily in which each partner brings children to the remarriage. The clinician obtains information during the telephone intake and from this information charts the genogram. In the case of the complex stepfamily, this diagram is especially useful to clarify visually this very complicated configuration. We then move through each step of the SfT model, demonstrating the family dynamics, concerns, and progress.

INTAKE INFORMATION

Couple presenting for treatment: David (35) and Eileen (39), married almost 2 years

Eileen's children (residential): Annie (15) and Kathy (13)

David and Eileen's child: Rebecca (1)

David's children (nonresidential): Joanie (11) and Sammy (9)

Employment: David is a freelance computer website designer. Eileen works as a beautician.

Eileen's ex-husband: Roy (40) and his new wife Vicky (35), married more than 1 year

Vicky's two children from a previous marriage: Barry (14) and Laurel (11)

Roy and Vicky's child: Shawna (1)

Employment: Roy is a doctor.

David's ex-wife: Linda (31), not repartnered

Linda's employment: Newspaper employee

Race, ethnicity, religion: White, /European American, Protestant

Parental hierarchies: David and Eileen, Roy and Vicky, and Linda

David makes the call for the couple, who come to therapy because they "cannot handle the situation anymore." There is "no money, no time, no privacy, no space." David feels he is ready "to explode."

Prior to their marriage, David and Eileen had an affair and carry residual guilt. The affair lasted a little more than a year, at which time they decided to leave their marriages and move their relationship forward. Eileen had a benign relationship with Roy; they grew apart because they never spent time together and had nothing in common. David also had a fairly good relationship with Linda until the divorce, at which time communication broke down.

Both ex-spouses are alive and in the vicinity. Linda did not have to move; however, both Roy and Eileen did. Roy has since remarried Vicky, who has two children, Barry and Laurel. Linda and Roy take an active part in the lives of their children, although Roy needs prodding and reminding about his visitation schedule. Custody arrangements state that David's children live with his ex-spouse, Linda, and come to stay every other weekend. Holidays are on an alternate basis as well.

Eileen has custody of her children. They go to their dad every other weekend and alternate holidays, but because of their dad's new baby, the visits often get cancelled. Annie does not like to visit Roy and Vicky because she resents Barry and Laurel, and does not get along with Vicky, who she says spoils 1-year-old Shawna. Annie also says that her dad tries to keep the peace by paying more attention to Shawna than to her. In fact, Annie doesn't see why she has to go to her dad's house at all, given that she seems like such a pain to everyone, although she admits that "the baby is OK." In contrast to Annie's belligerence, Kathy goes quietly along for visits, keeps to herself, and reads. Roy's children are half siblings to Shawna, the mutual child of Roy and Vicky, and stepsiblings to Barry and Laurel, Vicky's children. At home, they have their little sister, Rebecca, the mutual child of Eileen and David.

David has a conflictual relationship with Linda, mostly on the subject of money. Money is tight. Freelance website design is an unsteady source of income, which mostly goes to Linda. Eileen makes good money, which is sufficient for the expenses of the house for the most part, but she wishes that David were more able to help out with the money situation of the house where he lives. David rarely contributes to their household, and with Rebecca,

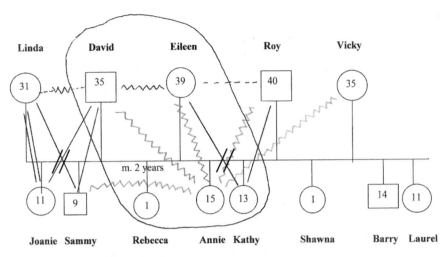

Figure 6.1. The Coleman family.

money is stretched so tight that there are arguments between David and Eileen on a daily basis. David's mom died 6 months ago and left some money, which mostly went to credit card debt.

Eileen's daughter Annie has never liked David, and now she is out of control. When she comes home from school, he is there because he works at home, so she just texts friends, gets on the computer, or takes off to hang with friends.

It seems that the situation is rife with chaos. People are constantly coming and going; David and Eileen feel like they live in the family car. They try to facilitate Annie's participation in sports and chorale. Kathy is a sedentary child who seems content to read and watch television. When David's kids are there, there is no space, and because they are younger, they are just seen as annoying. A question Annie often asks is "Why do they have to come?" There is no separate space for them to sleep, so Joanie usually sleeps in Kathy's room, and Sammy sleeps on the living room sofa. This creates separate problems because David likes to stay up late on weekends. Sammy has attention-deficit/hyperactivity disorder (ADHD) and gets on Eileen's nerves, also causing conflict between them.

The therapist makes a genogram (see Figure 6.1 and the legend in Figure 3.1) of the family and invites David and Eileen in for the first session.

APPLYING THE 10 STEPS OF STEPFAMILY THERAPY

In the sections that follow, the therapist applies each of the 10 steps of the SfT model to the Coleman family.

Step 1

Recognize the structure of the stepfamily (e.g., simple stepfather family, simple stepmother family, complex stepfamily in which both adults are stepparents). Use the initial telephone intake to look for systemic similarities within the context of the research literature.

This family is a complex stepfamily. Of new stepfamilies, 50% are complex stepfamilies with both the husband and wife bringing children to the marriage (Ganong & Coleman, 1994). Half of those couples have mutual children following the remarriage (Ganong & Coleman, 1994). Anne Bernstein (1989), author of *Yours, Mine, and Ours: How Families Change When Remarried Parents Have a Child Together*, stated, "How different to be born into this teeming complexity, peopled by explorers charting unknown territory, than to be born to a 'tea for two' couple" (p. 5). Decisions made in one family will influence the lives of the other; ties to the various parents and stepparents will modify relationships between siblings, half-siblings, and stepsiblings. Intertwined with these elements are visitation and custody arrangements affecting the residential and nonresidential children and mutual children born to the remarried couples.

The family is presenting in the Mobilization Stage, one of the Middle Stages, characterized by stepparents asserting themselves by voicing their complaints and feelings. It is a time when the stepparents (in this case) attempt to restructure the family for their own inclusion. Conflict and tension are conspicuously present (Papernow, 1993). Obviously, when a therapist takes an initial look at the binuclear family, it can appear chaotic and confusing. By charting a genogram of the entire family and dividing the configuration into subsystems, the therapist simplifies the picture, provides clarification, and reduces the seemingly overwhelming task of helping the family in treatment. These subsystems are more manageable units that can then be strengthened to produce a cohesive working whole, which is the concept of SfT as presented in this book.

From the intake, the therapist distinguishes problem areas common to complex stepfamilies.

1. There is no money, no time, no privacy, no space. Many demands are being made on the new stepfamily. The overwhelming needs of all of the different family members require money, time, privacy, and space. Money needs have increased because there are now three separate households, instead of one, on which to pay mortgage and maintenance. Quiet time or recreational time seems impossible to glean out of the divergent schedules, activities, and social engagements of the many children. Privacy

within the cramped spaces involves closing doors and being vigilant to who is where and at what time. Space, particularly on visitation weekends, becomes a source of discord between the children, with each parent understanding and advocating for his or her biological child's needs. This inborn parental protective and affirming mechanism just serves as fodder for a disagreement between the couple in which there is no invested gain for either member. The therapist knows that this chaotic situation needs some structure and a renegotiation of boundaries so the needs of the various family members can be fulfilled. To establish stabilization in the family, the work will need to be done one subsystem at a time.

2. Eileen had a benign relationship with Roy; they grew apart because they never saw each other and had nothing in common. David also had a fairly good relationship with Linda until the divorce, at which time communication broke down. Neither marriage was conflictual, volatile, or unstable; they were marriages in which there was dissatisfaction on both David's and Eileen's parts, which was the foundation for the affair. Two problems work against the couple from the beginning. The first is that when children are experiencing a nonconflictual marriage between their parents, adjustment to the divorce is difficult. If the marriage has been filled with explosive animosity, then the divorce seems to be a relief from the fighting and justified, and the adjustment of the kids to the divorce is better (Amato & Booth, 1997). Second, the fact that David and Eileen met and had a love affair while still married represents a betrayal not only to the mate but also to the children. The therapist needs to be aware of possible residual anger that may not be expressed overtly but in passive-aggressive ways.

   The couple is attempting to establish and strengthen the marital union in the presence of four children who have different degrees of anger toward and interest in the relationship. This is a task rife with anxiety and stress in the beginning stages of their marriage.

3. Roy needs prodding and reminding about his visitation schedule. Fathers have time and emotional obligations to their residential stepchildren, which divert their attention and energy away from their nonresidential children (Leake, 2007). The birth of Shawna can provide additional distraction from the nonresidential children, even though the birth of a mutual child can also be seen as a unifying feature for the binuclear

family of Roy and Vicky. The therapist needs to notice the state of the relationship between Roy and his nonresidential children Annie and Kathy and facilitate a more reliable and supportive connection, if necessary.

4. Annie is out of control. Annie was 13 years old when David and Eileen married. Children of this age have a particularly difficult time handling remarriage because of attachment and concurrent autonomy needs (Bray & Berger, 1993). Developmentally, the child is also experiencing physical and hormonal changes during an important stage of maturation; this complicates the already arduous task of managing her life while demands are made of her to fit into a new family configuration, one that she did not choose. For Annie, there are very arduous transitions related to the remarriage—moving to not one but two new homes, her father's remarriage, and new half siblings. The composition of the family keeps changing, and the boundaries, already more permeable in a stepfamily, fluctuate. Annie, as well as Kathy, finds herself in not one but two new complex stepfamilies.

It is entirely possible that because of Annie's recalcitrant behavior, the marriage has been under duress long enough to have increased conflict and confusion and raised the anxiety of the family members. Antagonism from a stepchild or poor behavior can have a negative effect on marital quality (Hetherington & Stanley-Hagan, 1999b).

Annie is angry with her mother, Eileen; her father, Roy; her stepfather, David; and her stepmother, Vicky. She finds her stepsiblings—all four of them—annoying, in particular Sammy. From the intake, one can surmise that she finds comfort in texting and visiting her friends. The therapist notes that Annie should probably be referred for individual counseling. Because she is a member of so many subsystems, her discontent and opposition provide a continuous destabilizing factor to any balanced resolution of an issue.

5. Roy tries to keep the peace by paying more attention to Shawna. When Roy concentrates on Shawna, he takes the attention away from Annie and diffuses the conflict between Annie and himself as well as between himself and Vicky. According to Papernow (1993), having a mutual child born into a complex stepfamily while in the early stages of remarriage can be very problematic to the adjustment of the family. Multiple transitions are challenging at the very least, but also the children may see the new baby as a realistic and tangible imped-

iment to their parents "coming to their senses and reuniting." For the stepparents, their own baby may certainly divert attention away from the task of building relationships with their stepchildren.

Step 2

Determine the membership of the first session—usually the marital dyad—and further delineate the unique concerns of the stepfamily.

David and Eileen are invited to the first session to cite their most urgent concerns. From the telephone intake, the therapist has noted that the couple is in crisis and the situation is perceived to be beyond their control. Reaffirming their commitment, defining their needs, and planning a strategy that will address them are therapist considerations. The marital dyad needs immediate reinforcement and strengthening; feeling more control and hearing their situation normalized as one common to complex stepfamilies will help to mollify the anxiety the couple is experiencing.

After initial dialogue, the therapist begins.

Therapist: After speaking with David on the phone last week, I heard him say that conditions are beginning to erode your relationship. Would you both agree with that?

David: Yes.

Eileen: I agree.

Therapist: David seemed to indicate that both of you were interested in working on the problems in the family situation.

David: For me, it feels like a monumental task.

Eileen: Impossible.

Therapist: The plan is to "divide and conquer." The situation looks impossible because you are looking it as a whole. We are going to work on one section of your family at a time and, I hope, plan a way to approach each difficulty and come up with a solution. It is important that you want to proceed with the process.

David: Yes, I do. I love Eileen, and it scares me to think that other people and stress could destroy what we have.

Eileen: I feel like we are on the brink of that happening if something isn't done; I want to save our marriage not only for us but also for all the kids. They have been through enough upheaval.

Therapist:	OK, then. Today we are going to hear what most concerns you about the current situation and what you feel are the most pressing issues in your family. I would like each of you to describe in turn your experience, with the other listening and really trying to understand each other's feelings. Who wants to start?
David:	It doesn't matter to me. I feel like I got a lot off my chest the other day.
Eileen:	All right. I don't know where to begin. I guess Annie is my main worry. She seems so angry. She does OK in school, but all she seems to want to do is hang out with her friends and not have anything to do with us.
Therapist:	So far, you seem to have described what adolescence is all about.
Eileen:	I expected that, but how do you tell whether it is just normal rebellion or anger from the situation?
Therapist:	Can you tell me a little more about it?
Eileen:	She doesn't want to be home; she hates going to her father's; she can't stand her stepmother; she picks fights with Kathy; she gets furious when David's kids come, especially Sammy, who drives her nuts. She gives David such a hard time, I am amazed he hasn't packed up and left.
Therapist:	Wow, I can see why you are worried. It sounds like she is very angry at the situation, on top of the usual adolescent discontent. In the research, it discusses how difficult all the transitions are on the children involved. She may wonder where she fits into a new situation that she did not choose. You see, she and Kathy are part of two complex stepfamilies with two new half siblings. Kathy may be having difficulty as well but is going along with everything. You may want to get Annie some individual counseling. It is very upsetting to see a child in so much pain, striking out at everyone. And it can have negative effects on your marriage. What else do you feel is a problem that you want to see change?
Eileen:	Money. We fight over it all the time. When David gets a job, I think, OK, this will relieve some of the pressure of the bills, but I never see it. It goes to Linda for not only child support but also extras like Sammy's meds, which should be included, and Joanie's skating lessons or new skates. Whatever . . . I am a beautician; I make good money and get some support from Roy, but we have a mortgage. Maybe money is my main con-

cern. I never thought I would see the day that I cared about every nickel and dime, but it has come.

Therapist: It must be very difficult to manage all the finances. Anything else?

Eileen: We never have any alone time, just the two of us. There is always someone around needing to go somewhere. All the coming and going—I feel like I live in the car. But I suppose that comes with the territory.

Therapist: It can get very busy and sometime very rushed, and one gets hassled with all the kids needing to go to doctors and activities and such. And you wonder when are we going to have time for our relationship?

Eileen: Exactly.

Therapist: Eileen, thank you. That really helps me understand what is bothering you. David, can I hear from you?

David: It is somewhat the same for me, only I am on the receiving end of the nagging about the money. I have court-ordered child support! I really don't want Eileen to be paying Linda. I mean your present wife paying your ex-wife?

Eileen: Well, it works into that whether you agree or not.

Therapist: We are going to try to reach some resolution about the money situation as we go forward. But right now I need to hear what concerns David.

Eileen: I'm sorry. This is really a hot issue.

David: She can't help herself. [sarcastically]

Therapist: I can see you are both very distressed and frustrated, but we are trying to get to the heart of what is troubling each of you. Then possibly there will be more understanding and consequently less anger. So money is a very sore subject and . . .

David: About Annie, I have just written her off because Sammy is such a handful, and I have my attention on him most of the time. I work at home freelance, so I have to kind of get stuff done in the morning because the kids (hers) are such a distraction. It is really hard to concentrate. And then right in the middle of something, I get called on to be a taxi, so I have the same complaint about Eileen, but I don't live in the car like she does.

Therapist: It seems like the pressure of everybody coming and going is really intense and wearing on you both. Anything else?

David: I think the romance has gone out of our marriage. I still love Eileen, but we seem to live for the kids and jobs and money. Our sex life is virtually dead. Sometimes we have a fight right before bedtime. It really makes for closeness. [sarcastically] There are always kids around.

Therapist: I can hear your frustrations, shared and individual, and your fears that they may erode your feelings for each other and derail your marriage.

The therapist has listened intently for and heard not only the actual verbal communication of complaints but also the periodic display of sarcasm on the part of both members of the marital dyad. Outside the therapist's office, the passive-aggressive anger is most likely aired, turning discussions into arguments that are bitter and personal. The relationship appears to be in crisis. There are pressing issues.

Eileen said that Annie was her main worry. A recalcitrant adolescent can put an enormous amount of stress on a marriage and even undermine a marriage bond. This is more the problem of the biological mother than a problem between David and Eileen. Their quarrels may be over the differential treatment she receives or the discipline issues—reining her in and getting her to be more compliant with chores and homework. Having Eileen assume the majority of the decision making regarding Annie and working out an optimal and unified parenting approach will address this issue to an extent. Annie may need individual counseling. However, Eileen may also be avoiding the central issue because it is such a trigger for arguments.

The therapist hears that money is a significant concern. With the family expanding to include more members, money often becomes a source of discord in stepfamilies. Having to support the additional households formed by remarriage and a new baby stretches the available money until the very thought of managing it produces anxiety and rancor. An extra stressor is David's freelance work, which does not produce a dependable bimonthly paycheck. So when completion of a job brings a "windfall" of money, Eileen watches as David fulfills the financial responsibility to his ex-wife and children while she pays the mortgage, taxes, maintenance, and necessities for the family by herself. The therapist notes that this is a more concrete problem, which provokes the more emergent dilemma. It also sets up a scenario for Eileen to begrudge Linda money even though she understands her needs.

In some cases, there may be a quasicompetition between the stepmother and the biological mother as to the loyalties and affections of the children (Ganong & Coleman, 1995a). Also, clinicians have noticed that often the remarried wife has enmity and anger toward the ex-wife on the basis of the description provided by the husband and vice versa. Not knowing each other may be opportunity to assume the worse and, thus, feel better about resenting each other.

In a complex stepfamily, logistics alone interrupt the relationship on a daily basis and account for a large portion of the disquietude in the marriage. The couple wonders what happened to the passion of stolen moments and the preoccupation to someday be together. The therapist hears this and makes a mental note that the negotiation for more time and a restoration of the excitement and mutual caring will involve organization of the family comings and goings. Basic changes in routine, purposeful planning, and a hopeful attitude need to be implemented on the part of the couple. Both members of the marital dyad remain committed to the marriage, and the feelings are still present. This is important for the therapist to hear because the therapeutic process can be complicated. Paramount to everything is the couple's investment in the work and determination to make a successful and contented stepfamily.

The topics of money, the couple's relationship, and the schedules and demands of so many children appear to be the principal issues in this stepfamily. The therapist can ascertain whether these are typical problems of complex stepfamilies and ease the couple's feelings of panic and loss of control by helping them to understand that the predicament in which they find themselves is more a function of this type of configuration and not necessarily attributable to the individuals involved.

Initial interventions can be suggested to diffuse some of the tension and begin the work. For example, the therapist might advise David to assume the role of parental monitor and enforce the rules of the house with his stepchildren but participate more actively in the care and supervision of his own children when they are visiting. A schedule of Annie's and Kathy's after-school activities will give David more advance notice of his driving responsibilities so that he can better organize his work and time constraints and not feel like a taxi, as he alluded to in the session. How the stepfamily applies and practices the intervention is important information for the therapist to have. It enables him or her not only to observe how earnestly the couple is participating in the process and but also to evaluate how much ability they have to exact change.

Step 3

Clarify the distinct subsystems in the stepfamily, and use this information to provide a direction for clinical treatment.

The clinician delineates the subsystems in this stepfamily.

1. The marital dyad: David and Eileen. The couple began their relationship while still married and had no idea of the complicated

path their lives would take by choosing to remarry. There are a plethora of stressors: children, ex-spouses, monetary needs, visitation and custody agreements, and more. The guilt from their affair, Roy's remarriage, and Sammy's special needs are putting pressure on the already circuitous family design.

Therapy has begun with the couple, who are in the center of the family configuration. Family loyalties, perceived preferential treatment, and/or the unfriendly or hostile attitudes of the children could cause friction and unexpressed tension between the couple, which need to be addressed and normalized. It is possible that the couple will require more than one session at the beginning of treatment to solidify the bond between them and further delineate problem areas. They can then be brought back after the therapist has met with other subsystems to check in and further reinforce their relationship.

2. The maternal biological subsystem: Eileen, Annie, and Kathy. This subsystem comprises Eileen and the two children of Eileen and Roy. Research indicates that a single mom with daughters is a difficult configuration for a man to join because of the often more collegial relationship between the members of a female single-family household (Coleman, Ganong, & Fine, 2000). Coleman and Ganong (1997) described a mother's "siege mentality" (p. 111) through the divorce, single parenthood, and remarriage. As a result, David may have endured resistance from Eileen and her daughters from the beginning, and because the remarriage had its origin in an affair, the situation is even more confounded.

This subsystem would be seen early in treatment to assure the girls that their mother, though she has remarried, has not abandoned them. David would not be a part of this session because of the danger of disruption of the session by the possibility of conflict or shutting down on the part of either David or Annie. Annie is angry with Dad, her stepmother, and Mom and David.

3. The paternal biological subsystem: David, Joanie, and Sammy. Often, the children of a nonresidential father need reassurance that there is a loyal, unwavering bond between them and their father. In this case, Joanie and Sammy watch from their home and perhaps perceive that even though Eileen's two girls aren't even related to their father, they are able to live with him and enjoy his company. They may feel displaced in his affections.

Also, Sammy's special needs require a lot of attention in behavior management, medication, and a very defined structure in the house, which the parents constantly have to monitor and correct. With the atmosphere becoming strained in the new stepfamily, Sammy may be inclined to feel even more like an outsider when visiting. So reassurance from his father that their emotional connection remains is necessary. A session with this subsystem would serve to validate and solidify the father's feelings for both of his children.

4. A former couple subsystem: David and ex-wife, Linda. Often in stepfamilies, there is friction between the couple that has divorced. If there is continuing acrimony toward each other, the children can be drawn into the dispute in various ways in an effort to complicate the life of the ex-spouse, sometimes passive-aggressively. In the literature, biological mothers are sometimes referred to as the *gatekeeper* of the children's other relationships, which also include their father, stepmother, and others (Kruk, 1992). For example, Linda knows that David and Eileen have theater tickets for a show that starts at 8, and she shows up to pick up the kids at 7:45 or cancels the arrangements at the last minute. David and Linda may have different ideas for bedtimes, curfews, and other household rules. Each of the ex-spouses may openly criticize the other to their kids and even advise them to not obey the other parent. Even if it seems that it will be difficult to arrange, most parents will come to a session if the therapist stresses that it is for the welfare of the children to come to a unified resolution on rules, visitation, and civility.

5. A former couple subsystem: Eileen and ex-husband, Roy, and his wife, Vicky. Most of what was discussed in the previous example is also applicable to this subsystem; however, there is an added consideration in this subsystem, that is, Vicky. Many times, the relationship may be too unpredictable or unsettled to bring the stepmother and the biological mother together. It depends on the situation, and the therapist can decide accordingly.

6. The stepsibling subsystem: Annie, Kathy, Joanie, and Sammy. The stepsibling subsystem has two important commonalities. They share a half sister, whom they seem to love, and a discontent with the fact that their lives have been irrevocably changed as a result of the circumstances. Annie and Kathy find themselves in a situation in which they cannot have their parents together and in addition have to live with a virtual stranger, David, who has intruded into their lives. Joanie and Sammy may

see themselves as lucky because they only have one stepparent and visit her only on weekends; otherwise they get to go home from their weekends to their mother and familiarity in routines and schedules. Annie and Kathy must leave their mother and stepfather, where they live, and go to their father and stepmother's home on weekends and some holidays, although the scheduled visitations have not always taken place.

The therapist could use a stepsibling session to help create more of a connection between them by talking about how difficult it must be to go back and forth and how annoying it is to have two places for their clothes and two different household routines. Discussing what is difficult about the situation in a neutral setting could be a unifying exercise. If there is conflict arising between Roy's children and Vicky's children, which, in turn, impinges on the rest of the binuclear family, then the therapist will have to take measures to quell the situation before it spreads throughout the family system. Because the couple presenting for treatment is Eileen and David, the focus of the treatment will be on that complex stepfamily, even though Roy and Vicky form an additional complex stepfamily.

7. The parental coalition: David, Eileen, Linda, Roy, and Vicky. In this case, the binuclear family involves three different households. Included in the parental coalition are all of the adults who are involved in the care of the remarried couples' children. Although the mutual children, Shawna and Rebecca, are important to workings of the households and have varying relationships with their half siblings, they are the offspring of married couples that are together and therefore are not the concern of more than one set of parents.

Step 4

Consider the research findings that normalize the experience of the stepfamily, and introduce them in clinical practice (when appropriate and meaningful).

Mavis Hetherington called the chaos and confusion in the early stages of remarriage *disequilibrium* (Hetherington & Clingempeel, 1992, p. 13), after which the family system begins to realign and redefine their roles in the new configuration (Hetherington & Clingempeel, 1992). The usual adjustment period is generally considered to be 4 to 7 years (Cherlin & Furstenberg, 1994; Papernow, 1993). Most couples are not thinking in terms of such a lengthy adjustment. Instead, many of them have misconceived notions that when they remarry, the new stepfamily will immediately become a family, based on their ideas about normative first-married family adjustment. These erroneous presumptions add to the anxiety they feel when children don't immediately welcome the new stepparent into their lives and, at the same time, become more distant with the biological parents. Anxiety increases with the shattering of each expectation. When a remarried couple presents for therapy, they are often somewhat astonished at the length of time it takes to adjust to stepfamily life, as described by scholars in the stepfamily field. Immediately, there is a sense of relief when any timetable for becoming a happy family is erased and they realize this is a shared experience among step-families.

Learning that there are more permeable boundaries in stepfamilies, which permit extra family members to come in and out of the different systems, is somewhat consoling. However, one of the outcomes of this, as found in the literature, is less cohesion than in first-married families (Pink & Wampler, 1985). The therapist encourages the couple to accept that things are going to be different and there is a need for flexibility to accommodate the additional members' schedules, routines, and needs. In addition, the stepfamily is not always going to feel unified and contained and understand their role in the process. There appears to be greater role ambiguity in complex stepfamilies, which causes more stress; it is assumed that this is due to each partner being both a biological parent and a stepparent (Fine & Schwebel, 1991).

The therapist could caution Roy that losing visits with his daughters could jeopardize his relationship with them in the future, and could also try to allay Eileen's concerns about her children's feelings when Roy cancels visits. Eileen would not have to alternately nag or cajole Roy to be more regular in his meetings if he could recognize that this is a common vulnerability for nonresidential dads. This could be shared in a subsystem meeting with Roy and serve as a reminder to him that a relationship interrupted by divorce and remarriage can continue with steadfast constancy, devotion, and love if the noncustodial parent is more dependable with the schedule.

Daughters often have more problematic adjustment in stepfather families than boys because boys tend to adapt more quickly to the remarriage and presence of a stepfather (Amato & Keith, 1991). Annie and Kathy have both a residential stepfather and a nonresidential stepmother; at the moment, Annie is externalizing the stress of the transitions, and Kathy may be internalizing. Preadolescent girls do not necessarily have as difficult an adjustment as an older sibling; however, when they move into adolescence, the discord will increase. Children's temperaments also seem to be a factor in adjusting to family transitions (Hetherington & Stanley-Hagan, 1999a). Those with problematic dispositions and behaviors usually bring out negative responses in parents and do not have adequate resources with which to cope with the stress (Hetherington, 1989, 1991). Conversely, those children with even-tempered natures who show accountability and maturity get more positive reactions (Hetherington, 1989). Does Annie have a problematic temperament? Her sister Kathy and her stepsister Joanie appear to be settling into the routine in a less trying way. Of course, they have been described as quieter and more sedentary. Annie may manifest her anger at her lack of control of events and rejection by provoking the adults even more intensely.

This is just a sampling of the research as applied to a complex stepfamily. Naturally, because of the complicated structure of this type of family configuration, there is more information available to apply. Stepfamily scholars overwhelmingly support the psychoeducational and normalization components of SfT (Papernow, 1993; Pasley, Dollahite, & Ihinger-Tallman, 1993; Pasley, Rhoden, Visher, & Visher, 1996; Visher & Visher, 1988), which bring about a reduction in anxiety almost immediately. "Overall, normalizing and educating members of stepfamilies to the realities of stepfamily living is an important key to successful clinical intervention" (Pasley et al., 1993, p. 321).

Step 5

> Actively assess and assist in the recognition of empathy when present, and increase the empathic experience between stepfamily members and subsystems.

In the first session with the couple, the therapist isolated the salient components of the problems in the stepfamily and heard that the couple is committed to the remarriage. A second session will address the empathic abilities of each of them because empathy, as stated previously, is indispensable in the treatment of stepfamilies.

The therapist begins the second session by asking how the interventions have been applied and what outcomes have resulted. Perhaps there is less discord between David and Annie because of less interaction; possibly the schedule for the "taxi" service has been helpful, so David knows how to apportion his work time. After checking in with the couple, the therapist begins.

> *Therapist:* In the last session, we discussed some of the problem areas: money; relationship issues; and the demands of managing five children with their individual schedules, activities, and comings and goings. I heard some anger and bitterness around these topics as well. So let us begin by hearing how each of you feels about the money issue. However, because there is a fair amount of animosity around this problem, I want you

	to make an effort to let go of your point of view and the anger attached to it when you are listening. Paying full attention to your partner's words, as if you are a third party, may be helpful. Who wants to begin?
Eileen:	I will. This really annoys me, this whole money thing.
Therapist:	We want to move away from the anger and talk about what is difficult for you concerning this issue.
Eileen:	OK. I'll try, but it is really difficult. We have been arguing about it almost from the beginning. I guess I feel like I am responsible for the entire workings of the house—taxes, mortgage, repairs, groceries, everything. It is exhausting; I just wish I had some support from David.
Therapist:	Can you help me understand what is most exhausting?
Eileen:	The fact that I feel everyone is feeding off me and depending on me for the roof over their head and the food in their mouth—it is just a lot of pressure. Some weeks are not as good as others. Whenever I have time free at the salon, I realize that I am not making any money, and I start getting panicky. I don't want to lose my home. I feel so anxious that by the time I get home, I am beside myself. I guess I get angry with him because I know that if he is about to get paid, I won't see a dime.
Therapist:	David, so you understand what Eileen is feeling?
David:	I can't help it. I am tied into the support payments.
Therapist:	You are getting a little ahead and moving into your point of view. Do you think you can describe how Eileen is feeling?
David:	OK. She feels exhausted because she is totally responsible for the bills and all. She wishes it didn't fall on her all the time. I guess she feels overwhelmed and pressured. We do never seem to be able to take a breather. She can't even get sick; then there is no pay.
Therapist:	So it must be very overwhelming for her to feel that if she doesn't produce, the whole household will collapse.
David:	Yes, it probably makes her very fearful and apprehensive.
Therapist:	And how would that play out?

David:	Probably she would get pretty irritated.
Therapist:	Does David have it right, Eileen?
Eileen:	Yes. I am very agitated most of the time, and then I lash out. I hate worrying about money. I'm not used to it.
Therapist:	So what you are saying, Eileen, is that before you never had to worry about money because there wasn't another household to help support. Not being used to having to deal with money may make matters worse, right?
Eileen:	Yes. And I knew what David did before we were married, so I shouldn't come down on him so hard.
Therapist:	Our expectations don't always prepare us for the reality. Eileen, I would like you to step back a moment and listen to David talking about how he feels.
David:	How I feel? I feel pressured—so pressured. I have these fairly hefty support payments and a mortgage. I fall behind when money isn't coming in and have to make it up when I get paid. Linda is pretty good about that, my being late, because she knows how the money comes in—in spurts. Then I have Eileen breathing down my neck waiting for some of the money that comes in, but there isn't any. What can I do? I am caught between a rock and a hard place. After all, I did leave Linda and the kids.
Therapist:	What do you wish could happen?
David:	Naturally I wish I could help Eileen. I feel awful that I can't. I watched last year when she got a really bad cold and had to work anyway through the whole thing. It really upset me. She was so strong. You could see that it would really help if she could just rest. I just know I will get in trouble if I don't pay the support. I feel so much pressure to help that it makes it worse almost.
Therapist:	From what David has said, Eileen, can you describe how David is feeling?
Eileen:	David is a really good website designer, so I think that is why he got a high amount of support to pay and their old mortgage.
Therapist:	So he is paying Linda a lot of money? How do you think he feels about that?

Eileen:	I am going to have trouble with this. OK. He feels awful that he can't help me. I know he wants to be honorable and responsible, so he feels he has to come through for them too. I guess I knew all along he must feel guilty, but he has never mentioned it. I feel guilty too. The guilt probably makes him even more anxious to make the support payments. When he has no money, what can he do? Maybe he just feels like he wants to escape from the whole situation.
David:	No, I don't feel that way. I sometimes wonder if that is the way you feel, when you were married to a doctor before and only had to work part time and had no money pressures.
Therapist:	Probably it wasn't as stressful for Eileen then in terms of finances, but there were other problems in her prior marriage.
Eileen:	Yes, we grew apart; we had nothing, and I mean nothing, in common, so all we talked about was the kids. Roy wasn't interested in me as a person or what happened to me at work.
Therapist:	You both have come into the present situation with different perspectives and pasts. You can't possibly see things the same way. When households divide, the same resources have to support two households; in a complex stepfamily, there are three households. One can understand that the money will feel very tight. But as the pressure mounts, the true feelings of self-reproach and contrition are hidden behind a wall of defensiveness and anger. You are really victims of the situation. No one is at fault or to blame, but you take it out on each other. Can you understand that this is equally difficult for both of you?
Eileen and David:	Yes.

The couple finds themselves oddly in the same position after they can empathically feel the other's dilemma. Both are feeling a lot of pressure concerning money and commitments because of the changes in the family configuration. The exercise in empathy not only helps them to understand each other but also may facilitate their having more of an empathic experience when listening to the plight of other family members. Empathy reduces opposition and defensiveness.

Another intervention can be suggested at the end of the session. To assuage the issue of the couple's lack of privacy, the therapist can recommend that the children's visitation schedules be coordinated so that all the children are away the same weekend. This will give the couple more alone time to nurture their relationship. The alternate weekends, when all the children are home, both residential and nonresidential, need to be planned and organized to better manage the children's activities and control the likelihood of contention between the stepsiblings.

Step 6

Identify and challenge unhelpful beliefs and specific miscommunication circulating in the stepfamily—the role of labels.

Unhelpful beliefs are especially dangerous in stepfamilies because there is no shared history. Stepparents and stepchildren meet each other and attempt to forge relationships with a myriad of impediments, for example, family loyalties, traditions, and rituals. When unhealthy beliefs are found in first-married families, they can coexist with love and loyalty; in a stepfamily, trying to form a relationship with someone else while assigning negative assumptions or intentions is difficult if not virtually impossible.

The therapist has been listening through the dialogue for unhelpful beliefs. In the end of the previous dialogue, there is a good example of an ongoing mind-set on the part of both Eileen and David that may confound or distort communication. Each partner is feeling like the other may just want to give up on the relationship because of all the financial pressures. This belief can generate additional stress or lead to an overall disheartened perspective on the stability of the marriage.

The therapist would also want to explore further attitudes concerning the issue of money. Because David defends his need to pay support to Linda, would Eileen feel that this is an indication of his prioritizing Linda's needs over hers? Research has suggested that there is an implicit rivalry between the biological mother and the stepmother (Ganong & Coleman, 1995a). Such an inclination in addition to an erroneous belief may fuel jealousy and discontent.

Annie could label David as a "slacker" because she watches her mother exerting herself in a struggle to stay ahead of the bills. This unfair label could diminish any likelihood that a relationship could be cultivated between Annie and David because the use of the label promotes disrespect and defiance. Annie does not have to get to know David because she has already "figured him out."

The symptoms of ADHD are pervasive across settings, and if Eileen is not aware of them, it can foster an unhealthy belief that Sammy is just trying to be a pain. Her responses, instead of being rational, would in effect be arbitrary and personal, as if fidgety and distracted Sammy was intentionally trying to upset her. Conversely, if Eileen treats Sammy with annoyance, even impatience, his symptoms may increase in severity and incur more negative responses. This may produce in Sammy a reluctance to come on visits and so forth. Providing materials on ADHD and the accompanying challenges to Eileen may redress her mistaken notions, thus interrupting potential reactivity and its damaging consequences.

As the therapist moves through the subsystems, he or she would identify and process the negative consequences of labeling and unhealthy beliefs held by the family members. Denoting and discussing the origin and influence of these beliefs on relationships would increase awareness, helping to eliminate these deterrents. Family members could then retain a more neutral than negative attitude toward each other and begin to build relationships.

Step 7

> Support the naturally connected subsystem (parent and child), and confirm that parent and child are capable of expressing mutual concern.

In a simple stepfather or stepmother family, there is one biological subsystem. In a complex stepfamily, there are at least two. These biological subsystems become unstable because of the modifications in family configuration brought about by the divorce. Children suddenly feel that the intractable changes may lead to a lessening of the bond between the remaining residential parent and themselves. Suddenly they are residing with a virtual stranger who usurps time and attention that "should" belong to them. SfT advocates reaffirming the existing bonds to reassure the children that nothing has changed in the relationship between them. Usually the biological parent is not entirely sure how to balance the needs of the new partner and those of his or her children. Kathy and Annie need reassurance that both Eileen and Roy are inexorably connected to them no matter what changes occur. David's children also need this security.

The therapist has learned from the intake telephone call as well as in first session that there are major disruptions in almost all of Annie's relationships. Most problematic to the remarriage and peace in the household is instability in the maternal biological subsystem. Annie and Eileen need to establish reconnection, balance, and unity between them to weather the family fluctuations and disharmony. Annie needs to be assured of Eileen's steadfastness. In stepfamilies, adolescents who have trouble accommodating to the entrance of a stepfather into the family system have poorer adjustment and lower achievement than do adolescents in first-married families (Hetherington

& Clingempeel, 1992). Eileen needs to guide her teenage daughter with parental firmness and love and not allow her guilt to interfere with this process. Thus, there is immediate work to be done in this subsystem because Annie has the potential to derail the couple relationship, as suggested in the literature (Hetherington & Jodl, 1994). Kathy, for the time being, is pleasant and essentially compliant; however, she may be internalizing her discomfiture. Her behavior and outward appearance may be obscuring her frustration and need of support. Therefore, Kathy will also benefit by shoring up the maternal biological subsystem and reinforcing the unity and attachment between them.

Eileen, Annie, and Kathy are invited in for the next session. After introductions and preliminary conversation, the therapist begins.

Therapist:	I asked you all to come here today to talk about how things are going and what it is like to be part of a stepfamily.
Annie:	I hate it.
Therapist:	What do you hate?
Annie:	Everything.
Therapist:	Well, can you pick, say . . . three things that are particularly annoying.
Annie:	Dad isn't with us, which isn't good, although I don't particularly like Vicky either. David is. That's two.
Therapist:	I am counting three. Dad isn't with you. Two—Vicky is with Dad, and you don't like her, and three, David is in the house where you live.
Annie:	I don't really care about Vicky. I see her on alternate weekends, well, that is the way it is supposed to be—maybe less often—and then Dad plans lots of activities with us. So I don't have much to do with her, fortunately. She is busy with her kids too and baby Shawna. So she doesn't count.
Therapist:	OK.
Kathy:	What about Sammy?
Annie:	Oh, he drives me crazy!! He is always yakking and disturbing things, and he can't sit still, and he comes into my room and picks up stuff.
Therapist:	So those are your three top problems?
Annie:	Oh, believe me, I can go on.

Kathy: Yes she can—you should hear her around the house.

Annie: You don't like this stuff either. Am I right or not? I just make more noise about it. Kathy is quiet and sticks her head in a book.

Kathy: I guess.

Therapist: Kathy, what upsets you the most?

Kathy: Well, I guess what bothers Annie, but I also miss our house and my friends.

Annie: I do too.

Therapist: Mom, how are you feeling about what Annie and Kathy are saying?

Eileen: I really can understand how they are feeling, although I thought David was the biggest problem. Her dad was often working late, so it was just the three of us a lot of the time and especially so after Roy and I divorced. But Sammy bothers all of us, even David. I think that I am put in the worst position because I have to deal with him sometimes when David is not there. It seems like he just tries to agitate me. I really get tense and yell occasionally. Thank God he is not with us full time. I miss my next-door neighbor too; she would come for coffee every morning. So—yes—I know what they are feeling. This has been difficult on all of us. But you don't plan to fall in love.

Therapist: Were you aware of how your mother felt, Annie, Kathy?

Annie: No.

Kathy: No, except I knew she missed our neighbor.

Annie: She is always telling me I have to be nice to David, so we are always fighting. I fight with everyone; nobody wants me around.

Eileen: I want you around. I love you—both—all of you. But you are really very disrespectful to David—you too, Kathy, sometimes—and it is unfair and it makes me angry.

Annie: I didn't ask him into our lives—you did!—and before you left Dad.

Kathy: Yeah.

Eileen:	I am sorry about that; we didn't plan it. It just happened. I do want to be with David. I love him, and you should be able to accept him and be nice to him. I feel like I am always defending him to the kids, especially Annie, and Annie to him.
Annie:	You never defend me—you always take his side.
Eileen:	No, I don't. You aren't in on every conversation, you know.
Therapist:	In stepfamilies, it is often a problem for the biological mother who has relationships with everyone because she feels caught in the middle. Do you feel like your mom doesn't love you anymore?
Annie:	No, but she always takes his side, and it isn't like it used to be when it was Dad and Mom and us—or even the three of us together—that was fun too.
Kathy:	Yeah.
Eileen:	Again, I don't always take his side, and second, your Dad and I—well, our relationship had changed into friendship, and that does not make a marriage. How can I stress it enough? I really love David.
Therapist:	Can we all agree then that your mom loves you very much?
Annie and Kathy:	Yes.
Therapist:	Can you understand that she feels very torn between all of you because she also loves David?
Annie and Kathy:	Yes.
Therapist:	We can also agree that you all don't feel the same about David, which is all right, but you really love your mom.
Annie and Kathy:	Yes!
Therapist:	I am sure, as the mom, you want everyone to get along and to like each other and maybe even expected it to be like that.
Eileen:	I did. I mean it wasn't as bad before we got married when he was just my boyfriend.
Therapist:	There is something about marriage that changes relationships. This is a common phenomenon that we see in stepfamilies. The kids didn't really have a say

	in the change, so it might take time for the relation-ship to build. Eileen, can you accept this?
Eileen:	If that is the way it is, I suppose there is nothing else to do but accept it, but they should at least be civil.
Therapist:	Girls, what do you think of what Mom is saying?
Annie:	I don't have to like him or accept him?
Therapist:	No one can force feelings. I am talking about every-one being entitled to respectful treatment, even if they have to enforce house rules when Mom isn't there. And in turn, David should treat you and Kathy with respect.
Kathy:	He is usually nice to me.
Annie:	What does respect mean?
Therapist:	Eileen?
Eileen:	Respect means saying hello and goodbye and not grunting. It means no weird faces or rolling your eyes when he is around. It also includes following his instructions when I am not there and he is telling you about house rules, for example, no backpacks dropped on the floor where you come in. It means please and thank you. Let's start with that. OK?
Annie:	Well, he hasn't been telling me what to do lately. So I guess I can try to do that, but I don't have to like him.
Eileen:	Thank you, I really love you two, and I would be so happy if you could just do that. He is going to have to enforce house rules and be in charge when I am not here. So I realize that it might at first be different, but everyone deserves respect.
Annie and Kathy:	OK.
Therapist:	Eileen, do you think you and the girls could talk about some fun things to do over the weekends, just the three of you?

The therapist reaffirms the steadfast love that exists between Eileen and the girls before the work of the session begins. It is critically important that they be aware that this affection within the maternal subsystem will endure, even through challenging transitions. With the reestablishment of their bond, the therapist moves to Eileen's split loyalties. David is not discounted;

Annie and Kathy hear their mother confirm her feelings for him. To acknowledge and give permission to the biological unit to have different feelings about David will, it is hoped, reduce Annie's contentious behavior; this, in turn, should immediately ease the tension. Respect is the minimum standard of behavior. Expectations are more realistic.

The paternal biological subsystem is less agitated than the previous subsystem; however, the therapist needs to ensure that the attachment and relationship between David and his children is secure. If there is any distress or disconnection, this can be delineated and processed. For example, a session might begin as follows:

Therapist: I am wondering how you are all doing with the changes in your lives over the past 2 years.

David: I think we are all doing pretty well.

Therapist: What do you think, Joanie and Sammy?

Sammy: I miss spending time with Dad. I mean we get to see him every other weekend, but it isn't the same. Annie and Kathy have him most of the time; he even took them to Champions on Ice.

Joanie: I don't like to go there even. There is no place for us to sleep. And then there is Rebecca. It really makes me mad. I mean she is our sister just as much as she is Annie's and Kathy's, but Annie doesn't let me hold her or play with her or feed her or anything. She is really mean about it and tells me I don't know how to take care of her. Rebecca is really cute too.

David: I didn't realize . . .

Joanie: That is because I have just stopped making a fuss about it. I mean Eileen and you haven't ever noticed really. The first few times it happened, I said something, but then I was kind of scared that maybe I would hurt Rebecca or something. But I am just 1 year younger than Kathy, and she gets to take care of her; I think I could too.

David: I didn't know you felt that way. I thought you were all right with that. You seem to get along with Kathy.

Joanie: Kathy is OK, but she likes to read and stay to herself. She doesn't watch TV.

Sammy: Yeah—she's nice. She and Rebecca are the only ones that don't yell at me over at Dad's. Even Dad yells.

David: Well, you don't know when to stop. I have to tell you to sit down or be quiet 10 times. I don't know what gets into you.

I mean I know you have a lot of energy, but you never used to be this way. Actually [turning to therapist] between Annie and Sammy, we have about 75% of the noise in the house. It's incredible.

Therapist: Joanie, we will come back to your situation with Rebecca in a moment, but for now I hear a lot of stress, which is leading in a different direction. Is that OK with you?

Joanie: Yes.

Therapist: Thanks. You sound very stressed, David. And it sounds like it came on pretty quickly just now. Is that what Sammy is talking about?

David: I guess. It's just hard—all the problems. I guess I shouldn't blame anyone. Well, that's not right. I am not blaming anyone. I guess I am tense a lot of the time, and then when I am trying to finish a project and Sammy is getting into stuff and then Annie flips out . . . I just lose concentration, and I have pressure on me about child support and stuff so I have to work. Well, we have talked about this before— then I start yelling.

Therapist: Sammy, do you understand what Dad is saying?

Sammy: Yeah.

Therapist: Can you tell us?

Sammy: He's telling us that he is really uptight because of money. I have heard him shout that before. It is really about that and work and just that we make a lot of noise and he is trying to get things done. I guess I know that already because Mom used to shush us when we got too loud when he was with us. She had videos she would put on if we were finished with our homework, and then we would all eat dinner together when he would take a break, so we could hang out then. I really liked that. We don't do that now. Sometimes I have to eat with them.

Therapist: Them?

Sammy: Yeah. Eileen, Annie, and Kathy.

Joanie: What about me?

Sammy: Well, you sit there and don't say anything, and they yell at me and tell me I am the pain!

David: Eileen, too?

Sammy:	No—not really. She will tell me to sit still and stop fidgeting in my chair. I get told that a lot by Mom too, so that is nothing new. Annie is the biggest pain. She is so mean.
Therapist:	OK. I heard two things I want to go to. David, you are under a lot of pressure to get your projects finished. Kids don't always understand grown-up concerns very easily. How do you feel Sammy did in explaining how you feel?
David:	Very well, as a matter of fact.
Therapist:	I heard him go on to say that he misses your time at dinner together. So I am curious how we could figure out a solution that would get you the time you need and, at the same time, be able to join your kids for dinner. That would benefit all of you.
David:	That would be good. I used to spend a lot more time with both of them. I miss it. I guess everything has gotten a little busy. Yeah, that sounds like a good idea.
Joanie:	Do you really miss us, Dad?
David:	Of course, I haven't stopped loving you just because I married Eileen. That will never change. You do know that?
Joanie:	It just seemed like things were different. It felt like all you would do some days is yell at us. It felt like you didn't love us anymore or want us there. I thought you loved them more.
Sammy:	Yeah.
Therapist:	Often in stepfamilies, the stepfather ends up spending more time with the stepchildren just because of driving them to activities and going shopping, and this may cause hard feelings. This is not in your family alone.
David:	Oh, I am so sorry. I didn't know. It's the pressure. I really love you both.
Therapist:	It sounds like your dad really loves you, and things have just gotten a little mixed up. So, kids, do you have any ideas that would take care of what you want and your dad could get his work done?
Sammy:	I guess we could find something else to do—or a video—for how long, anyway?
David:	It is not every weekend I have a deadline. Some are less pressured than others. But on days I have a deadline—wow—I just really need to concentrate.
Therapist:	So some days, you could take time to have dinner or help them with their homework or take them to a movie or a

show. But when you have to work, then it's stressful. Let's work out a plan. And then we will talk about Rebecca, Joanie.

The children were feeling insignificant and disconnected, which their father did not realize. The therapist's job in this case is to reinforce the loving bond of the members and then make concrete plans to correct the problems that have caused the distance. Although this is just a small intervention, it supports the idea of stabilization for that biological subsystem.

The other biological subsystem of interest to the treatment of this stepfamily is composed of Roy, Annie, and Kathy. This represents a parallel set of dynamics transpiring with the two siblings visiting their father and his new wife, with a baby who is half sister to both of them. This subsystem may be struggling with the same issues as David and Joanie and Sammy—not enough time with Dad. Roy has been working as a doctor, which entails long hours and an on-demand schedule. This only exacerbates the limited time outlined in the visitation agreement. The goal of unifying and reinforcing this subsystem entails helping the girls to feel more connected to their father when they visit, which might promote less recalcitrant behavior in Annie. This subsystem would be seen in this step as well.

The couple subsystem has been seen twice and have recommitted to their marriage; they also have shown an empathic concern for each other and have applied some recommended interventions to ease the relational and logistical strains, for example, having Eileen take the majority of the direct management of the children. Having stabilized the biological subsystems, the therapist can again invite the couple in to check on the progress of the family and to help enlighten them as to their part in the circular dynamics of the family. It may be premature to have the entire stepfamily present for the next session. Stepfamily work sometimes requires sufficient time for the interventions to become consistently applied and produce positive results, so that the fluctuating relationships and ill feelings are assuaged. It is unusual to establish an instantly smooth path to a success.

Step 8

Teach the family about its own systemic functioning.

When there is still actively contentious interaction within a subsystem, there is the potential to destabilize other subsystems. A good opportunity to address this discord is within this step. The therapist evaluates the progress of the family. When the couple reports that there is a lot of dissension among the children, the stepsibling subsystem is invited to a session. The four children share commonalities that they probably haven't noticed or considered. Enmity

and estrangement are easier alternatives to choose than friendship and cama-
raderie because the latter entail accepting the remarriage and the children who
come with it. The four children have not had the freedom to choose each
other as friends, or more drastically, as siblings. Thus, in bringing this subsystem together and teaching them about family interaction, the therapist assists
them in understanding their role within the family, synergistically.

Annie, Kathy, Joanie, and Sammy all reluctantly enter the therapist's
office. They are encouraged to sit wherever they like. Annie sits somewhat
apart from the other three. The therapist attempts to put them at ease with
light conversation about school, activities, and their grade levels and ages.
The session begins.

Therapist:	So you are all different ages?
Sammy:	Yep! I am the youngest.
Annie:	And he acts that way too.
Therapist:	Annie, we are here to talk about what you all can do to make the situation easier. Everyone has a part in what is happening. It is a situation that none of you chose, but it looks like this is the way it is going to be; so for your sakes, we want to work out what would be best for all of you. So can we all agree to be more positive?
Joanie, Kathy, and Sammy:	Yeah.
Therapist:	Annie, what is the most difficult part of this change in your life?
Annie:	Can someone else go first?
Therapist:	OK—who would like to begin?
Kathy:	I think the most difficult part is not having Mom and Dad together.
Joanie:	I agree.
Sammy:	Me too.
Kathy:	. . . although they didn't seem very happy. Dad worked at the hospital late hours and had to go for emergencies. So she was alone a lot. When I see Mom now, when she is not stressing about money, she and David have fun together.

Therapist: I think that they have come to see me because they wanted to make things better for everyone. They want everyone to be happy, and so I think they are committed to making things work. Even though everyone might want things the way they were, we have to move on and see what each of you can do to improve the situation as it is.

Kathy: Going back and forth is the biggest pain. There is not really room in the other house for us. Annie hates going there because she has to sleep in the living room on the couch, so she complains like crazy, and everyone gets upset. I sleep in Laurel's room.

Sammy: I have to sleep on the couch too!

Therapist: So you and Annie have that in common. Annie, what do you do when you are upset?

Annie: I get really mad, and sometimes I throw things.

Therapist: Wow—it sounds like you get pretty angry. Then what happens?

Annie: Then they tell me I am grounded and can't see my friends until I learn how to behave. They also say they are not going to convert the attic into a room for me until I am less "temperamental." When I get mad they don't trust me around Shawna. It is just not fair!

Therapist: What would happen if you didn't get mad?

Annie: I don't know.

Therapist: It sounds like you all are revolving in a big circle. You get mad because you have to sleep on the couch, then you behave badly, then they get angry and ground you and are afraid you might not handle Shawna in a gentle way and won't let you see your friends. Then you get angrier and then they get angrier, and it just gets worse and worse. It sounds pretty hopeless to me, unless someone does

	something. And you are all moving around in a circle.
Annie:	Well, I feel like I don't belong.
Therapist:	And that hurts.
Annie:	Yeah.
Therapist:	Sometimes when one person does something different, everything changes. Do you understand what I am saying?
Annie:	Yes.
Therapist:	Would you like things to change?
Annie:	Yeah.
Therapist:	Maybe we can figure out what you could do differently to change things.
Annie:	I am not going to make nice! But I suppose I could keep my mouth shut.
Kathy:	I don't think you can do that.
Annie:	Excuse me! You are such a . . .
Therapist:	So you don't think Kathy is right?
Annie:	No! She doesn't know anything. She just sits around and reads.
Therapist:	What do you think your father would do, if you didn't get so angry?
Annie:	I don't know. He might let me see my friends and play with Laurel.
Therapist:	And maybe after a while, he would convert the attic into a bedroom for you.
Annie:	I don't know.

If Annie can become more accountable and understand her part in the consequences she receives, she might not feel so out of control. Then she can elect to alter her responses when she is visiting Dad and his new family. The stepsibling subsystem can also share their commonalities and complaints about the new family configuration and possibly improve empathic reciprocity.

Other systemic revelations can be processed in this step as well. For example, Eileen may be extremely concerned about Annie's misconduct. As a result of the stress of having to manage Annie and Sammy at the same time,

Eileen may feel more comfortable inflicting harsh and reactive discipline on Annie. After all, Annie is her daughter. Eileen may not recognize her disproportionate treatment of the two children and wonder why Annie's behavior is escalating. Annie, in turn, may watch the preferential treatment of her stepbrother and feel unjustly punished, fueling her anger. Helping Eileen to understand how her daughter feels may prompt her to monitor her fairness and be clear about the unacceptable behavior while trying to keep order. Earlier in the chapter, we also reviewed the necessity of Eileen having an informed idea about the symptoms of ADHD, predominantly hyperactivity, so that she will be mindful of what Sammy's needs are and what behaviors he can control.

It is critical for the family members to understand their actions and reactions and their histories and present challenges around the issue of money. The therapist has already worked with Eileen and David on an empathic awareness of each other's feelings on this issue, but further enlightening them as to their interactions and impact on one another and the other family members would be very beneficial.

Eileen and David focus much of the time on Rebecca's needs, obviously, because she is a baby and needs more care. This reverberates throughout the family system with all the different children. It is most difficult for Annie and Kathy, who have two half sisters who are 1 year old in two separate houses. Accommodating to different roles and relationships in both locations is difficult to manage. If they are proprietary about Rebecca, about which Joanie has complained, it may be that they are overcompensating for their seemingly less important status with Shawna. Parents need to process this with the therapist, perhaps in the next step when they all come together to become unified on the routines and expectations for the children.

This step—helping the stepfamily to understand their systemic functioning—proves to be a valuable process. The hope is that the family members, through awareness of their own response and conduct in conflictual and futile interactions, will effect a change in them, which will be reflected in healthier behavior patterns for everyone.

Step 9

Assist in coparental work between any and all involved parental figures, including the binuclear family.

Moving toward the final step of integration, the therapist has to facilitate consensus between all of the parents who are caretakers of the children directly affected by the divorce: Annie, Kathy, Joanie, and Sammy. Matters such as visitation, discipline and boundary issues, and time with the babies Rebecca and Shawna should be processed, and expectations of behavior for

Annie should be coordinated to provide structure and a sense of cooperation among the parents. Annie's behavior is most likely caused by a sense of chaos, fueled by loyalty to "the way it was" as well as rebellion at her lack of control of the situation. But whatever the motivation, her behavior needs to be contained. With the parental coalition being decisive and in charge, Annie may acquire a sense of safety and control.

The covert and confounding factor preventing a strong parental coalition is David and Eileen's affair, which led to the demise of the marriage. The residual guilt of the remarried couple and the anger of their ex-spouses loom as enormous obstacles to having the parental coalition gather together. This determinant, which has not been acknowledged or processed to any degree, can undermine the possible convening of this subsystem.

It is probable that the therapist will begin this step by seeing the parental coalition as two separate subsystems in two different sessions, that is, Eileen and Roy, preferably without Vicky in the beginning, and David and Linda. To establish accord between the ex-spouses would be the first step in moving toward agreement in the entire parental system. Again, the therapist has to advance the notion that the purpose of this subsystem coming together is the benefit of the children; however, clinical experience has demonstrated that this is not always possible to achieve. It is delicate work that requires balance and empathy on the part of the therapist, as well as keeping the session focused and restrained. One positive component may be the amount of time that has passed since the indiscretion. Although Roy has moved on with a new wife and baby and Linda is still a residential single mother of two children with financial pressures, the therapist cannot naturally assume that one session will be easier than the other. As most therapists know, the anger that a client silently harbors is difficult to gauge and sometimes not expressed until the safety of a therapeutic session is provided. For example, one cannot, because of the circumstances, anticipate more acrimony in a session with David and Linda than in one with Eileen and Roy. The therapist hopes that after both of the former spousal subsystems have had their sessions, communication is more facile and impediments to future harmony have been fully processed. This is easier said than done. However, for purposes of applying the model, we have assumed that this has been accomplished.

To approach the subject of a conjoint session and to prevent any members of the parental hierarchy from feeling threatened by a session together, the therapist would have to present a goal of reducing conflict and arranging rules and boundaries around discipline and visitation for the children. Bringing together the parental coalition is a complex and challenging objective; just one member refusing to participate or convincing his or her partner that it serves no purpose can interrupt the process. It is important that the therapist anticipate any potential obstacle, use judgment on the proper timing to achieve this goal, and take measures to assure the emotional safety of the participants.

The therapist then invites the entire parental coalition in for a session: David and Eileen, former spouses Linda and Roy, and Roy's present wife Vicky. There may be a palpable sense of discomfort or awkwardness among the family members; however, the therapist redirects the adults to consider the objective of the session for the benefit of all the children who are directly affected by the divorce, principally, Annie, Kathy, Joanie, and Sammy.

After preliminary introductions, the session continues.

Therapist:	How does it feel being here together today?
David:	Uncomfortable.
Roy:	Awkward.
Linda:	I agree.
Therapist:	No one said has said this would be easy; but we have gathered together here to get to know one another better so it will be easier to communicate and work with each other for the benefit of the children. This is a difficult time for the children because of the multiple transitions that have occurred; they are struggling with many pieces of their lives. You, as adults, need to help them through this by reducing conflict and acting as role models for transitioning and getting along. In that way, they will feel less worry and anxiety when you meet each other for visits and other events at school for example. We need to talk about how we can manage to do that.
Linda:	I think things go OK as long as I don't have to spend a lot of time with them. [looking at David and Eileen]
David:	What about Annie's game coming up? That is a fair amount of time.
Linda:	We don't have to sit together.
Therapist:	So you don't want to sit together, but what kinds of things do you think you could you do, Linda?
Linda:	Well, it is different when David is alone than when she is with him.
Roy:	I kind of agree with Linda on that one. I mean I really don't want to see him. [looking at David] I said that when Eileen and I met in session; I don't mind admitting that here too.
Eileen:	Well, you don't get free for all that much time anyway.
Roy:	I have a schedule that makes many demands on my time, unlike some people.

Therapist:	Can we slow down for a minute and remember what we are here for? We are here concentrating on looking forward to the future to see how we can help the children feel less tense and anxious in general. They have new people in their lives, stepsiblings, half siblings, and stepparents; it is a challenging situation for them to get used to. The past is behind us. It holds many hard feelings, and we need to move on for the sake of all the kids. Children watch very closely. Even subtle expressions are noticed. Can we agree that we need to prioritize?
All clients:	Yes.
Therapist:	OK, Linda, we were asking what kinds of things could you do instead of avoiding Eileen or not speaking to her?
Linda:	Is it just me, or does everybody have to do this?
Therapist:	Well, I want everyone to answer that question in his or her head, but I am just continuing where we left off in our conversation. I don't mean to single you out. Maybe I can ask a simpler question. What do you do now?
Linda:	I avoid her.
Therapist:	How about the rest of you?
Roy:	The same, I avoid David.
Eileen:	I don't really have a problem with Linda or Vicky.
Vicky:	I don't have a problem with anyone.
Eileen:	Me neither.
David:	I really don't either, but I don't think that Roy and I will ever be friends.
Therapist:	You don't have to be friends, polite acquaintances would do. Anger shows to children. They are very adept at sensing things. I heard three of you, David, Eileen, and Vicky, say that they didn't have a "problem with anyone." But obviously others have problems. I can guess that the circumstances of the divorce were painful for all of you, and I am asking that you put aside those feelings for now so we can have some sort of dialogue. Do you feel that it is possible to do that?
Everyone:	I guess.
Therapist:	Can we all agree that the children come first?
Everyone:	Yes. [more emphatically]

> *Therapist:* Can we all agree that they need a balanced, nurturing environment, which is essentially drama-free? Sometimes we are not aware of our own body language or facial gestures, and unwittingly these displays hinder the process of cordial communication. Can you all focus on what you can do to make the situation less stressful for the children?
>
> *Everyone:* Yes.
>
> *Therapist:* That is half the battle. You'd be surprised how many adults are unable to do this . . . or maybe not. But these are your lives. If you agree on those points, then what remains is to figure out how you can provide that for the children by doing your part. So who would like to begin?

The therapist hopes that each parent will understand that he or she "owns" part of the problem and will recognize his or her need to demonstrate adult behavior and treat each other with respect. The parental coalition needs to accomplish this goal before it can progress to issues involving the discussion of house rules, discipline, visitation schedules, and playing with the babies. Of course, in each home there will be differences in parenting, routines, and more; however, when the children go back and forth between houses, there should be consensus on expectations for conduct, respect, honesty, and accountability, which are to be consistent across the entire parental coalition.

Step 10

> Increase communication among all stepfamily members available, and move toward integrating the various subsystems into a functioning and satisfied stepfamily.

This unwieldy family configuration has been divided into and seen as subsystems to clarify and stabilize the family process. It is in this step that the therapist hopes that family members can come together without rancor or insensitivity to communicate freely about the needs of the children. Realizing and acting on the idea that there should be no competition between parents and stepparents and demonstrating to the children accord in parenting strategies and rules will enable the children to feel a return to a new normalcy.

If the therapist assesses the growth of the family in moving their adjustment forward and feels it is possible to have a session involving the children, then an effort can be made to do this. The mutual children Rebecca and Shawna could be included, which would necessitate Vicky's attendance; however, their presence has the potential to enhance the session in a positive way because of their connection to so many of the members of the binuclear system. There is always the possibility that Rebecca and Shawna could be a distraction, so planning to include toys in the session optimizes the chances that it will go smoothly.

The goal of the session would be to (a) communicate to the children that the parents have met and decided to establish common rules for behavior and doing chores across all of the households and that they will need the input of the children to do this; (b) model adult behavior and unity; (c) ask the children to communicate in respectful ways about what they need and how they feel; and finally (d) affirm that in spite of the circumstances and all the changes that have taken place, the children are loved, each and every one of them, and that is not going to change.

The therapist can best serve the family by smoothing out the interrupted relationships and restoring affectionate connections between the children and the family of the ex-spouses. Thus, attending to the old ties as well as the incipient steprelationships can bring the binuclear family system into equilibrium, increase its ability and resilience to manage the inevitable complications, and foster a solid foundation for the future.

7

THE EXTENDED FAMILY
IN A STEPFAMILY

If one were asked to design the perfect stepfamily, what would be the total membership? Would the stepfamily of one's design have an extensive series of relations from every adult involved, or would one restrict it to a small number of relatives? This is, of course, an impossible task because no one can predict with complete accuracy what will always work well and what will always work poorly. But it does highlight the complexity of extended family in a stepfamily. Given that a stepfamily involves more people who are connected as family in a nontraditional manner, it is by definition a complex family form.

STRUCTURAL COMPLEXITY INVOLVING
EXTENDED FAMILY MEMBERS

Does this increased complexity always make things more difficult, or are there some advantages to this family form? Although the research evidence points toward increased complexity resulting in more stress (Pasley & Lee, 2010), it would be inaccurate to label extended family as only a burden. Support may arrive from an unexpected source. Clinical work with stepfamilies highlights that on occasion an underused extended family member is interested in making a positive contribution. When a sense of family is increased to include more people, the strength of a good connection may offset the negative effects of increased complexity.

Gender is an important factor in creating a stronger sense of family. When the family has at least two women who live in close proximity it is more likely that these family members have some connection to one another (Weaver & Coleman, 2005). Therefore, on a therapeutic level, the clinician should notice whether there is a good chance that a bond can be established between a stepmother and a stepdaughter or stepgranddaughter. Women and girls are simply better, on average, at keeping relationships moving forward, even if there are some bumps in the road (Schmeeckle, 2007).

These positive aspects of stepfamily life, however, are certainly not assured. Research on the effect of a larger family on both stepfamilies and single-parent families suggests that larger, thus more complex, systems correlate to more negative child outcome (D. Kerr & Beaujot, 2002). The research suggests that the child's needs are not addressed as the number of people in the family increases. For many, the extended family in a stepfamily offers little additional support, and often the increased complexity is simply regarded as an avenue to greater tension and stress. As Pasley and Lee (2010) suggested, becoming "a stepfamily through marriage (or cohabitation) is similar to moving to a foreign country" (p. 239). Although there are many aspects of this new family to adjust to, the wider the circle of relationships becomes, the more chaotic the adjustment is likely to be. Therefore, the clinician considers ways to make the complexity more manageable. Because chaos is usually connected to a misunderstanding that leads to an emotional outburst or rejection, the clinician is looking for areas in which the addition of extended family causes tremendous stress within the stepfamily itself.

The clinician does not want to separate the stepfamily from the extended family, except in the most dysfunctional scenarios; rather, the clinician observes what relationship or relationships can be improved. Frequently there is some dyad that can be made stronger without having a negative ripple effect throughout the system. It is the job of the clinician to suggest a series of subsystem sessions that can help to achieve the desired change. Therefore, the initial subsystem invited in for a session will be that one that can be made stronger; following that session, other subsystems are invited. The rationale is to understand how these other subsystems benefit or may be negatively affected by the strengthening of the initial subsystem.

For example, when a clinician requests that the stepmother have a session with the 25-year-old stepdaughter who has a 3-year-old child, the first step is to find what type of relationship would be mutually satisfying. In other words, might both women, in this case, benefit from a relationship with each other? A bond may form that, at first, is based on helping and enjoying the

3-year-old child. If both women feel that something is gained from their connection, it is likely to continue. Because there are always other family members affected by a new relationship, any systemic impact should be discussed. For example, might the stepdaughter's own mother feel displaced if the stepmother becomes involved with the 3-year-old child? The clinician must keep a positive attitude and always remind those involved that the goal is actually rather modest, just a mutually satisfying relationship that might only reach the polite cordial level.

Another problem that occurs when the extended family increases is the growth of loyalty binds. As the complexity of various relationships continues to grow, the likelihood of loyalty conflicts also increases (Carlson & Furstenberg, 2006). In some ways, this complexity may be the reason that many models of stepfamily treatment did not advocate the involvement of extended family members. However, it is our opinion that the confusion exists, and the best manner in which to address it is to directly advocate communication among the various subsystems, even when engaging these people also adds to the overall complexity of the stepfamily or binuclear family. Pasley and Ihinger-Tallman (1982) pointed out that this lack of clarity regarding the appropriate behavior among these various subgroups of a family can significantly raise levels of stress in the family. Therefore, the clinical direction involves creating clarity around the boundaries and interactions of these interdependent relationships. This is done with the clear idea that one does not want children to be the mediators of adult issues. When former spouses have difficulty speaking to each other, the children are often inducted as mediators. This is a particularly bad position for a child to be in (Ahrons, 2004).

STEPGRANDPARENTS

In the past 20 years, many aspects of stepfamily life have become clearer as a result of increasing research. One area that remains very important, but critically understudied, is the area of stepgrandparents. Ganong and Coleman (2006) articulated the concern that neither researchers nor clinicians were addressing the growing numbers of older stepfamilies. They wanted to find out what was already known about stepgrandparents and what further research was necessary on the topic. Two years later, Ganong (2008) addressed this issue by establishing the following: (a) The number of stepgrandparents is growing as a result of longer life spans and later marriages; (b) three distinct life patterns can result in the presence of stepgrandparents; and (c) these various family constructions have key implications. The purpose of this section is to discuss possible clinical responses to challenges that affect these stepfamilies. Brief case examples are used to demonstrate some clinical issues; however, the full

10-step model is not used in these examples. The three "pathways to step-grandparenting may be distinguished based on who is remarrying or repartnering" (Ganong, 2008, p. 397).

The Late-in-Life Stepgrandparent

The first pathway includes those stepfamilies that are created when one gains a stepgrandchild because one's new spouse or partner has a grandchild. With this population of stepgrandparents, the family is less likely to define this new stepgrandparent as kin (Ganong & Coleman, 2006). This family type can create a deep impasse that can be quite destructive to the overall family harmony. The following example portrays a rather simple construction of an older stepfamily, but the impasse does not require extraordinary complexity to be problematic.

In this case example, the Richards Family (see Figure 7.1 and the legend in Figure 3.1), we present a scenario that can be very difficult to help clinically, but not impossible. Rhonda is deeply hurt and angry at Callum for leaving her after 26 years of marriage. She is completely opposed to Mathew, her son, or his family having any contact with Callum's new wife, Alexis. This reaction by Rhonda is possible even if there is no suggestion of Alexis and Callum having had a relationship prior to the divorce. It is also probable that Mathew will respect his mom's wishes and choose to refrain from forming any relationship with Alexis.

Callum has been a warm and loving grandfather to Samuel, so when he asked him to come over to meet Alexis, Samuel did so, even though his father,

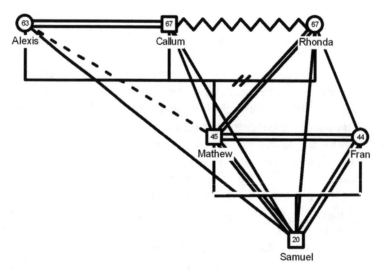

Figure 7.1. The Richardson family.

Mathew, asked Samuel to avoid her. Samuel is a college junior, very independent thinking, and he feels that his dad is wrong about this request. In fact, when Samuel returned from going to his granddad's house, he stated that "Alexis is perfectly friendly and makes Granddad happy; what's the big deal?" Mathew, having met Alexis at his father's wedding, does not disagree, but the pressure from his mother is constant and intense. For the sake of this example it is important to understand that Rhonda is quite normal. She is not ranting and throwing fits; she is simply sad and angry at Callum, and though she knows that Alexis did not "steal" her husband, she does not want Mathew (or his family) to make it any easier on his dad than it already is.

Callum and Mathew meet for lunch once or twice a week. This was an agreement they made so that they could stay in each other's lives while still respecting Rhonda's request that Mathew have nothing to do with Alexis. The clinician is approached by Callum and Alexis, who are starting to have fights over the fact that Alexis now feels that Callum should stop seeing Mathew for lunch unless he is willing to come to the house or she can come to the restaurant. Callum is dumbstruck by Alexis's request. He too is very angry at Rhonda for making her demand, but he does not feel that his relationship with his son should be affected. The couple is requesting that the clinician bring in Mathew with the two of them so that they can figure this out like adults.

Although this clinical suggestion may sound peculiar, the subsystem that we recommend bringing in to treatment is Callum and Rhonda. The initial appointment is with Callum and Alexis, but the clinician may want to hypothesize that until Rhonda and Callum have less anger between them, no one in this binuclear family can move forward. Alexis may resent being asked to leave treatment for a short while; Callum may feel genuine fear at having to face Rhonda's wrath; and Rhonda may feel that she will be forced to compromise, which may make the prospect of treatment unappealing. Even with all of these caveats, this subsystem offers the best chance for significant healing. If Rhonda and Callum do attend a session together, the clinician must be in charge. The purpose of the session, which must be made crystal clear, is that some arrangement must be created that takes Mathew out of this insidious triangle. This is a family that raised a loving man and to force him to suffer by having to hurt either parent is simply unjust. There are times that such an intervention is too sophisticated and demands a level of maturity that the client cannot reach, but when it works it allows for extraordinary progress.

The "Inherited" Stepgrandparent

In this situation, an older person "inherits" a stepgrandchild because an adult stepchild is now in a relationship with someone who has a child. There are factors that influence the adjustment of these stepfamilies. We use a case

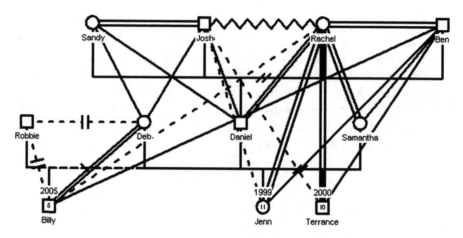

Figure 7.2. The Otto family.

study of the Otto stepfamily (see Figure 7.2) to understand some common problems and the clinical interventions that may be useful in supporting selected intergenerational relationships.

Daniel and Deb have been married for 1 year. Deb made the appointment for therapy because she is (a) concerned for her son, Billy, and (b) feels that she and Daniel are "not as together" as she had hoped. The two concerns are related in that she feels the marriage to Daniel might be making things a little harder on Billy than they were during the lengthy single-parent period. Deb is concerned that Billy is very shy, has few friends, and has not "even formed a strong bond with Daniel." Deb feels that Daniel should "step up and really fill in as a dad." Daniel believes that he has tried with Billy, but he feels that Billy is "very difficult to get to know well."

Deb is also concerned that Billy has no significant relationships with any grandparents. Deb's mom, her only surviving parent, lives 1,000 miles away in a large Midwestern city. Robbie's parents never made much of an effort when Deb and Robbie lived together, and once they broke up, Robbie's parents made no attempts to stay in contact with Billy. Therefore, Deb has been particularly impressed by how involved Daniel's mom Rachel has been with her two grandchildren. This too has become an issue of disagreement between Deb and Daniel. Daniel has requested that his mom and stepdad, Ben, really embrace Deb and Billy, but Rachel is very close to Samantha, her original daughter-in-law, and her two grandchildren (Jenna and Terrance). She has made it clear to Daniel and Deb that she does not intend to take time away from her visits with her grandchildren to get to know Billy. She is happy to see them once a month for dinner, but she reserves the right to continue having Jenna and Terrance come for weekly sleepovers (especially because Samantha needs "some down time"). This position has only made Deb feel more hurt and desperate to make family connections for Billy's sake.

The possibility of opening new family connections by applying a subsystem focus becomes apparent with this case example. Just because Rachel has been the "gold standard grandparent" does not mean that she is the only person potentially capable of bonding with Deb and Billy. In fact, as the clinician reviews the genogram, there is a subsystem very worth investigating to soften the argument between Daniel and Deb and possibly fulfill Deb's wish for Billy. Josh and Sandy, Daniel's dad and stepmother, live only 8 miles from Daniel. Sandy has also shown an interest in becoming more involved in Billy's life. Sandy was never a mother, and she was made aware early in her relationship with Josh that his grandchildren were very close to Rachel and not so close to him. However, with Deb and Billy, a variety of factors make this relationship worth pursuing.

The first factor that points toward the viability of the proposed relationship is proximity. Proximity is an important factor in trying to build relationships, and although being across the street might be better, 8 miles is not too far to begin to have regular visits. The second important factor is Billy's age. The fact that Billy is young makes it more likely that both he and his stepgrandparents will make the investment in this new relationship (Cherlin & Furstenberg, 1986). Another feature is that although Josh does have other grandchildren, he is not particularly close to them, and Sandy has no other grandchildren that divert her attention. And finally, as mentioned previously, because this case happens to involve two women who are particularly interested in forming a relationship, it is more likely to occur. Women are more likely to create and maintain ties with other family and stepfamilies (Weaver & Coleman, 2005).

A further subsystem session that helped this family involved the three children together, Terrance, Jenna, and Billy. With Deb becoming calmer as a result of Sandy's involvement, it was possible for the children to discuss a project they could do together when they came to visit with their dad. Although the older kids were generally involved in their own activities, they did interact with Billy, for which Deb was grateful. Although she did not overemphasize her pleasure in their behavior to the children, she let Daniel know that she thought they were good kids, a comment always appreciated by a parent. In addition, as time went on, Daniel became more comfortable with Billy, still seeing him as "slow to warm," but their mutual fondness grew. As expected, Deb relaxed her panic about Billy's welfare, and the stepfamily dynamics became less troubling.

The Long-Term Stepgrandparent

The third pathway to stepgrandparenthood is, in some ways, the most similar to traditional grandparenthood. In these situations, the stepparent was

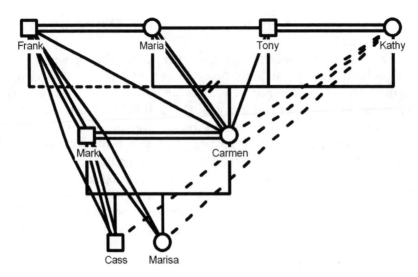

Figure 7.3. The Lange family.

involved in the life of the person who now has a child. Therefore, this step-parent has a history with the adult who is now a parent. As Kornhaber (1996) stated, the middle generation is the gatekeeper of information between the older generation (the stepgrandparent) and the younger generation (the stepgrandchild). The quality of the relationship between the older generation and the middle generation is a crucial element in predicting the issues that may need to be addressed with these stepgrandparents.

The Lange family, for example (see Figure 7.3), exhibits a relatively common dynamic. Kathy has been Carmen's stepmother since Carmen was 11 years old. Kathy and Carman had a relationship that was hostile during Carmen's teen years and then become largely distant but cordial as Carmen grew into a young adult and got married. Now that Carmen has two children, she has noticed that Kathy is actually very nice to both her son, Cass, and daughter, Marisa.

This case came to the attention of the clinician only because Cass was having panic attacks at school. Although stepfamily issues were not a major part of the problem per se, this case is useful in demonstrating the importance of simply opening the door to a relationship that the client is already interested in pursuing.

Maria, Carmen's mother, is a devoted grandmother, and she is not concerned about "sharing" her grandchildren. Maria wants what is best for her grandchildren, and although she and Kathy are not best friends, there is no tension when they see each other at important family events. The reality of multiple grandparents makes this situation quite natural. As discussed earlier, loyalty issues are always possible, but the clinician does not have to search for problems if they are not readily apparent. In most cases, if there is a loyalty conflict, it is discussed openly. Therefore, in this case example, the clinician is not worried about assisting one subsystem to improve because no one else resents or feels challenged by this proposed relational improvement between Kathy and Carmen. An added feature of this case is that Kathy experienced anxiety attacks after an automobile accident in her late 20s; therefore, she is particularly interested in helping Cass learn how to expose himself to what he fears (the chaos of the cafeteria) and learn relaxation techniques. As this case continues, the improvement in the relationship of Kathy and Carmen is noticeable, but not dramatic. Carmen is glad to have Kathy more involved; she views her stepmother as a good person, but they never became terribly close, just close enough to create no impediment for Cass and Marisa to have an additional loving grandmother, this one a stepgrandmother.

REMARRIAGES THAT FOLLOW BEREAVEMENT

When a couple's relationship ends because one member dies, the survivor and any children from that union have a unique challenge if a remarriage or repartnering occurs. This challenge involves acceptance by any children and the involvement of extended family. A particular challenge involves the parents of the deceased spouse, who now often increase their involvement in the lives of their grandchildren. In addition, when a couple divorces, or breaks up in the case of a cohabiting couple, it is likely that the couple is not in love. However, although the death of a spouse does not guarantee that they were still in love, there is no reason to assume that the surviving spouse does not have positive associations with marriage or long-term cohabitation.

Certainly, the first and overwhelming reaction in such a family is mourning. As experts on bereavement point out, everyone grieves at his or her own pace. Although there are stage models that often assist people in understanding their reactions to the death of a loved one, the time line for how long it takes to "recover" varies widely depending on a range of factors. Again, because of the sheer complexity inherent in conceptualizing the potential issues that a clinician may face if the survivor chooses to remarry or repartner, we use a case example.

The Trevosky Family

Sam Trevosky was referred to therapy by a therapist running the bereavement group that he had been a member of for 2½ years. Sam had been married to Victoria (see Figure 7.4) for 18 years until she died of cancer. The marriage,

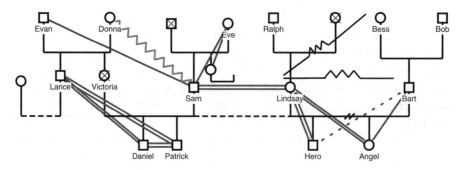

Figure 7.4. The Trevosky family.

according to Sam, was great. He reported that they had the normal number of disagreements but were always in love and never had any crisis that threatened them "until the disease won." Sam and Victoria had two sons, Daniel and Patrick. Sam was very involved in work throughout his marriage. He was the owner and president of a water purification firm that both provided a good income and kept him at work a great deal. He stated that he "always made time for the marriage, but I probably short-changed the boys a bit." Victoria, on the other hand, was "a great mother, loving, and a good disciplinarian." When Victoria died, Sam and the boys were understandably devastated. Sam became very involved in bereavement counseling, both individual counseling and a support group. His sons went to a couple of sessions but never found the bereavement work comfortable. Given the pressures of his business and his own insecurity about his ability to raise the boys on his own, Sam moved into the neighborhood of his in-laws, Victoria's parents, Donna and Evan.

Sam admits that if his mother had not been chronically ill, he might have leaned on her during the early period after Victoria's death, but she was not capable of helping him. In addition, Donna insisted that she should help out for Victoria's sake and for the boys. Sam moved into the new neighborhood, and the boys practically moved into their grandparents' home. Although they each had a bedroom in Sam's house, they actually spent more time with Donna and Evan, between meals, homework, and regular sleepovers. For the first 6 months, Sam believed that he had done the right thing. The boys were doing well in school, and from all reports by Donna and Sam, they were making friends in the neighborhood. However, Sam was starting to feel that he was losing his connection with his sons; in addition, he honestly started to question if he was a good father.

Victoria's brother, Lance, who had a separate residence, had a long-term girlfriend. He felt that he really wanted to stay close to the boys because it made it possible to feel that Victoria was still present, at least through the boys. So, when the boys were not with Donna and Evan, they were out doing fun things with Lance and sometimes Lance's girlfriend. This pattern continued for a little less than 2 years, at which time Sam started to date Lindsay. Lindsay was divorced, was also financially secure, and also had two children, a son, Hero, and a daughter, Angel. Because Sam was often alone in the house if he was not at work, he had begun to meet people online, and Lindsay was the first person from that arrangement whom he dated.

The reaction to Lindsay was swift from Donna, Evan, Lance, and both boys; they refused to meet her and felt that Sam was being entirely disrespectful to the memory of Victoria. The timeline in this case was as follows: At the time Sam was referred to therapy to address relational issues, not only bereavement, Victoria had been deceased for close to 3 years; Sam had actively been in bereavement counseling for over 2 years, and he still loved Victoria deeply (keeping her photo in his wallet and going to the cemetery regularly) but was lonely and believed in his heart that Victoria would not have expected him never to find another person to love. So, although he knew that introducing Lindsay would be challenging to the boys, he did not expect a full-scale rebellion.

Sam came into therapy claiming that he intended to bring the boys into a session and demand that they get to know Lindsay because "she is really important to me and someone they will like." Instead, the clinician lobbied for Sam to work on restoring his relationship with his boys and on regaining a sense of parental competence. This was achieved by being available to discuss issues about driving and potential college applications. In addition, as the boys began to complain about Donna, Sam did not add fuel to the fire; rather, in therapy he had learned that simply listening to his sons meant that they would not start to argue with him about Donna's positive points. As his sons began to recognize that they could approach him and he would not become defensive, they began to open up to him. Interestingly, as this began to occur, the boys started to spend more and more time at home with their dad. Although they still did their homework and had some meals with Donna and Evan, they rarely slept there. As a result of the unusual power that the boys had thanks to their second home across the street, Sam was unable to demand that the boys meet Lindsay. But a step that Sam could take was to assure Lindsay that she was the woman he desired. She feared that Sam was not challenging the boys because he was afraid to commit; in fact, he felt able to commit but was unwilling to lose his sons in the process. As treatment progressed, Sam expressed to Lindsay his intention to marry her in a couple of years and to start having her over for meals at which the boys would be asked to stay.

As Sam become a more confident father, the boys, especially the older son, Daniel, started to build back a relationship with him. As Daniel began to date, Sam was able to draw the comparison that he would never want to interfere in such a way as to hurt Daniel's girlfriend. Finally, Sam, Patrick, and

Daniel sat home one night and went through all of the photos from the earlier family life. Sam made it clear how much he still loved their mother. Within 3 months, the boys were willing to meet Lindsay, even going to her house for one meal and meeting her children. Although the couple was still not living together, something they both wished for, they knew that they were heading to a fuller commitment, and the boys were not fighting this idea.

Sam finds that he has little reason to interact with Donna at present. Although he and Evan still chat a little, his relationship with Donna remains strained, but this relationship was always strained and only strengthened for a short period around Victoria's illness and death. Lance still has get-togethers with his nephews, but both he and the boys are finding that they are too busy to do this often.

Moral Authority

There are few instances in which someone can claim moral authority in a situation that for all intents and purposes is ambiguous. However, children who have lost a parent to death have a sense of moral authority that empowers them to reject the notion of someone sharing a bed with their surviving parent. This is not to suggest that either the child or the parent is correct. In fact, given the opportunity, both parties can offer a very convincing argument to support their position.

The parent makes it clear that he or she still loves the deceased mate, but living without the love and affection of a partner is too lonely and unsatisfying. The child, who in fact may be an adolescent, may acknowledge that he or she is powerless to stop his or her parent from remarrying, but he or she does have the power to reject this new person. The impasse that follows can be most unpleasant. This situation is not universal. There are occasions when a stepparent is welcomed into such a home, but one cannot assume a smooth transition.

In most cases, the child has little recourse if the surviving parent chooses to remarry or repartner. But in some cases, the child can move in with other family, and this is one power play that is difficult to counter. Although the clinical intervention in this situation is dependent on some mutual desire on everyone's part to stay together, it can be difficult to achieve. The job of the clinician is twofold: (a) assist the family member in understanding the concern of the other, even though they do not agree, and (b) keep this discussion between the child and parent. In other words, at this time it is best not to involve other family members or the new romantic interest. This is a discussion between the parent and the child or children interested in moving. Often, the larger issue is to respect the memory of the deceased parent and provide a forum for the surviving family members to reaffirm a sense of commitment.

To achieve these goals, the clinician usually needs to see the parent alone and then the child or children alone. These early sessions are explicitly geared to assess (a) the developmental level of grieving, (b) the family environment prior to the death of the parent/spouse, and (c) the current relationship between the surviving parent and his or her child.

The degree to which one has grieved is individual and often difficult for another to interpret. Therefore, the grieving partner may show an overt and profound reaction, which may actually scare his or her children if it continues for a long time. On the other hand, one may successfully hide one's grief or simply have a very modest grief reaction. For a child observing his or her parent having a very subdued mourning, the emergence of a new romantic partner will, on occasion, trigger a reaction that the deceased parent has been forgotten. At these times, clinical intervention can sometimes be quite helpful.

Although there are exceptions, surviving spouses are usually deeply bereft, so although there may be some guilt if they begin to love another, it may be couched in a belief that they are embracing life again not only for selfish reasons but also for the sake of their children. They feel that the children need to see an example that even when one's life is torn apart, it can, to some extent, be mended. It is clinically important for the surviving parent and his or her children to have a discussion about their loss, establish how they still show respect, and be given permission to recognize that each individual is moving at his or her own pace. It needs to be reinforced that the mourning process does not have an exact timetable. These interventions may take place in the clinician's office or simply be planned there and then executed at home. In most cases, this process is restricted to the surviving family, but if a new person is being invited into the family, a ritual (after this initial process occurs) can be designed to reduce the sense that the new person, by association, represents forgetting the deceased parent. This ritual generally involves presenting the deceased parent through stories and photographs. The new person is privileged to view this family event, and the family should be encouraged to design this presentation to honor, not compare.

It is important to understand the family environment that existed prior to the death of the one parent. In particular, what was the nature of the relationship between the surviving parent and the child? This legacy can strongly influence a surviving parent's sense of competence. For example, the surviving parent may state that "Dad was the fun one; I can still make sure that the homework is done, but he was that one that got us to play together." There may be a great deal of truth in these legacies, and there is little benefit in openly challenging one. Rather, the clinician is looking for an indication that all members of the family are interested in the possibility of expanding the current parameters of the parent–child relationship.

The current relationship between parent and child is not necessarily unchangeable. Although a parent may have a style that emphasizes loving support, discipline, or being the financial provider, most can expand their range to exhibit some other trait. This is not to suggest that the serious business-minded mom will suddenly become a barrel of laughs, but leaving one's comfort zone is easier if one believes that the other would welcome one's effort.

Therefore, clinically, the primary intervention in these circumstances is to challenge the absolute. Whenever someone portrays him- or herself as "all business" or "all heart and no head," there is inevitably some exception. The important factor when a client views him- or herself in absolute terms is to determine why this surviving parent feels the necessity to accent only one side of him- or herself. Often these surviving spouses talk about the idea that the other side of their style died with their spouse. It is sometimes easier for people to compartmentalize in order to reassure themselves that they can soldier on. The clinician does not wish to challenge the evident strengths but rather suggests that restricting one's range does not pay tribute to the person lost. Instead, such behavior only represents one's fear of being fully whole again. With this in mind, the current relationship between a parent and a child is supported by bringing back some aspects that have been missing since the death of the loved one.

Family of One's Deceased Spouse

The bond that grows between a surviving spouse and his or her in-laws can be profound. On occasion, this bond provides genuine support and comfort both through the period just following the death, and sometimes, as a permanent extended family. However, as indicated previously, many relationships have a way of becoming strained and unpleasant when the complexity of the situation is increased.

It is of course folly to predict the course of any relationship. However, connections with one's in-laws after one's spouse has died consist of a couple of variables that can often influence the course of a relationship. When an adult loses a mate, he or she will often bond with in-laws in the aftermath of the death. The spouse or partner knows that with calls to the in-laws, they will find someone always willing to reminisce or express sadness about the tragic loss. In this way, a bond can be established that is deeper than the relationship that might have existed before the death. This is a relationship that, in large part, is now defined by mutual support and understanding.

In time, however, the grief is usually not enough to sustain the relationship, and the focus either shifts to any children from the original union or the bond starts to fade. There may be a sincere desire on the part of all involved to perpetuate this new closeness, in part to keep the memory of the deceased alive.

But for many, the gaping hole created by the death is repeatedly reopened by this relationship, rather than healed.

When one is told, "You will always be part of this family," this statement is often entirely sincere. However, there are also times when this commitment is tested by a new romantic partner entering this grieving system. If either the child or parents of the deceased object to the introduction of a new love interest, they can seek support from the other, and this support is generally forthcoming. In other words, even if an in-law is resigned to the possibility that their daughter-in-law may someday fall in love again, when their grandchild plaintively asks, "Doesn't it seem too soon?" it is the rare grandparent who will still give their blessing to a union that seems to erase the last vestiges of their son's life.

The clinical intervention in this situation is focused on understanding the motivation behind different people's actions. Although few clients seek treatment explicitly to address negotiating a new marriage with former in-laws, the clinician will hear from one member of the stepfamily about the current disagreement. Sometimes clinicians are not in a position, nor should they be, to negotiate or lobby for a particular standpoint; rather, clinicians may serve their clients best in this situation by simply removing negative bias. The in-laws are unlikely to desire that their daughter-in-law suffer; rather, they are concerned about the kids feeling angry and sad. The daughter-in-law, in this example, is not trying to replace the man who died; she is just ready to love again. Therapy in this situation is less about getting people to change their views or their behavior and more about softening the worst assumptions, proclaiming each person's desire, and recognizing the feelings of the other as legitimate. Because of the potential for deep hurt and disappointment in the scenario described here, there are times when the relationship with one's in-laws is bound to simply fade following a death.

Experience of the New Person

When one falls in love with someone who has lost a previous mate to death, there may be a swirl of conflicting feelings. Although the dominant issue revolves around falling in love, secondary issues often enter the consciousness of one getting involved with a widow or widower, especially when children are involved.

As is so often the case in stepfamilies, even the name used to label someone is often imperfect. The *new wife* or *new husband* seems appropriate for a few weeks, not years. One is not a *replacement* because everyone makes it clear that the intent is not to replace the former spouse. The term *second wife* can be similarly problematic; often people simply state, for example, "I am Sally's husband," avoiding entirely the idea that there was a previous husband who is now deceased. This pattern works well enough until a child or an in-law feels the need to remind this husband that "Sally had another husband too, remember?" In many cases, the spouse who lost a mate to death may still feel love for that person. It does not mean that he or she loves the new spouse less, but he or she did not shed the earlier love on meeting the new person. This level of confusion is part of the experience of the new spouse. The new spouse is not sure how he or she is perceived by the children, the in-laws, or the old friends of the couple—the couple that no longer exists.

Even how this new couple met is under scrutiny. Were they friends prior to the death of the spouse? If so, how much support was offered during the difficult time of mourning? Were they family friends? At times it is the deceased spouse's best friend who falls in love after going through such a traumatic period. And although these arrangements are often completely innocent, they cause a sense of intrigue that can be easy for children to use as evidence against this new union. Just because a child really liked someone who was Mom's best friend, this does not translate into his or her remaining fond of that person as a stepmother. For instance, if the new partner is from work, then Dad's previous comment that work was the only thing that kept him sane during the early days after his wife's death also becomes suspect. Clinicians are not detectives; the facts of the case are not as relevant as the perceptions held by family members and the reaction to those perceptions. At times the clinician is trying to assist people in juggling two contradictory actions: accept the perceptions of others and continue to establish the truth. However, it is important to help clients to recognize that a judgment will never be handed down to confirm guilt or innocence. People continue through life with perceptions and misperceptions; they must find a way to build the relationship they wish to have, even when that relationship is being challenged.

One significant challenge these relationships face is around the topic of children. If the new spouse enters into the family with the notion that he or she will offer to be the "other parent" and that offer is soundly rejected, a tremendous strain will occur in the couple's relationship. But, as discussed earlier in this book, a parent is unable to request that his or her children accept the parental overtures of the new spouse. Interestingly, there are times when this new adult slowly assumes more and more parental authority and provides love to the children, and the children accept this relationship with gratitude. There is no clear pattern that distinguishes the instances when children seem open to the love and guidance of another adult after the death of their parent and the times when children fight with every fiber of their being against accepting this new person. Anecdotally, cases have presented in which the relevant variables seem identical, yet one family is having a terrible adjustment and the next seems to be making the best of the situation while still mourning the loss. It is understandable that the reader might find such a comment frustrating; however, it is important to recognize that some situations are simply profoundly difficult, and no one person deserves the blame. It is equally important to recognize that sometimes when things are going well, there seems to be a modicum of good fortune attached. Although there are clinical concerns that can be addressed, some of these dynamics appear to be greater than clinical intervention.

One possible variable that might make the difference between acceptance or rejection of a new parental figure is successful mourning. If a child has gone through a grieving process and appears to be willing to consider showing some affection without feeling guilty, that family is likely to look less tense. However, some of the angriest young people are those who feel that they are being pushed to grieve in order to accept the new person. In this situation, the good intentions of the adults who are recommending to the child that he or she seek some assistance to continue forward in life backfire strongly when the child explicitly refuses to consider mourning because to do so would exhibit disrespect to the deceased love one. At times this message seems to be coming from the grandparents, but at other times this belief appears to be completely the child's own decision. Therefore, the dilemma is that the child needs to grieve, but the child (or adolescent or young adult) refuses to do so and begins to connect successful grieving with forgetting his or her parent. In these cases, all that can be done is to have the new person back off any pressure and allow the relationship to build very slowly. Although this sounds relatively easy, it is not. The surviving parent is often perceived as somehow endorsing this attitude of his or her child, causing the new spouse to feel even more alone. But just as one starts to recognize the pain of the new spouse, there is a flash of remembrance that this child lost a parent to death, and the pain of that experience understandably dominates. The clinician may find that trying to assist both parties to gain empathy for the other does not usually work when the level of anguish is too great for each party. Therefore, the clinician needs to think of the subsystems that can be addressed to aid in this situation.

If the child is willing to be seen, that is a crucial variable. The phrase *willing to be seen* is used intentionally here. Often in family therapy, the child is willing, but even if he or she is reluctant, the parent uses his or her influence to bring the child into treatment because the latter's behavior is part of the problem. In this circumstance, forcing the child might make the child's reluctance to move forward even more formidable. In the child's eyes the problem is not his or her nonacceptance of this new adult in his or her life; the problem is, in fact, the mere presence of this person. The child believes that things were great before his or her parent's death; things became tolerable after some period of adjustment to single-parent life and only became intolerable when Mom or Dad got married again. Therefore, pushing the child toward treatment should only be done if it is aimed at helping the parent and the child talk about their relationship and the loss of the parent. Any discussion of moving toward acceptance of the new person is premature if the child is seething with resentment. Usually, the anger will begin to subside, but that occurs when the child really believes that his or her parent remains available and this new partner is neither replacing the deceased parent nor stealing away the surviving parent. So these cases often involve parent–child sessions, followed by couple sessions. The couple sessions are intended to explain some of the issues that are affecting the family, reinforce the bond between the couple, and reduce expectations of significant relations between the new adult and child, at least for a time.

This discussion of the new adult has been premised on the idea that this person has an interest in having a parental role, at least to some extent. There are, however, those people who enter these relationships with little interest in anything other than being married or cohabiting with the surviving adult. The involvement of children is considered unimportant. These cases are not as likely to come to treatment, but they do represent an interesting subset. The new adult is basically a roommate and often sees the children as either annoying or as buddies. When the parent is comfortable carrying all the responsibility for child care, this model can be functional; however, usually when the child reaches adolescence, the system becomes strained. The clinician's task in these situations is to determine what role the "new" (the new person may have been around for 10 years) partner wishes to take and what role the parent wishes this person to have. This is a *discussion* because there is no correct model. Although it might be difficult to remain only a roommate when dealing with adolescent stepchildren (for they are the person's stepchildren or stepchild), it is possible to do so if the couple can withstand the pressure of the totality of parental power resting in one person. Usually, most couples that want to shift to a more egalitarian model find that the years of the one adult being a buddy have seriously undermined any parental authority. Although the idea that they can now become an equal coparenting team is unlikely, some adjustments, which largely involve establishing house rules with a clear consequence to be delivered by either person, are a start. The clinician needs to encourage the couple to begin with very basic rules that fall under the coparenting arrangement. It is extremely easy for the child or children to flummox this system if it is too strict or places too much authority in the newly empowered adult. It is a baby step approach to authority that demands that the relationship still be more important than the discipline.

Above all, it is critical for the new spouse in a bereaved family to attempt to avoid defensiveness. Whether or not this new adult wishes to be parental, there will be challenges to the legitimacy of his or her presence. It is valuable to understand the child's concern but not to spend too much time trying to counter the logic of someone who is experiencing loss. The steady presence, although challenging and requiring patience, is the stance that appears to most often establish a place in these homes.

CONCLUSION

The extended family in a stepfamily is important. As a clinician works with a stepfamily it is crucial to understand the roles that these members play. Because of the subsystem emphasis of this model, it is possible to benefit from the involvement of people who might normally not be associated with treatment but who can play a significant role in the stepfamily becoming healthier. These extended family members include grandparents, aunts, and uncles. Additionally, this sphere can expand to stepgrandparents and in-laws after the death of a mate. Although there is no single intervention that can be applied to these situations, there are steps that reduce the confusion and increase each member's understanding of the systemic effect of this exceptionally complex family arrangement.

8

STEPFAMILY DIVERSITY

THE IMPORTANCE OF UNDERSTANDING
THE ROLE OF DIVERSITY

Psychotherapy continues to evolve in numerous directions. One area that has become far more sophisticated is the importance of understanding diversity as related to building effective clinical relationships. Whereas early discussions emphasized how selected cultural or racial groups differ from the majority culture, such a focus now seems far too limited. The American Psychological Association (APA) has explicitly recognized that psychologists need to be aware of "age, gender, gender identity, race, ethnicity, culture, national origin, religion, sexual orientation, disability, language, and socioeconomic status" to exhibit "respect for people's rights and dignity" (APA, 2010, Principle E).

Most clinical discussions on diversity attempt to inform in order to lessen the level of misperception or faulty assumptions that are placed on people culturally or racially distinct from the clinician (Sue & Sue, 1999). This use of scholarship, often sociological in nature, is quite helpful in addressing diversity at a clinical level. However, as the field has increased the array of people who need to be understood, the process of being competent with diverse populations has also expanded. There are other writers (Green, 2002; Hong, 2009) who have attempted to expand diversity studies beyond making the argument that diversity must be understood politically as well as sociologically. In other words, although it is necessary to recognize the sociological and demographic reality of diversity, theoreticians must incorporate a fuller understanding of how these wider populations fit into the psychological theories themselves. Without this effort, these theoretical models are tantamount to continuing oppression unintentionally.

In this chapter, we clarify factors that are distinct about stepfamilies of various ethnic and cultural groups, and more important, we provide a fuller understanding as to why an awareness of diversity is an ethical requirement and a necessary process for any clinician. In any discussion of therapy, it is important to embrace an awareness of diversity. This perspective was, for many years, relegated to an afterthought rather than being seen as central to the clinical process. There are, however, philosophical, ethical, and clinically practical imperatives that impel this topic to the forefront.

The APA (2010) "Ethical Principles of Psychologists and Code of Conduct" was created to establish a benchmark for psychologists and other mental health professionals who adhere to the APA standards. A clinician complying with the ethical standards of his or her field is making a commitment to be mindful of the need to benefit the person seeking treatment. To do that, the clinician must overtly respect those who are different.

Although the notion of respecting difference has become an automatic refrain, for many making such a leap is not so automatic. Ethics assist in the process of really accepting "the other" because following the ethical standards of one's field forces one to examine the situation with an allegiance to serving justice. And striving to be just increases the likelihood that one is not permitting subjective beliefs to dictate one's actions.

The practical advantage of displaying competence in diversity is directly related to an improved clinical relationship. One essential factor in forming a relationship is to have the other feel understood. To feel misunderstood is not neutral but rather represents a missed empathic opportunity (Comas-Díaz, 2006). When this occurs, there is a negative effect on the building of trust between people. Empathy is particularly dependent on the sense of a shared vision. For example, two people need to be able to see why this situation was so hurtful or why that interaction was so important to form an empathic bond. If the clinician is confused by the other and believes that their worldviews share no overlap, then the attempt to achieve an empathic connection will usually fail.

One might challenge this premise by suggesting that the well-educated White clinician may have no overlap with the Latino gang member. However, the strength of empathy does not rely strictly on the overt similarity between two people but rather on the connection that is attributed to shared humanness.

A debate exists in the field as to whether one can achieve true cultural empathy (Ridley & Lingle, 1996). Some argue that the best one can achieve is a form of cognitive empathy that can be augmented by empathic witnessing (Kleinman, 1988). Ridley and Lingle speculated that one can achieve a true empathic connection, even across cultures, by engaging in vicarious affect. In other words, clinicians use experiences and feelings from their own lives to more fully comprehend the experience of the other, even the culturally distinct other. If, in fact, clinicians were not able to create an empathic bond with those dissimilar from themselves, the research on ethnic matching would not be so inconclusive (Comas-Díaz, 2006). Although the findings still support that people will stay in clinical relationships longer if there is a cultural match between clinician and client, there is no significant proof that treatment in this context is superior (Karlsson, 2005; Winterstein, Mensinger, & Diamond, 2005). Fortunately, clinicians who are not matched with their clients can make efforts to be responsive and aware of relevant cultural and racial issues (Chang & Berk, 2009).

John Norcross (2001) researched what to attribute psychotherapy's effectiveness to, and he determined the percentages of various factors in order to specify what appears to be important. Although his findings suggest that unexplained variables and client contribution constitute the greatest percentage of outcome, 24% has been found to be attributed to the therapeutic relationship, the individual therapist, and the interaction between therapist and client. Although these three components of effective therapy cannot be linked to a sensitivity to diversity alone, it would be naïve to suggest that such a sensitivity is unnecessary for a positive clinical connection. Therefore, one could argue that a dedication to understanding diversity is an important factor in the quality of a relationship and thus an important factor in effective psychotherapy.

If one accepts the importance of sensitivity and understanding of diversity, it is necessary to explore why diversity is so complex. Each person brings his or her own frame of reference to every situation. That frame of reference is determined by a wide range of factors: age, culture, ethnicity, gender, sexual orientation, physical ability, neurological uniqueness, socioeconomic status, and religious belief. On one hand, there is significant reason to believe that a clinical bond can be formed with anyone; however, the logistical challenge of preparing a clinician for all the potential variables of diversity is truly daunting.

The first step in the process of becoming aware of the other is to become self-aware. It is with this in mind that we acknowledge that we are both White, are primarily of Northern European descent, and reside on the East Coast of the United States. One of us has been a stepparent, and both of us have lived in the context of a stepfamily as a child or as an adult.

The process of disclosure serves to highlight the frame of reference each of us brings to our thinking and emphasizes those arenas in which we need to be aware of what we do not know by experience. The benefits of White privilege, especially White male privilege, are such that the practice of self-examination must be honest and unflinching. Awareness does not remove the perks that come with society's acceptance. Rather, awareness of privilege heightens the clinician's acceptance. It is this acceptance, partially born from a commitment to ethical standards based on justice, that reduces a clinician's natural defensiveness. This acceptance and increased patience can be an important step in building trust and reducing stereotypes in both directions. When a clinician experiences anger from a particular family member during treatment and that anger does not seem connected to the therapy, awareness of the possible reason behind projected anger permits the clinician to reserve any clinical move for the time being. For example, a White male therapist is often granted a great deal of respect, but on occasion, may be perceived as a member of the oppressive class. It is at that moment that he must acknowledge (largely to himself) that he is a member of a category (White and male) that has derived power on the backs of diverse populations. The clinician does not need to flagellate himself for being a member of this oppressing class. The clinician can take some comfort in working actively to end some of the mistakes that have been made toward diverse people, often people of color. But it is the ability to respond with no defensiveness that is of critical importance. A young male African American, for example, has every right to request an acknowledgement of the historical reality of oppression. It is a matter of justice.

Painters describe *negative space* as that part of a canvas that forms the background, either because there is no paint or only a neutral shade is present. The eye of the observer is drawn to the image painted, but the true artist sees everything, including the negative space of any canvas. In much the same way, the more fully aware clinician sees the negative space around the client: the burden of oppression and societal expectations. In keeping with this metaphor, although the client is the focus of the painting, and therefore receives the primary attention, the therapist from a majority culture must examine the entire canvas.

Another factor that adds to the complexity of working with diversity is that such understanding is multidisciplinary. Scholars of diversity recognize that they cannot cite only a single field of study when discussing the issues relevant to any population. It is necessary to have a familiarity with cultural anthropology, history, psychology, sociology, demography, and often theology to gain a sophisticated view of the other. It is this challenge, along with the difficulty of recognizing one's our own biases that makes the work of being competent with diversity so difficult and so necessary.

ENGAGING THREE DIMENSIONS TO INCREASE
COMPETENCE IN CLINICAL PRACTICE

Addressing clinical practice in light of cultural dimensions involves at least three overarching perspectives: (a) recognition of the way in which any cultural group differs from the majority culture; (b) recognition that level of acculturation and racial identity development (Sue & Sue, 1999) will influence the role of power dynamics and effects of oppression; and (c) recognition that research, even sophisticated research, may suggest a clinical direction that is poorly matched with the stepfamily in treatment because certain psychological concepts are not universal in nature. For example, although much of the research regarding good parenting may be useful to an Asian stepfamily, it is possible that there will be some general recommendations that flow from the research that are actually unhelpful to this Asian stepfamily.

How Populations Differ From the Majority

By engaging these three perspectives, the clinician will not be addressing all possible issues that may be relevant to the diversity of the stepfamily he or she meets, but awareness of these perspectives encourages the clinician to be certain to do no harm. The initial perspective motivates the clinician to use the wide array of information published that addresses how any one group is different from the majority population. The differences reported originate from the various fields that produce research on issues related to the family. This information may concentrate on demographics, such as how large this population is in America. Or the information might establish that this population tends to be more communal and not interested in individuality. It may also report on this population's general attitude toward authority, family roles, the medical profession, religious faith, or any of the innumerable topics that have been chronicled. This material has been well covered by authors such as Sue and Sue (1999) and Comas-Díaz (2006) and should be reengaged whenever a clinician is meeting with a family from any culture that he or she does not share. It is also within this first perspective that the clinician should determine if there is evidence of efficacious treatment with this particular group.

Level of Acculturation

The second perspective, level of acculturation, is of critical importance and has received less attention in the diversity literature. Although it has been well articulated by Hong (2009) and Green (2002), it remains an area in which many clinicians do not fully appreciate the therapeutic implications. This perspective involves the evaluation of the client's comfort with his or her own identity. Cultural, racial, or ethnic identities are connected to one's level of acculturation. As theories of identity development suggest, one's level of acceptance of one's own identity is tied to one's comfort with the majority culture. In fact, in the early stages of identity formation, it is developmentally necessary to reject large aspects of the majority culture. For example, the process of *coming out* and accepting oneself as gay will usually demand a rejection of the traditional cultural standards. A newly self-actualized gay man may seek out environments in which being gay is typical and celebrated. This does not mean that he has become antiheterosexual but rather that identity formation propels him to more fully engage the group he feels part of. Again, identity formation theory suggests that as one becomes more fully integrated with one's identity, one may also feel fully comfortable engaging in activities of the majority culture.

A clinician needs to gauge where a client stands on his or her own journey of identity formation. This question is relevant for two reasons. The first is that the clinician needs to assess how relationally based the therapy should be. A client may be in a stage of identity formation in which a rejection of the majority culture, which the therapist represents, is a necessary and appropriate step in the client's own mental health. The type of therapy being practiced affects the bond between therapist and client. For example, although one could argue that a clinician relying on behavioral interventions still needs to establish a relationship, there is little doubt that the relational factor is overshadowed by the specific intervention, such as exposure. Although a combination of cognitive and affective interventions is generally best, in a sense mirroring the balance of content and process, a continuum often is present in which the clinician is determining what types of intervention fit best with this client. In fact, some models of therapy clearly steer toward one type of intervention specifically because that theorist believes that to concentrate in one arena, the behavioral, for example, is the best treatment in certain situations with certain clients. That same continuum can be used as the clinician assesses the client's stage of identity development. In other words, if the clinician feels that attempts toward emotionally connecting with this client only cause a push back, an intervention that helps explain their experience will often help. For example, for a White therapist working with male African American adolescents, there are occasions when an adolescent is deeply immersed in celebrating his racial identity and a strong therapeutic bond is unlikely. In this situation, rather than offering little to this client, the clinician can support his identity formation by helping him articulate what he wants as an African American man and how he sees himself. Certainly it is also appropriate to make reference to African American writings and role models and, on occasion, to refer the client to an African American therapist if it appears that being matched is necessary for this person.

If a client is so acculturated that he or she rejects his or her own identity and defers to the clinician, it is important not to use that power in a way that undercuts the client's search for his or her own identity. For example, a Korean teenager who was adopted at birth by a White American family might reject his own identity as Asian. He knows he is of Korean descent, but he has no contact with other Koreans or even Asians. In fact, he goes so far as to say, "When I look in the mirror, I actually do a double take sometimes because I feel so White." The White therapist makes no effort to rely on the therapeutic relationship to support a challenge to the client. Rather, the challenge is purely intellectual; the therapist must make it clear by discussing identity development that his client's desire to reject his heritage will necessarily lead to greater distress. This intervention is conveyed less as a warning and more as a clear statement that identity formation is a relatively universal phenomenon.

The other dynamic that needs to be understood regarding the issue of acculturation and identity is an awareness of power. A White therapist might see using first names as a respectful joining style, whereas some people may see the use of first names in this context as disrespectful. Therefore, a clinician needs to be alert to any area in which a misuse of power is occurring, even if it is entirely unintended.

In any discussion of cultural diversity, place is of exceptional importance. For example, Mexican scholars can study stepfamilies and build an important research base; however, the topic automatically includes diversity when Mexican stepfamilies are studied while living in the United States. A focus on differences is important, but it is equally necessary to determine the ways in which psychological science is universal, regardless of the population with whom it was tested. It may be the case that any concept that has not been tested directly on a particular population may not have a perfect overlap, but it is vital to remember Harry Stack Sullivan's comment that "All of us are much more human than otherwise" (Sullivan, 1953, p. 32). In other words, although it would be unethical and arrogant to apply most concepts that have only been studied with a White middle-class population, it might be equally divisive to abandon all psychological premises because clinicians do not have research findings that represent the exact population sitting in front of them in their offices.

The Usefulness of Large Psychological Concepts

A third perspective used in the service of respecting diversity involves the clinician evaluating five important dimensions of assessing a case. These five dimensions can mistakenly be interpreted as stable, but in fact they can present differently when observed in diverse populations. The five dimensions are hierarchy, parenting style, differentiation, diagnosis, and respect for psychotherapy.

This does not imply that the clinician needs to dismiss psychological benchmarks as not being robust enough to explain people beyond the research sample but rather that the clinician should be aware that the template being used to explain some behavior may not be as accurate for different populations. Parenting style is a particularly good illustration of this dilemma. Many clinicians would cite Dianne Baumrind's (1996, 2005) work, which points to the advantages of authoritative parenting, as quite universal. Yet, recent evidence suggests that some ethnic and racial groups, in fact, seem to benefit more from either authoritarian or even indulgent parenting (Greenspan, 2006; Lamborn, Mount, Steinberg, & Dornbusch, 1991). In other words, for years clinicians felt that they could, with confidence, advise parents to use authoritative parenting practices, and in many cases this form of parenting is still considered the best single approach. However, as the topic continued to be researched, it became clear that the cultural issues and the needs of certain children were better served by other parenting styles.

Because this section is dedicated to examining those psychological concepts that need to be viewed through the lens of diversity, the five concepts discussed clearly vary when examined through the lens of different cultures or races. There is, however, one concept, attachment (Ainsworth, 1967), which although not exactly universal, can be considered less susceptible to the effect of diverse populations. Although there still are pockets of debate, attachment is perceived to be experienced by all people. Researchers studying attachment assert that the core mechanics—the instinct, the experience of it, and the outcome—appear to be universal (Grossman, Grossman, Huber, & Wartner, 1981; Posada et al., 1995). Grossman, Grossman, and Kebler (2005) have theorized that the universal drive may present differently in different cultures as a result of ecological factors, and yet the system of how attachment operates is universal (van Ijzendoorn & Sagi, 1999). Therefore, if the clinician considers the client's behavior to be the result of poor attachment, the clinician would not necessarily be culturally biased to view this as a valid concern regardless of which race or culture the person represents.

Hierarchy

Assessing the role of hierarchy is critical in understanding the structure of a stepfamily. How is power situated in this stepfamily? Although first-marriage families are not a monolith, generally the most significant variable regarding power and control is gender. As feminist scholars (Hare-Mustin, 1978) have pointed out, men in many families are granted power for no reason other than gender. Stepfamilies must take gender-based issues into account, but an equally critical factor in held power relates directly to the biological versus nonbiological family relations. The biological or adoptive mother of a child, explicitly as a result of her maternal connections, carries more relational power than a stranger. Therefore, the clinician needs to assess how power and control are exhibited and how effective the manner of power sharing seems to be.

Investigating this dynamic does not suggest that the clinician is entering this assessment with a predetermined idea of one correct system for sharing power; however, there are some hierarchical patterns that are more likely to fail, at least this is true with a largely White client population. The clinician needs to assess if a stepfamily, for reasons of diversity, exhibits a style of power and control that may look problematic but, in fact, works well. For example, an Asian American stepfamily may present with the stepfather assuming significantly more authority than the mother.

The issue of hierarchy in the home is fascinating and complex. A variety of factors must be taken into account when examining this issue with a stepfamily. Although the research (Bray & Hetherington, 1993) supports the idea of the stepparent taking a less active role as a disciplinarian in the first few years, this research has involved primarily White subjects. The ethnic, cultural, and religious dimensions of a stepfamily may make such advice unwelcome and inaccurate. Similarly, Deal (2006) discussed the tightrope that a clinician may need to walk in working with a devout Christian stepfamily. There is an inherent contradiction between the research findings and the religious teaching advocating that the man is to be the leader of the home. Deal encourages stepfathers to lead through the relational influence he has through his wife.

However, having a body of research on this topic, or any topic, neither confirms nor disconfirms that this information is useful for the stepfamily in treatment. But the likelihood that the information may be useful to a stepfamily understanding their own trials and challenges is certainly increased if the research in question comes from research subjects who could be considered matched with the stepfamily in treatment. Therefore, if one assumes that all interventions that are based on a comparison with research findings demand some clinical finesse to determine relative suitability, then research findings shared with diverse populations must be even more closely considered.

In the case under discussion, the clinician makes a judgment as to whether sharing information about the research on parental and stepparental power would be useful. If the clinician determines that the problems evidenced in this case suggest that this information might be of use, the information must be presented as a possible hypothesis rather than as a norm not being achieved by this stepfamily. When information is shared but a clear caveat is provided to emphasize that this research may not be transferable, the stepfamily is empowered to consider the implications without perceiving the information to be a recommendation.

Parenting Style

For many years, it was taken for granted that authoritative parenting was universally superior to the other parenting styles. However, even Steinberg (2001), who for years advocated the superiority of authoritative parenting, stated, "Authoritative parenting is associated with certain developmental outcomes, not all of which are adaptive in all contexts" (p. 13). Other authorities on the effects of the interaction of parenting style and successful adolescent outcomes have also noted that when examining parenting style, the cultural background makes a significant difference (Chao, 2001; Greenspan, 2006).

In fact, when researchers examined academic outcomes with both African American adolescents and Asian American adolescents, they found that these two populations may in fact have superior performance when living in an authoritarian home rather than in an authoritative home (Steinberg, Dornbusch, & Brown, 1992). The rationale given is that these two populations of adolescents may benefit from more structure and less warmth than do White adolescents in the United States.

Therefore, when examining parenting style in a stepfamily, the clinician must be aware of both the issues that relate to the coparenting dynamic between remarried couples and the cultural issues that may challenge any preconceived idea of best parenting practice. This does not mean that the clinician does not attempt to discuss parenting, for this is an area of intense frustration in many stepfamilies, but the conversation should not be too simple. The complexity of the issue demands that the therapist weigh all the factors and have a collaborative discussion of the couple's parenting preferences combined with the therapist's informed consultation.

Differentiation

Murray Bowen (M. E. Kerr & Bowen, 1988) developed a concept that for many years was perceived to be the most salient dimension of mental health when considering the individual within the context of a family system. His concept of *differentiation* is now understood to be more culturally bound than was once believed. The process of differentiating from one's family still deserves attention because it remains a force in the maturation of many young adults. However, clinicians must be careful to consider the appropriateness of the concept before assuming it to be a positive in any stepfamily.

Bicultural or multicultural families may find this concept to be the source of tremendous misperception. For example, a biracial couple, a White man married to a Latina American woman, may perceive the mental health of a young adult in distinctly different ways. The White man, who in this example is a stepfather, may feel that a differentiated young adult, one who is not overly emotionally involved with his family of origin, is healthy and secure. His mother, on the other hand, sees that behavior in her son as a sign of his lack of love, disconnection from the family, and lack of respect for the older generation. The clinician must be able to assist both members of the couple to see the reason their views are so distinctly different. Western White culture particularly views the differentiated young adult as mentally healthy; many other cultures, including the Asian American and the Latino American, see a strong emotional connection combined with active attention to the family as appropriate.

There are primarily two ways that the issue of differentiation may be problematic, especially with diverse stepfamilies. The first is when the remarried couple views the young adult very differently as a result of distinct cultural mores regarding differentiation. The second is when the therapist advocates a particular opinion as to the "proper" emotional distance a young adult should take, especially when cultural differences are not taken into account.

Therefore, the clinician needs to be alert to both potentially problematic scenarios. The first is dealt with by teaching the couple about their differing perspectives. In practical terms, people who view differentiation through separate lenses can, at best, understand why they differ from the other. Rarely does someone change his or her opinion on this issue, but one may become less dogmatic as one understands the worldview of the other. The second scenario, the one in which the clinician applies an inaccurate template, must be addressed by self-reflection, supervision, and awareness. Assisting therapists to gain a respect for the importance of cultural, racial, and religious sensitivity remains an important goal.

Diagnosis

The goal of a diagnostic system is to create an objective method by which people can be labeled to access the best treatment specific to the disorder in question. However, this laudable goal is not always achievable. The *Diagnostic and Statistical Manual of Mental Disorders* (4th ed., text rev.; DSM–IV–TR; American Psychiatric Association, 2000), the essential reference for psychiatric diagnosis, is again under revision. The revision of the manual results in changes in criteria based on changes in the science of understanding the etiology and presentation of a condition. In some case, a diagnosis is removed from the manual itself, indicating that something once judged as pathological is no longer seen in that light and, in fact, should not be labeled as *abnormal*. Homosexuality was, until 1973, a diagnosis in the DSM–II (American Psychiatric Association, 1968). The Board of Directors of the American Psychiatric Association determined to remove homosexuality as a diagnosis. This decision was later reaffirmed by a vote of the membership of the association. For an interim period, the *DSM–III* (American Psychiatric Association, 1980) used a new diagnosis, ego-dystonic homosexuality, until finally in 1986 the diagnosis was removed completely (Herek, 2001).

Another factor that affects diagnosis is knowledge. When a specific population is made more aware of a diagnostic category as well as possible treatments, the number of people receiving that diagnosis will often increase (Bailey & Owens, 2005). Sometimes physicians need to be alerted to the perception of their professional organizations that some condition may be underdiagnosed or the diagnosis needs to be generated earlier to assist in early treatment benefits. This occurred recently when the American Academy of Pediatrics revised information to encourage physicians to be alert to the signs of a child potentially being diagnosed on the autism spectrum. They warned their membership that the public knowledge of the symptoms of autism spectrum disorders was expanding rapidly as a result of information in the media and that physicians needed to be prepared to respond to these increased concerns (C. P. Johnson, Myers, & Council on Children With Disabilities, 2007).

Two additional factors that need to be considered when discussing diagnosis are gender and culture. When considering the behavioral symptoms to be used in making a diagnosis, gender may serve to tip the balance from one diagnosis to another. For example, men exhibiting symptoms that would likely result in a woman receiving the diagnosis of borderline personality disorder are more likely to be considered for posttraumatic stress disorder (Layton, 1995). In regard to culture, evidence suggests that if a male adolescent is African American, his behavior is more likely to result in a diagnosis of conduct disorder than if the same behavior is exhibited by a White male adolescent (Walls, 2003). Giving someone a diagnosis is a powerful and important action. If diversity issues are relevant in the assigning of a diagnosis, it would be ethically suspect (APA, 2002) to ignore such pertinent information. Therefore, for various reasons, it is important to use diagnostic criteria with careful attention to the objective benchmarks established. Although bias cannot be erased, it can be reduced.

Respect for Therapy

No culture is a monolith, but influential belief systems exist within any group. Research suggests that therapy, in general, benefits people from any race or cultural group to some extent. However, those people more acculturated to a Western industrialized lifestyle will more likely view attending therapy as a reasonable option when in distress. Other groups take a distinctly less open position regarding psychotherapy, seeing it either as contrary to religious teachings or only useful for the treatment of insanity. Therefore, the stigma felt by those who are uncomfortable with therapy is a significant hurdle. People acculturated in a Westernized country may still see therapy as a mystery, but many will know someone who went to treatment for a condition and reported some benefit from the process.

Clinicians need to be respectful of how difficult going to therapy can be for someone. It can be challenging for a clinician to remember that many people feel ashamed to be in therapy or that they truly do not understand how the process is expected to work. Because clinicians see themselves as members of a helping profession, the notion that the process is either shame inducing or a fraud is completely contrary to a clinician's worldview. Therefore, it is important for the clinician to listen carefully, be aware of and reduce personal defensiveness, and adjust his or her treatment style to one that does not feed the negative assumptions of the client being seen.

For example, an Asian American family that comes to treatment because of a school referral may be uninterested in a highly emotive process. There may be serious reservations, often unexpressed out of respect, about sharing family problems "in public." This concern is so powerful that the clinician who ignores this perception is not being responsive to the needs of the family.

TWO DIVERSE AMERICAN STEPFAMILIES

In the sections that follow, we present a discussion and case examples of two American stepfamilies with diverse ethnic backgrounds.

The African American Stepfamily

The African American stepfamily is far more common than is generally perceived. In fact, African American children are more likely than White children to reside in a stepfamily if the definition of what constitutes a stepfamily is enlarged to include the great variety of ways in which an adult is involved in a parental manner with a child who is not biologically related. However, because African Americans are less likely to marry (Stewart, 2007), the number of families that could be considered African American stepfamilies has been underestimated.

In general, in the African American family, the roles and boundaries are more fluid than in White families in America. Stack (1974) reported that there is a history of Black families including *fictive kin*, people with no biological or legal ties who are accepted and respected as family members. This more open system appears to make transitions to stepfamily living less unusual in that children in African American families are more used to responding to adults as if the person speaking has parental authority.

Certain features of the typical African American experience work to make stepfamily life easier; whereas some features appear to make it more difficult. Additionally, some characteristics are difficult to assess for their overall effect on stepfamily life for African Americans. This ambiguity regarding certain features comes from the fact that the number of variables involved can be so great that it is impossible to predict the effect, and the research literature on African American stepfamilies is still very limited.

Research does suggest that African American men are often quite comfortable with their stepchildren and may actually read more to them than do biologically related fathers (Fagan, 1998). Also, the African American couple has been found to be more egalitarian in regard to household tasks (DeGenova & Rice, 2005). Although this finding appears to be positive because of the general support for egalitarian unions, it might also cause an unexpected problem. If the man, for example, who has remarried a woman with children is working equally hard on household tasks, he may be more frustrated about a child's unwillingness to help out around the home.

Interestingly, African American men tend to stay on friendly terms with the women with whom they have had a child (Hamer, 1998; Stewart, 2007). In the majority of situations, this more positive relationship allows for easier transitions for a child living in two homes. However, these studies commented on those who remained in the child's life and not those who discontinued contact. In contrast, Ahrons (1994) studied a largely White population, finding that 50% of divorced parents were not on friendly terms. The wide spectrum of experiences within each racial group makes a direct comparison of postdivorce relationships across racial lines impossible; however, the apparent détente among many divorced African American couples should be studied further to determine the implications.

Although some of the common features associated with African Americans appear to serve a positive function for stepfamilies, a couple of dynamics that have been identified by research in the African American population clearly limit the success of these remarried families. African American couples, in general, have relationships that they rate as lower in quality. In addition, spouses in these couples rate their spouse's behavior in more negative terms than do Whites (Broman, 2005). Findings such as these may partially explain why African American couples have a higher rate of marital dissolution than do White couples in the United States (Bramlett & Mosher, 2002).

The following case example is not intended to present the African American stepfamily as an archetype; rather, this stepfamily represents simply one stepfamily. However, some of the issues raised in this case are typical of African American stepfamilies. We therefore encourage therapists to use a dual lens, one to examine stepfamily issues in general and a more refined

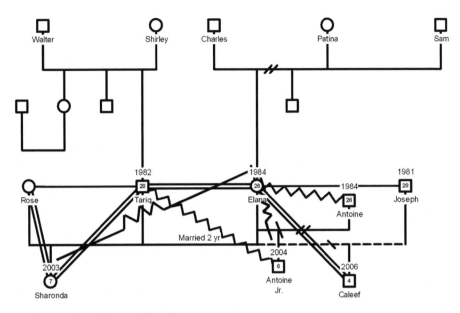

Figure 8.1. The Edwards family.

lens to highlight those issues affecting this family in part as a result of their cultural presentation.

The Edwards stepfamily (see Figure 8.1) came into treatment to (a) keep the loving couple from becoming conflicted over parenting differences, (b) assist Antoine Jr. (called Junior by the family) with his behavioral problems, (c) reduce the arguments between Elana and Sharonda, and (d) create a more positive relationship between Tariq and Junior. The course of treatment for this example is restricted to eight sessions. Although there is no number of sessions that is considered optimal, many stepfamilies stay in treatment long enough to move past the crisis stage they feel necessitated the initial call. Because of some learning issues that were found when Junior was assessed, he continued in tutoring past the end of therapy, and both his mother and Tariq received some additional coaching around this issue. In addition, many stepfamilies engage in occasional follow-up sessions (some months after the "end" of treatment) that serve as a "booster shot" to the stepfamily.

Session 1

Session 1 was focused on the remarried couple. In particular, this session was intended to allow the couple to hear each other and present their separate points of view of the current situation in the home. When the therapist was confident that each person's position was understood, the empathy exercise was initiated. In this case, as had been recommended in Step 5 of the stepfamily therapy (SfT) model described in Chapter 3, each member of the couple was able to express the perspective of the other in a manner that exhibited an empathic understanding and some level of care about the children around whom the tension was building, Junior and Sharonda.

Tariq was able to empathize with Elana about her feeling bossed around by Sharonda, and Elana was able to express understanding that Tariq found Junior to be "mouthy" and very rejecting of Tariq's efforts to bond with him. The couple was comforted by not needing to convince the other as to the absolute correctness of either person's opinion. The only assignment was for Elana to get specific information from Junior's teacher about his problems and learning style in class.

Session 2

In Session 2, Tariq and Elana were again seen together. The intention was to assist them to function as a team to best chart a course of action regarding Junior's academic problems. The therapist highlighted that with the feedback from the teacher, they would have a full perspective on whether Junior needed an educational evaluation. In this case, it was determined that there was enough evidence to request an assessment of Junior's learning issues. Although it is possible that Junior has attention-deficit/hyperactivity disorder (ADHD), such a diagnosis should be made only after the learning issues have been assessed. This care should be taken in all cases, but when discussing an African American adolescent, one needs to be aware that this population is concerned with the perception that teachers use the diagnosis of ADHD as a means of avoiding looking for more complex learning issues (Bailey & Owens, 2005). Interestingly, ADHD is actually underdiagnosed and undertreated in the African American population possibly because of a bias that underemphasizes medical problems and pushes blame over to assumptions of poor parenting and socioeconomic factors (Kendall & Hatton, 2002). Therefore, one would want to fully assess the possibility of ADHD in the case of Junior, following the standard tools for such a diagnosis.

Session 3

The overarching goal for this session is to tangibly reconnect Elana and her son Junior. Elana was helped to soften her view of Junior's behavior as not being so easily defined simply as bad. Rather, his behavior, even before the findings of the assessment, is reframed to couch his actions in a fuller, more complete context. This is not to say that Junior does not exhibit some bad behavior or that discipline should not be used. In fact, as stated earlier, African American youths often greatly benefit from structure. However, the reframe is to acknowledge that Junior is likely to have some learning issues, has an absent father, has made a bond with Joseph (Caleef's father), feels a constant tension with his mom, and is not sure that he is ready to try to get to know Tariq yet. A reframe does not give Junior a free pass, but it makes it likely that the simplistic explanation of his behavior is no longer satisfactory. Both Junior and Elana took the opportunity to reaffirm how important they were to each other.

Session 4

Elana was alone in this session to examine a number of interpersonal relationships in her life and determine which ones needed to be addressed. Some questions were entertained, for example: Is Antoine Sr. able to be an asset in any manner? How involved does Joseph want to stay with Junior? If Joseph is interested in being available to both Junior and his son Caleef, how does Tariq respond to that? Also, does Elana feel that she can connect with Rose enough to form a collaboration so that Sharonda's visits are less conflicted? This session was helpful in that Elana was able to clarify, both for herself and the therapist, the benefit of involving other people in treatment for the good of the entire binuclear family. As it turned out, both Joseph and Tariq were willing, according to Elana, to be involved for the sake of the boys. It is not unusual in African American stepfamilies to have nonbiologically related adults form a community, and this occurred in this stepfamily.

Session 5

It was time to concentrate on the couple. After doing the work of stabilizing some of the subsystems and beginning to address the child-based issues, the clinician put the relationship between Elana and Tariq front and center. This session dealt with some psychoeducation on coparenting and some of the positive steps that have been taken, but most of it was dedicated to discussing the ways in which the couple could support each other, have fun together, and be less thrown by the vicissitudes of stepfamily life.

As with many African American couples, Elana and Tariq were very egalitarian in their distribution of household tasks. Tariq was open and willing to be involved in tasks around the kitchen while Elana completed many of the physical tasks around the yard. Although the strengths of such an arrangement were highlighted, the couple was asked to list some aspects of this style that caused frustrations. This was not about teaching the couple about their own culture, which would have been insulting; rather, it allowed the therapist to offer a more focused question than might have been raised without the therapist's understanding of the cultural literature. In this case, because Tariq felt that he was very engaged in working around the house, he was quick to pounce on Junior for not helping out enough.

Session 6

Session 6 was a binuclear adult session. Four of the five parents, Elana, Tariq, Joseph, and Rose, were invited in with the specific understanding that this meeting was intended to assist everyone involved in helping all the children. Antoine Sr. had been phoned, and messages had been left, but these messages were never acknowledged.

Sessions of this nature are interesting. The first 15 minutes are often an experiment in keeping people from wading into sensitive topics and in beginning the process of learning to tolerate and maybe even like each other. The focus then shifted to a discussion of schedules, the needs of the children, and improving necessary adult communication. We have found that although such sessions are often useful with White stepfamilies, in the African American community, the general comfort with fictive kin often makes these sessions even less contentious.

Session 7

Session 7 was explicitly intended to be a split session, one in which there were two short sessions, each of 25 minutes. The split session is useful for a couple of reasons. Sometimes the clinician simply wants to introduce an idea to a subsystem and give them enough time to see some positive aspects of working together. It is not that the clinician is avoiding the real issues, but rather, some relationships only need a little structure and encouragement to improve on their own.

In this case, Tariq and Sharonda were seen first. The purpose of this time together was to affirm the importance of their relationship, give Sharonda some time to really talk to her dad about her feelings, and introduce the idea that Tariq really wanted Sharonda and Elana to have fewer battles during Sharonda's visits. This was not posed as Sharonda's fault or Elana's fault, simply as a systemic reality of sharing Tariq. Tariq made it very clear to Sharonda that he was able to love her, his daughter, and love his wife at the same time. The second shortened session was reserved for Sharonda and Elana. They were given time to begin to talk about how they might have some fun together and avoid topics that lead to bad feelings. In addition, both were given a chance to acknowledge that at times Junior's behavior did raise the general tension of the home and that they each needed to not interpret things personally.

Session 8

Session 8, the final session for the purpose of this case study, was a stepfamily session with Elana, Tariq, Junior, and Caleef. Given all of the subsystem sessions that had preceded this session, the emphasis was on giving everyone a chance to talk about what was working at home and what was still difficult.

Because of Caleef's age, a stepfamily drawing was done in which everyone worked together to create what he or she wanted the home to look like. Using art projects at these times offers a chance for the discussion to remain somewhat metaphorical, in this case a stepfamily that could have a big room to be together and little rooms so they could find peace when it was needed.

A Latino American Stepfamily

Latino American families bring with them an exceptionally powerful issue that relates directly to acculturation, power, and economic diversity, and that issue is language. Although Spanish is increasingly common in the United States, being unable to speak English continues to have huge ramifications (Falicov, 2009).

Although the research literature on Latino American stepfamilies is still quite limited, there is evidence that intergenerational differences in acculturation are occurring, but a commitment to intergenerational assistance is still greater in the Latino American family than in the White American family (Coleman, Ganong, & Rothrauff, 2006). Therefore, clinicians need to consider both the norms of the culture they are working with as well as the effect of differing levels of acculturation between the generations.

It is worth noting that among Latino Americans, there are differences in parenting issues that are likely to influence stepfamily life as well. Given that Latino parents are more inclined toward being protective parents (Domenech-Rodríguez, Donovick, & Crowley, 2009), the clinician needs to be very aware of parenting differences in granting autonomy to adolescents. In other words, if the stepparent and parent are in strong disagreement as to the level of appropriate autonomy, a clinician from a different culture should be wary of making a recommendation.

Adler-Baeder and Schramm (2006) pointed out that members of Latino American families are less likely to identify themselves as a stepfamily than are members of either White or African American families. When interviewed, most responded that they are a family, a married family, with no indication that this family has gone through divorce and remarriage. This perspective may offer some benefits to the family; however, it may also attempt to hide a reality that is best acknowledged. The data at this time cannot answer whether this pattern of rejecting the self-identification of stepfamily is a factor to be addressed, but the data certainly suggest that clinicians should be respectful of the manner in which these families identify themselves.

The Lopez stepfamily (see Figure 8.2) was referred to treatment by a Department of Human Services worker after the family has been investigated for child abuse, a claim that was found to be unsubstantiated. The initial report to the Department of Human Services had been made by a teacher who had a

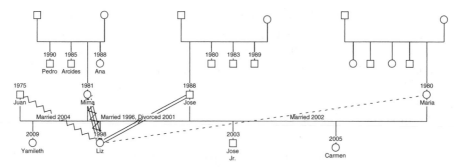

Figure 8.2. The Lopez family.

good relationship with Liz Santiago, the daughter of Mirna Lopez. Liz, age 12, had reported to her teacher that her stepfather, Juan Lopez, "beats her." Although the teacher saw no bruises, she was concerned because Liz seemed unusually aggressive with the other students in school. In fact, Liz had been suspended from school for aggression on three occasions in the past 2 months.

Although Juan was very upset about having been reported to the Department of Human Services by Liz, he was willing to attend treatment with his wife, Mirna, but he was reluctant to speak much in front of Liz, whom he no longer trusted. Mr. and Mrs. Lopez feel that Liz is out of control. Liz's father, Jose Santiago, lives within 20 miles and is willing to take Liz on occasion when Mirna feels that Juan and she are unable to control her. However, at the Santiago home, where her stepmother, Maria, and two stepsiblings live, Liz's behavior is considered too difficult, and she is usually returned within 2 weeks.

Although this case was addressed using the tenets of SfT, there were unique features in which an awareness of Latino culture proved very important. In particular, issues of parental authority, acculturation, and interfamilial postdivorce relationships were all adding to the clinical problems presented. In this case, the issues of gender and parental authority made clear the necessity of being respectful of cultural norms while recognizing the dynamics that influence stepfamily functioning. Mrs. Lopez believed that Liz needed to treat her stepfather, Juan, with the same respect that she accorded her father, Jose. It is an admirable goal to expect Liz to show equal respect to both her father and stepfather; however, as clinicians who have worked for years with stepfamilies and have read the research literature understand, the evidence suggests that such respect, when it occurs, comes gradually as part of a positive relationship. It may be that unintentionally Mirna has made it even harder for Juan by putting him in charge of Liz and so completely abdicating her own authority. This pressure led Juan to use more physical discipline than he wished. (Although he continues to deny that he ever beat Liz, he admits that he did use spankings.) In addition, Liz admitted feeling angry with her mother for leaving everything up to Juan and being, as Liz described, "totally lame." Although the clinician respected the desire Mirna had for Juan to be "the strength in the home," it became clear that Liz would not allow this to occur if it meant that Mirna, her mom, had no power whatsoever. In meeting with Mirna and Juan in a couple's session, it was quickly apparent that Mirna's limited English skills were a major factor in her feeling insecure and unable to act with authority. Juan, having very good language skills in English, was perceived by Mirna as the better choice to serve as an example to Liz.

When Liz was sent to her father's house, she was reasonably polite to him, but she was not respectful to Maria, her stepmother. In addition, Liz was quite physical with her two younger stepsiblings. Although neither child was ever really hurt by Liz's rough play, Maria had become increasingly anxious about leaving Jose Jr. or Carmen alone with her. This pattern defeated one of Jose's desires, which was to be able to let Liz babysit so that Maria and he could go out on a short date away from the kids. Jose would get increasingly angry at both Maria (for her fear that Liz was dangerous) and Liz, eventually just giving up and sending Liz back to her mother and Juan.

The therapist proceeded to address this case with the following goals in mind: (a) Mirna must gain enough self-respect to reach the point at which she wishes to be parental; (b) Juan needs to be viewed as a respected stepfather and not just the disciplinarian; (c) the four primary adults (Mr. and Mrs. Lopez and Mr. and Mrs. Santiago) need to coordinate a schedule so that Liz is not always leaving or coming under duress; (d) Liz needs to attend a class to learn how to be a babysitter so that she can be seen as capable with her stepsiblings (to whom she claims a desire to be close); (e) Liz needs to be given access to her own counselor for her to work out her frustrations with school and home; and (f) Juan and Mirna need to attend a stepfamily education class to address communication and discipline styles. Although it will not be mandated, Mirna will also be encouraged to pursue some additional instruction in English because, she says, this issue "makes me feel bad every day."

A CROSS-CULTURAL RESEARCH PROJECT: ITALIAN AND AMERICAN THERAPISTS

A collaboration between the Universita Cattolica del Sacro Cuore in Milan, Italy, and Chestnut Hill College in Philadelphia, Pennsylvania, resulted in a cross-cultural study that investigated (a) the interventions and theoretical assumptions of Italian therapists treating stepfamilies and (b) how American and Italian therapists differ on a number of factors related to treating stepfamilies (Browning, Accordini, Gennari, & Cigoli, 2010).

The Italian research team was headed by Professor Vittorio Cigoli, researcher Marialuisa Gennari, and doctoral student Monica Accordini. The American research team was headed by Professor Scott Browning and doctoral student Rebecca Shaffer. The study was approved by the institutional review boards of both institutions and included 125 Italian therapists and 45 American therapists. The instrument for surveying the therapists was designed by the Italian research team in consultation with Dr. Browning. The instrument was then translated by Monica Accordini, who distributed it to the Italian subjects.

The findings suggested that both the Italian therapists and the American therapists view the stepfamily as having unique characteristics. However, very interestingly, the Italian therapists appeared to be less sure of how to approach these cases, which they perceived as having far greater complexity than those of first-union families. Because the Italian therapists had very little training on the treatment of stepfamilies, they tended to retreat to traditional tenets of whatever model of treatment they had been trained in, rather than find specific interventions and theoretical approaches unique to stepfamilies. The Italian therapists recognized that stepfamilies are unique but found their treatment of these families to be disorienting because they had no map to survey the landscape of stepfamily life. American therapists, on the other hand, who saw more stepfamilies in their practice and had attended a greater number of continuing education programs that highlight this population, had a clearer idea of special interventions to be used. Again, American therapists were just as likely as their Italian counterparts to view stepfamilies as complex, confusing, and having ambiguous boundaries, but they were more likely to have specific interventions that they relied on to assist them with the issues presented.

GAY AND LESBIAN STEPFAMILY FORMATION

Gay and lesbian stepfamilies can be formed when a biological parent or a parent who has either adopted or used donor insemination brings a child into a newly formed partnership. Most common are the stepfamilies formed when a biological mother or father with children from a heterosexual union enters into a relationship with a lesbian or gay man. Most of the gay father households are less inclined to have children living with them and are therefore nonresidential households (Ganong & Coleman, 1994), whereas lesbian mother households are likely to be residential.

In most cases, there are no rituals marking the beginning or formalization of a relationship and no "symbolic gestures" (Lynch, 2000, p. 93). Often, prospective partners simply move in together or maintain separate residences but either way form a relationship. If one or both partners are leaving a marriage, they have to gauge when to tell spouses, when to come out, when to move in together, and when to explain what others consider to be the "choices" they have made. With the lack of any normative guidelines to direct one through these issues (Cherlin & Furstenberg, 1994), there may be a tendency for individuals to feel "a denial of identity and an isolation and invisibility" (Lynch, 2000, p. 93). For each partner, determining how to go from heterosexual and married or cohabiting to lesbian and cohabiting or from unattached and lesbian to stepparenthood is unimaginable.

Just as in heterosexual stepfamily formation, there is an inclination to hold false expectations and myths about the imminent change (Visher & Visher, 1979); the logistics of the new arrangement pale in comparison with the profound disillusionment that will take place. So although they share similar features of stepfamily structure with heterosexuals, "They share gender composition with other lesbian and gay families, and the juncture of structure and gender composition produces a distinct family form" (Lynch, 2000, p. 82).

Implications for Treatment

When working with gay and lesbian stepfamilies, it is of critical importance to be aware of one's attitudes concerning homosexuality and to monitor one's countertransference for any indication of homophobic viewpoints. "Gay and lesbian clients whose therapist is straight will have their antennae out for signs of homophobia and heterosexism" (Bernstein, 2000, p. 449). Being honest about deficiencies in knowledge and at the same time sensitive to cultural differences are qualities that add to the therapist's proficiency (Nealy, 2008). The most vital attribute, according to Green (2008), is the "therapist's own comfort with love and sexuality between two women and two men" (p. 308).

In the sections that follow, we address four topics of importance: the coming out process, relationship issues, parenting, and dissolution and legal issues.

Coming Out

In both gay and lesbian stepfamilies, the biological parent has had to contend with going from the socially approved role and respected status of heterosexual father or mother to a less esteemed homosexual parent identity (Lewin, 1993; Lynch, 2005; C. A. Thompson, 1992), which has also been termed "the loss of heterosexual privilege" (Lynch, 2005, p. 49). For example, the biological mother who leaves a heterosexual relationship and enters into a lesbian relationship may be facing coming out, with all the ramifications and responses from friends, family, and community; this is accompanied by the myriad and considerable changes she is making in her life and the lives of others. Lynch (2000) quoted a parent who described this period:

> There are so many levels on which we're trying to reinvent the wheel . . . we've got all the stepfamily issues overlaid with all the coming out issues, overlaid with all the parent and child, gay and lesbian issues, overlaid with all the divorce issues. (p. 91)

At the same time they are also having to contend with "accepting one's homosexuality," termed *internalized homophobia* (Green, 2000, p. 301) and external disclosure. The expectation of heterosexuality is nowhere more compelling than in the parent–child relationship (Patterson, 1995).

The stepparent, on the other hand, probably has addressed and is already comfortable with her lesbian identity. Instead, her challenge will be to adjust to the ambiguous and often misunderstood role of the stepparent and the entrance into her life of stepchildren, who will be in most cases residential. The two viewpoints expressed in the paragraphs that follow are not similar.

From the biological mother:

> My husband agreed to the divorce and said "Just don't tell the children the reason." When I was finally allowed to tell them, they said, "We knew." My son Jonathan hugged me; Emily had more of a problem. She was upset about the divorce. My husband was upset about the coming out. Everything was so difficult; I mean you are exhilarated because you have found your love, but guilty and depressed because of the divorce and tearing the family apart.

From the stepmother:

> I wish I had had more time. On top of that, the realization came to me— she has been married for 12 years and—oh my gosh—she has kids! I was not ready for that piece of it, and it was hard to negotiate those relationships from the beginning.

The gay couple may have the same types of struggles; however, as mentioned previously, the significant difference is that the biological father's children are predominantly noncustodial because the courts usually favor the biological mother in custody cases (Erera, 2002), maybe even more so when the case involves a homosexual father. Because gay men are primarily seeking only visitation, rather than custody, there is often less bias in the courts (Erera, 2002).

The Relationship

Same-sex love defies one of the most fundamental normative gender rules of our society (Green, 2008). Beginning very early in their lives, gay men and lesbians hear messages about the impropriety, immorality, and aberrant nature of same-sex relationships. These values are internalized and form a value system that is dissonant with one's natural inclinations. The therapist has to be aware of this and facilitate the deconstructing of all the various ideas and communications, overt or covert, that they have received in their lives (Green, 2008, p. 301). If one member of the couple dyad is hesitant to explore these feelings in front of the other, then a referral for individual counseling should be given; continuing this process together may lead to discord between the couple (Green, 2008). A support group has also been found to be helpful. Left unaddressed entirely, these disparities could affect the well-being of the relationship.

Yet, most of the literature that addresses the relationships of lesbian or gay couples discusses the more egalitarian division of household tasks, the shared decision making, the congenial and stable lifestyle, and the extensive and loyal support system of gay and lesbian friends, often called a *family of choice* (Green & Mitchell, 2008; Cherlin, 2004; Weeks, Heaphy, & Donovan, 2001), and in many cases, biological family members. Frequently, the family of origin is less of a steadfast and dependable source of support than the gay community (Crosbie-Burnett & Helmbrecht, 1993; Demo & Allen, 1996; Green, Bettinger, & Zacks, 1996). With the entrance of a child or children into the household, the stepparent suddenly realizes that the biological parent has other, perhaps more important, priorities. For the most part, stepparents are in agreement that the children are priorities for their partner; some would not want a partner who would be any other way (Lynch, 2005). Although, according to Bozett (1987), many gay men without children do not comprehend the attachment that a gay father feels for his children and family (Crosbie-Brunett & Helmbrecht, 1993). To add to this, gay fathers may feel more comfortable with heterosexual friends who have children and with whom they spend more time and have more things in common (i.e., children's activities and events) than with gay friends who are not parents. For both lesbian and heterosexual mothers, the "centrality of motherhood" not only formulates a woman's identity but also her circle of friends (Lewin, 1993, p. 141).

In a heterosexual stepfamily, the biological parent often complains of being caught in the middle between his or her biological children and the new partner; the stepparent does not know what is expected regarding his or her role. In a gay or lesbian stepfamily, similar feelings have been reported (Lynch, 2000). The therapist must intervene to help the couple clarify expectations, ease role ambiguity and anxiety, and realistically accept the givens: the parent–child bond, the loyalty to the ex-spouse or partner, and the loss of the previous family arrangement.

To achieve a comfort level and openness about one's gender identity is always a goal. Balsam, Beauchaine, Rothblum, and Solomon (2008) found that the more out and open a couple is about their relationship, the better its quality. Psychological well-being in the biological mother is associated with openness about her lesbian identity with children, ex-husbands, and employers (Rand, Graham, & Rawlings, 1982).

Parenting

Because the predominant homosexual stepfamily form is the lesbian stepfamily formed with children from a heterosexual union, many studies and journal articles have been published on the various aspects of this experience. Researchers have devoted relatively little time to studying the role of fathers in general, so the prospect of gay fathers commanding attention is small (Flowers, Barret, & Robinson, 2000). The authors go on to quote Margaret Mead, "Fathers are a biological necessity but a social accident" (Flowers et al., 2000, p. 158).

In new heterosexual stepfamilies, it is generally indicated that the stepparent step back and allow the biological parent to have the majority of the responsibility of the child or children, which includes parenting, discipline, and scheduling. Suzanne Johnson and Elizabeth O'Connor (2001) used various measures in The National Gay and Lesbian Family Study to examine variables involving relationship quality, parent practices, and abilities. Four family types were studied—primary gay and lesbian families and gay and lesbian stepfamilies. In gay stepfamilies, according to their findings, only a small percentage (9%) felt there was equity in child care, whereas half of all sampled in the three other family types reported that there was equity in child care. Gay stepparents therefore were less likely to be equally involved in child care. They also reported that gay stepfamilies, of all the four family types investigated, were the least open with children's doctors, teachers, and friends' parents. Gay stepfamilies scored high on a scale measuring parental alliance, but Johnson and O'Connor suggested that this may be a function of the lower level of involvement by the stepparent, which leads to less of an arena for discord. In lesbian relationships in which there is a natural inclination in each partner to be caring and nurturing, there is great stepparent role ambiguity and anxiety over this natural inclination. This heightened involvement leads to a lower score on parental alliance, more disagreements between partners, and less positive feelings about each other. All four family groups scored as well or better than heterosexual families on relationship adjustment measures and interaction about their children. All the groups reported very limited use of spanking or hitting (15%), lower than the general heterosexual population (Johnson & O'Connor, 2001).

In one study, when compared with heterosexual mothers, lesbian mothers were found to be more child-centered (Miller, Jacobsen & Bigner, 1981). On the other hand, sometimes lesbian stepparents find themselves deliberately restraining their tendency to be warm and affectionate because of role confusion and acceptance of the biological parent as the expert on parenting

(Levin, 1993), leading to a tendency for the biological parent to be more involved with the children (Patterson, 1995). Lesbian stepparents have been found to be most helpful to the children in processing their place in the world and disclosure; accommodating their new living arrangements into their lives, which include their friends and others; and finally, encouraging the stepchildren to adopt "stigma management strategies" with which they are at ease (Lynch, 2005, p. 57). A stepmom who was sympathetic and empathetic could be most helpful with the child's or children's adjustment to these issues.

Dissolution

Gay and lesbian marriage and civil unions are legal in a number of states. Yet in the majority of states, there is no ritualistic, defined beginning to gay and lesbian relationships that is similar to heterosexual cohabiting partnerships. There are also no parameters for the dissolution of relationships. When the relationship includes children, dissolution becomes far more painful for all involved. Because there is no body of laws covering custody, visitation, or support and no protection for a nonbiological stepparent, he or she finds that there is no recourse in the courts to fight for the right to continue a relationship with a child who is neither biologically related nor legally adopted. Because there is no divorce in a same-sex relationship (in most cases) and no attendant legal maneuverings, there is no clarity, no authenticity, and no community verification. This may lead to stress, confusion, and an incredible sense of "ambiguous loss" without resolution (Boss, 1999). If the stepfamily is unable to resolve their differences, then the therapist needs to help them prepare for the unstructured and nonnormative dissolution process to minimize pain and stress for everyone.

Diversity is modifying the appearance of the typical family configuration. Not only are there conventional heterosexual families with parents in normative, explicit gender roles and behaviors but also gay and lesbian stepfamilies—"diverse family forms with increasingly fluid and negotiated relationships" (Williams, 2004, p. 18). A therapist who works with acceptance, flexibility, and creativity, the very strengths of gay and lesbian stepfamilies (Lynch, 2000), has a good foundation to join with the clients. By acknowledging their own informational limitations and empathizing with the clients about the negative societal forces impinging on gay and lesbian stepfamilies, therapists show genuine respect for their client population.

Case Study

In this case study, we present a lesbian stepfamily because the most common gay and lesbian stepfamily is formed when a woman brings children from a previously heterosexual relationship into a new relationship with another lesbian. Therapeutic issues are similar to those of stepfamilies in general, with the aforementioned sexual orientation complications. For this case study, we return to the 10 steps of the SfT model in an abridged format.

Intake Information

> **Biological mom:** Kim
> **Stepmother:** Sarah
> **Biological father:** Vincent
> **Children:** Johnny (18) and Melissa (12)
> **Jobs:** Kim is an events manager. Sarah is a restaurant server. Vincent is a lawyer.

Kim makes the call to the therapist. She and Sarah have been together for 1½ years. Kim was previously married to Vincent, with whom she enjoyed an easygoing, collegial relationship; the couple was able to balance parenting, jobs, and individual interests. Kim reported being happy with Vincent, although she felt that something was not right. Vincent, as her loving husband and friend, recognized Kim's discontent as well and talked about it with her, although it was too vague for either to identify. When Kim met Sarah, she experienced strong feelings of attraction and had an "aha" moment. She recognized the possibility that this was what she had been missing. She disclosed her revelation to Vincent; the two women moved in together 6 months later.

Kim says that lately her daughter has been giving Sarah such a hard time that she is having trouble watching it. Any consequences Kim wants to mete out to Melissa are interrupted by, "of all people, – Sarah!" Then they find themselves arguing. Sarah feels that Kim should just let Melissa's animosity run its course rather than continue to confront it. Kim feels that she is the mom and is responsible for the children's upbringing and insists that Melissa be respectful of Sarah. Melissa will not discuss any of this with Kim and just becomes sullen and withdrawn when approached. She also refuses to go to counseling. Kim is afraid this will undermine her relationship with Sarah, who has expressed a lot of guilt for causing Kim's marriage to break up. Johnny appears to be adjusting well in the family but spends a lot of time out of the house.

The extended family has mixed feelings. Sarah's parents are further along in terms of accepting her sexual orientation because she came out at an earlier age; however, her brother-in-law Chuck is disgusted with and embarrassed by what he considers to be Sarah's "choices." Kim's parents are confused but supportive of Melissa and feel that she has a "right" to be angry. Vincent's parents are very angry with Kim for many reasons: breaking up the marriage, leaving Vincent and the children, "becoming" a lesbian, and entering into a relationship with another woman.

The therapist makes a genogram (see Figure 8.3) of the family and invites Sarah and Kim in for the first session.

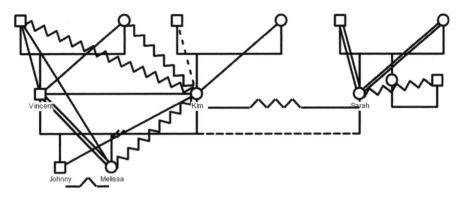

Figure 8.3. The Elliott family.

APPLYING THE 10 STEPS OF STEPFAMILY THERAPY

In the sections that follow, the therapist applies each of the 10 steps of the SfT model to the Elliott family.

Step 1

Recognize the structure of the stepfamily (e.g., simple stepfather family, simple stepmother family, complex stepfamily in which both adults are stepparents). Use the initial telephone intake to look for systemic similarities within the context of the extant research literature.

The structure is a simple stepmother family in which one partner brings children to the relationship. The difference obviously is that the biological parent in this case is a woman. In the intake interview, the therapist should listen carefully to the presenting problem to consider whether the issues are stepfamily related or gay and lesbian issues. He or she surmises that the various stepfamily issues are parenting issues, which include Sarah's disagreement with Kim over Melissa's disrespect, an estranged and troubled biological subsystem, Sarah's role confusion, and poor adjustment to the stepparent on the part of a preadolescent girl.

Step 2

Determine the membership of the first session—usually the marital dyad—and further delineate the unique concerns of the stepfamily.

Kim and Sarah will be invited to the first session. The obvious rationale for this is the necessity to shore up the couple subsystem and protect it from the barrage of possible issues emanating from not only the stepfamily configuration but also the same-sex relationship. Problem areas regarding the stepfamily that need further scrutiny are the residual guilt of both Kim and Sarah for the dissolution of the marriage, Sarah's role confusion, and parenting strategies.

Step 3

Clarify the distinct subsystems in the stepfamily, and use this to provide a direction for clinical treatment.

The identified and distinct subsystems in the family are as follows:

1. The partner dyad: Kim and Sarah. The stepfamily issues have been teased out of the array of confusion and anxiety that Kim and Sarah feel and can be addressed by using the Sf T model. It appears that the basic relationship is sound. The problematic interaction between Sarah and Melissa appears to be the sole stressor, although Sarah may be experiencing role confusion within the family, a typical stepmother struggle. The therapist may refer the couple for either individual or couples counseling for issues having to do with coming out. For Kim this process has just occurred, whereas Sarah has been out since college days. Both may be feeling internal dissonance and guilt related to being lesbian and raising children. There is most likely disquiet and worry over the children and their respective peer groups and their parents. Extended family may be complicating the partners' adjustment with negativity and judgment.

2. The biological subsystem: Kim, Johnny, and Melissa. This subsystem is in distress, and there is alienation between Kim and Melissa, which is an oft encountered problem in stepfamilies. Again, the therapist has to differentiate between the two central factors. Melissa is obviously troubled by the breakup of the marriage, her mother finding a new partner immediately, and her mother's new status as a lesbian. She is saddened and angry. Even though she holds less resentment for Sarah, she attributes some of the "fault" to her and becomes even more incensed when Sarah is nice to her. Johnny is on his way to college and removes himself both emotionally and physically from the family by hanging out with his friends most of the time. He says he is "cool with Mom's situation" and to show this has joined the gay and straight alliance at his school.

3. The sibling subsystem: Johnny and Melissa. Johnny and Melissa are not having any problems between them as defined from the

intake or the first couple session. Johnny is protective of Melissa and is disturbed by her troubles. However, attempts to alleviate some of her anxiety by listening and reassuring her conclude in disagreement and added tension. She does not feel that Johnny is supportive of her.

4. The parental coalition: Kim, Sarah, and Vincent. This subsystem meets to generate a unified parental stance for the sake of the children. Is Vincent able to watch his wife leave the marriage, disrupt his life and the lives of the children, and move into a lesbian relationship, all without lingering bitterness and passive-aggressive anger? These feelings and possible homophobic attitudes on the part of Vincent, whether expressed or restrained, could confound resolution and the process of moving on. Acrimony between spouses is the most injurious impediment to the adjustment of children.

5. The paternal biological subsystem: Vincent, Johnny, and Melissa. This subsystem may be in distress because of Johnny and Melissa feeling despondent for their father and anxious that he may feel lonely or depressed. These benign feelings may be fueling the anger at their mother. Just as in a heterosexual stepfamily, the goal in meeting with this subsystem is for Vincent to assuage the children's concern for his well-being. Reassuring them that he is accepting of their mother's choices, feels fine, and intends to resume his life is of overriding importance.

6. The stepsubsystem: Sarah, Johnny, and Melissa. This subsystem is troubled by Melissa's bitterness toward Sarah for the demise of her parents' marriage. Blaming Sarah is a simplistic yet natural sentiment because of a child's need to keep his or her parents in a positive regard. Sarah is not clear in her role toward Melissa. Should she try to be a friend and/or a confidante to Melissa, or should she give her distance and time? Can she openly display affection for Kim? How should she introduce herself to Melissa's friends and others in the school and in the community? If this subsystem is ready to meet, then the desired outcomes should be for everyone to understand that the present situation contains stress and challenges that affect everyone and to devillainize the stepmother.

7. The extended family: three sets of grandparents and Sarah's sister and brother-in-law. The therapist needs to determine which extended family system is bringing the most stress and oppositional behavior to the stepfamily unit and invite them in for a session first. Revealing feelings and quelling negativity can

transform a subsystem's impact into a source of support. The grandparent subsystems have their own idiosyncratic issues, yet they also share the commonality of being closely related to the central subsystem. There are myriad possibilities and an opportunity to be creative in setting priorities to bring maximum relief to the stepfamily subsystem.

Step 4

Consider the research findings that normalize the experience of the stepfamily, and introduce them in clinical practice (when appropriate and meaningful).

The research on gay and lesbian stepfamilies is growing. However, having a therapist separate the stepfamily dynamics per se from gender-related issues is helpful, as is processing the interplay of these two criteria. The normalization of these issues in stepfamily literature and what is known about lesbian dynamics will serve to increase the clarity of the stepfamily's internal experience and ameliorate self-doubt and guilt in the individual family members. For example, according to stepfamily research, Melissa's anger at Sarah can be expected because it illustrates the difficulties that preadolescent girls have in adjusting to a new stepfamily (Brand, Clingempeel, & Bowen-Woodward, 1988). The idea that parents are divorcing after enjoying a benign relationship is more confusing for the children than a divorce coming from extreme marital conflict (Amato & Booth, 1997). Loyalty issues common in stepfamilies, manifested by worry about a father's welfare or strict adherence to old rituals, for example, compound Melissa's response to Sarah. There is then an overlay of attitudes toward homosexuality. The therapist should also become conversant with the literature that is available on the gay and lesbian family and stepfamily to best serve the client family.

Step 5

Actively assess and assist in the recognition of empathy when present, and increase the empathic experience between stepfamily members and subsystems.

As previously stated, the couple is the foundation on which the stepfamily is built. The therapist will invite the couple in for an additional session before attending to the other subsystems simply to ensure that the members communicate to an optimum level with the use of empathy. With the multiple factors intruding into their lives, it is essential that empathic understanding between the couple be identified and affirmed to strengthen this subsystem. Eventually, by extending the use of empathy throughout the subsystems, stepfamily members will recognize the pressures that are brought to bear on each of them from extended family, peers, and other social forces in the community.

Step 6

> Identify and challenge unhelpful beliefs and specific miscommunication circulating in the stepfamily—the role of labels.

From the telephone intake and initial therapy sessions, the clinician has identified two unhelpful beliefs that need attention. The miscommunication between Kim and Sarah is a function of Kim's proprietary attitude toward her daughter, Melissa, and what she sees as Sarah's excessive tolerance of Melissa's behavior. The overt feeling of the need to give respect to everyone in the household has been voiced by Kim and can be seen as a universal goal in all family structures and as treatment to which everyone is entitled. However, Kim may be overlooking the more nuanced aspects of Sarah's emotions. That is, Sarah may not only be troubled by causing strife between Kim and Melissa on the obvious grounds of seemingly causing the demise of the marriage but also by covert feelings of which she may not even be aware. Sarah's tolerance of Melissa's behavior might be due to her feelings of guilt over and empathy for the awkward position in which Melissa finds herself. Sarah may wonder if Melissa's behavior is a reaction to the presence of someone in the stepmother position or to the same-sex feature of the relationship. To speculate further, is this then an unhelpful belief and projection on the part of Sarah? Melissa could simply be angry at her mother and/or the situation, and this anger expands to include other members of the stepfamily. She may even be discontented with Johnny for spending time out of the house with his friends and not standing with or supporting her while she struggles in distress. These elements need to be investigated and clarified.

Step 7

> Support the naturally connected subsystem (parent and child), and confirm that parent and child are capable of expressing mutual concern.

Bringing the biological subsystem in for a session is necessary in all stepfamily work. The fragmentation of this subsystem can be seen as having ample potential to derail the new stepfamily. Melissa and Johnny need to understand the full scope of Kim's decision to leave the marriage. Processing Kim's personal choices and separating them from the relationship between Kim and her children and that of Kim and Vincent is essential, as is reassuring the children of her love and steadfastness.

The therapist would then meet with Vincent, Melissa, and Johnny. It would be important for Vincent to make clear that his presence in their lives is assured and his love is enduring. Because he and Kim enjoyed a positive and close relationship in the past, there is no reason to assume that this will not continue or that he is going to absent himself from their lives. Vincent can also voice his previous conversations with and concern for Kim about her bewilderment and ineffable discontent during their marriage and how discovering the source of her restlessness is gratifying for him. Above all, he wants Kim and the children to be happy and to assure them that he will always be there to support and help in any way. He can confirm that he holds no bitterness toward Sarah. This may sound unrealistic and improbable to attain, but it would be the goal in any stepfamily, gay, lesbian, or straight, to ensure optimum conditions for the stepfamily and other important extended family members to move forward. Loyalty issues on the part of the children could be a serious roadblock toward stepfamily formation and development in the future. To promote this scenario, the therapist may want to meet with Vincent, either alone or with Kim, prior to this session to ensure that Vincent feels amenable to such a goal.

Step 8

Teach the stepfamily about its own systemic functioning.

In Step 6, the clinician concentrated on unhelpful beliefs; however, these ideas, once elucidated and processed by the couple and eventually the rest of the subsystems, can be used to demonstrate the family's systemic functioning. Kim gets upset with Sarah, which generates tension between the couple and internal unease in Sarah, which in turn causes Sarah to withdraw from Melissa. Melissa may see Sarah's behavior as rejection, which may exacerbate a view that Mom has connected with not only another woman but also a cold, dismissive one as well. These speculative ramifications need to be processed for greater understanding about the process in the stepfamily.

Step 9

Assist in coparental work between any and all involved parental figures, including the binuclear family.

Kim, Sarah, and Vincent, the parenting coalition, would be invited in for a session, just as in a heterosexual stepfamily, for the purpose of establishing and solidifying a more unified set of household rules and parenting strategies across the coalition. Now would also be the appropriate time to bring to the surface any residual bitterness, unspoken feelings, and considerations for harmony and well-being in the future. For example, how is the stepfamily going to present itself in the community, in the school, or at church? How and when will disclosure occur? Who is Sarah—Kim's partner, friend, or roommate? Melissa's aunt? The parenting coalition could process these concerns as a preliminary discourse to a conversation that could eventually include the kids. Decisions do not have to be made; however, research finds that adolescents have better adjustment when mothers are honest about their sexual orientation (Rand, Graham & Rawling, 1982). Vincent would most certainly want for the stepfamily the smoothest assimilation into the community setting.

Step 10

> Increase communication among all stepfamily members available, and move toward integrating the various subsystems into a functioning and satisfied stepfamily.

The extended family, that is, grandparents and Sarah's sister and brother-in-law, is invited in after the stepfamily subsystems have been strengthened and there is improved communication throughout the parental coalition and sibling subsystem. Because each set of grandparents is in a different mind-set regarding the new stepfamily, it is probable that the therapist cannot meet with the entire extended family subsystem at once. However, being mindful of the goals of Step 10, the therapist knows that the supports already in place (Sarah's parents) need reinforcement, and the various impediments to integration of all the subsystems need to be addressed.

REFERENCES

Ackerman, N. W. (1966). *Treating the troubled family*. New York, NY: Basic Books.

Adler-Bader, F., & Schramm, D. (2006, May). *Examining and building the empirical knowledge of African-American and Hispanic/Latino stepfamilies*. Symposium conducted at the meeting of the National Council on Family Relations, Minneapolis, MN.

Ahrons, C. (1979). The bi-nuclear family: Two households, one family. *Alternative Lifestyles, 2*, 499–515. doi:10.1007/BF01082682

Ahrons, C. (1981). The continuing coparental relationship between divorced spouses. *American Journal of Orthopsychiatry, 51*, 415–428. doi:10.1111/j.1939-0025.1981.tb01390.x

Ahrons, C. (1994). *The good divorce*. New York, NY: HarperCollins.

Ahrons, C. (2004). *We're still family: What grown children have to say about their parents' divorce*. New York, NY: HarperCollins.

Ahrons, C. R., & Wallisch, K. (1987). Parenting in the binuclear family: Relationships between biological and stepparents. In K. Pasley & M. Ihinger-Tallman (Eds.), *Remarriage and stepparenting: Current research and theory* (pp. 225–256). New York, NY: Guilford Press.

Ainsworth, M. S. (1967). *Infancy in Uganda: Infant care and the growth of love*. Baltimore, MD: Johns Hopkins University Press.

Amato, P. R., & Booth, A. (1997). *A generation at risk*. Cambridge, MA: Harvard University Press.

Amato, P. R., & Keith, B. (1991). Parental divorce and adult well-being: A meta-analysis. *Journal of Marriage and the Family, 53*, 43–58. doi:10.2307/353132

Ambert, A. (1986). Being a stepparent: Live-in and visiting stepchildren. *Journal of Marriage and the Family, 48*, 795–804. doi:10.2307/352572

American Psychiatric Association. (1968). *Diagnostic and statistical manual of mental disorders* (2nd ed.). Washington, DC: Author.

American Psychiatric Association. (1980). *Diagnostic and statistical manual of mental disorders* (3rd ed.). Washington, DC: Author.

American Psychiatric Association. (2000). *Diagnostic and statistical manual of mental disorders* (4th ed., text rev.). Washington, DC: Author.

American Psychological Association. (2010). *Ethical principles of psychologists and code of conduct (2002, Amended June 1, 2010)*. Retrieved from http://www.apa.org/ethics/ code/index.aspx

American Psychological Association. (2005). *Policy statement of evidence-based practice in psychology*. Retrieved from http://www.apa.org/practice/resources/evidence/evidence-based-statement.pdf

Anderson, H., Goolishian, H. A., & Windermand, L. (1986). Problem determined systems: Towards transformation in family therapy. *Journal of Strategic & Systemic Therapies, 5*(4), 1–13.

Arditti, J. A. (1999). Rethinking relationships between divorced mothers and their children: Capitalizing on family strengths. *Family Relations, 48,* 109–119. doi:10.2307/585074

Axinn, W., & Thornton, A. (1992). The relationship between cohabitation and divorce: Selectivity or causal influence? *Demography, 29,* 357–374. doi:10.2307/2061823

Bailey, R. K., & Owens, D. L. (2005). Overcoming challenges in the diagnosis and treatment of attention-deficit/hyperactivity disorder in African-Americans. *Journal of the National Medical Association, 97*(Suppl. 10), 5S–10S.

Balsam, K., Beauchaine, T., Rothblum, E., & Solomon, S. (2008). Three year follow-up of same-sex couples who had civil unions in Vermont, same-sex couples not in civil unions, and heterosexual married siblings. *Developmental Psychology, 44,* 102–116. doi:10.1037/0012-1649.44.1.102

Banker, B. S., & Gaertner, S. L. (1998). Achieving stepfamily harmony: An intergroup-relations approach. *Journal of Family Psychology, 12,* 310–325. doi:10.1037/0893-3200.12.3.310

Bateson, G. (1951). Information and codification: A philosophical approach. In J. Ruesch & G. Bateson (Eds.), *Communication: The social matrix of psychiatry* (pp. 168–211). New York, NY: Norton.

Bateson, G., Jackson, D. D., Haley, J., & Weakland, J. (1956). Toward a theory of schizophrenia. *Behavioral Science, 1,* 251–264. doi:10.1002/bs.3830010402

Baumrind, D. (1996). The discipline controversy revisited. *Family Relations, 45,* 405–414. doi:10.2307/585170

Baumrind, D. (2005). Patterns of parental authority and adolescent autonomy. *New Directions for Child and Adolescent Development, 108,* 61–69. doi:10.1002/cd.128

Bell, J. E. (1975). *Family therapy.* New York, NY: Jason Aronson.

Bernard, J. (1956). *Remarriage: A study of marriage.* New York, NY: Russel & Russel.

Bernstein, A. C. (1989). *Yours, mine, and ours: How families change when remarried parents have a child together.* New York, NY: Norton.

Bernstein, A. C. (2000). Straight therapists working with lesbians and gays in family therapy. *Journal of Marital and Family Therapy, 26,* 443–454. doi:10.1111/j.1752-0606.2000.tb00315.x

Booth, A., & Edwards, J. N. (1992). Starting over: Why remarriages are more unstable. *Journal of Family Issues, 13,* 179–194. doi:10.1177/019251392013002004

Booth, A., & Johnson, D. (1988). Premarital cohabitation and marital success. *Journal of Family Issues, 9,* 255–272. doi:10.1177/019251388009002007

Boss, P. (1999). *Ambiguous loss: Learning to live with unresolved grief.* Cambridge, MA: Harvard University Press.

Bouchard, G. (2006). Cohabitation versus marriage. *Journal of Divorce & Remarriage*, *46*, 107–117. doi:10.1300/J087v46n01_06

Bowen, M. (1978). *Family therapy in practice*. New York, NY: Aronson.

Bowerman, C., & Irish, D. (1962). Some relationships of stepchildren to their parents. *Marriage and Family Living*, *24*, 113–121. doi:10.2307/346999

Bozett, F. W. (1987). Gay fathers. In F. Bozett (Ed.), *Gay and lesbian parents* (pp. 3–22). New York, NY: Praeger.

Bramlett, M. D., & Mosher, W. D. (2002). Cohabitation, marriage, divorce, and remarriage in the United States. *Monograph of the National Center for Health Statistics: Vital Health Statistics*, *23*(22).

Brand, E., Clingempeel, W. G., & Bowen-Woodward, K. (1988). Family relationships and children's psychological adjustment in stepmother and stepfather families. In E. M. Hetherington & J. Arasteh (Eds.), *Impact of divorce, single parenting and stepparenting on children* (pp. 299–324). Hillsdale, NJ: Erlbaum.

Bray, J. H. (1988). Children's development thorough early marriage. In E. M. Hetherington & J. Arasteh (Eds.), *Impact of divorce, single parenting and stepparenting on children* (pp. 279–298). Hillsdale, NJ: Erlbaum.

Bray, J. H. (2001). Therapy with stepfamilies: A developmental systems approach. In D. D. Lusterman, S. H. McDaniel, & C. Philpot (Eds.), *Integrating family therapy: A casebook* (pp. 127–140). Washington, DC: American Psychological Association. doi:10.1037/10395-010

Bray, J. H., & Berger, S. H. (1993). Developmental issues in Stepfamilies Research Project: Family relationships and parent–child interactions. *Journal of Family Psychology*, *7*, 76–90. doi:10.1037/0893-3200.7.1.76

Bray, J. H., & Hetherington, E. M. (1993). Families in transition: Introduction and overview. *Journal of Family Issues*, *7*, 3–8.

Bray, J. H., & Kelly, J. (1998). *Stepfamilies: Love, marriage, and parenting in the first decade*. New York, NY: Broadway Books.

Broman, C. L. (2005). Marital quality in White and Black marriages. *Journal of Family Issues*, *26*, 431–441. doi:10.1177/0192513X04272439

Brown, A. C., Green, R.-J., & Druckman, J. (1990). A comparison of stepfamilies with and without child-focused problems. *American Journal of Orthopsychiatry*, *60*, 556–566. doi:10.1037/h0079208

Brown, S. L. (2000). Union transitions among cohabitors: Significance of relationship assessments and expectations. *Journal of Marriage and the Family*, *62*, 833–846. doi:10.1111/j.1741-3737.2000.00833.x

Brown, S. L., & Booth, A. (1996). Cohabitation versus marriage: A comparison of relationship quality. *Journal of Marriage and the Family*, *58*, 668–678. doi:10.2307/353727

Browning, S. W. (1987) Preference prediction, empathy, and personal similarity as variables of family satisfaction in intact and stepfather families. *Dissertation Abstracts International: Section B. Sciences and Engineering*, *47*(11), 4642–4643.

Browning, S. W. (1994). Treating stepfamilies: Putting family therapy into perspective. In K. Pasley & M. Ihinger-Tallman (Eds.), *Remarriage and stepparenting: Current research and theory* (pp. 94–104). New York, NY: Guilford Press.

Browning, S. W., Accordini, M., Gennari, M., & Cigoli, V. (2010). How therapists view stepfamilies: An analysis of Italian clinicians' representations. In V. Cigoli & E. Gennari (Eds.), *Close relationships in community psychology: An international perspective* (pp. 15–33). Milano, Italy: FrancoAngeli.

Browning, S. W., & Bray, J. H. (2009). Treating stepfamilies: A subsystems-based approach. In M. Stanton & J. H. Bray (Eds.), *The Wiley-Blackwell handbook of family psychology* (pp. 487–498). West Sussex, England: Blackwell.

Browning, S. W., Collins, J., & Nelson, B. (2004). Creating families: A teaching technique for clinical training. In D. L. Berke & S. K. Wisendale (Eds.), *The craft of teaching about families: Strategies and tools* (pp. 185–204). New York, NY: Haworth Press.

Buchanan, C. M., Macoby, E. E., & Dornbusch, S. M. (1991). Caught between parents: Adolescent's experience in divorced homes. *Child Development, 62,* 1008–1029.

Bumpass, L., & Lu, H. (2000). Trends in cohabitation and implications for children's family contexts in the United States. *Population Studies, 54*(1), 29–41.

Bumpass, L. L., Raley, R. K., & Sweet, J. A. (1995). The changing characters of stepfamilies: Implications of cohabitation and nonmarital childbearing. *Demography, 32,* 425–436. doi:10.2307/2061689

Bumpass, L. L., Sweet, J. A., & Castro Martin, T. (1990). Changing patterns of remarriage. *Journal of Marriage and the Family, 52,* 747–756. doi:10.2307/352939

Bumpass, L. L., Sweet, J. A., & Cherlin, A. (1991). The role of cohabitation in the declining rates of marriage. *Journal of Marriage and the Family, 53,* 913–927. doi:10.2307/352997

Carlson, M. J., & Furstenberg, F. F., Jr. (2006). The prevalence and correlates of multi-partnered fertility among U.S. parents. *Journal of Marriage and the Family, 68,* 718–732. doi:10.1111/j.1741-3737.2006.00285.x

Carter, E. A., & McGoldrick, M. (1988). *The changing family life cycle: A framework for family therapy* (2nd ed.). Boston, MA: Allyn & Bacon.

Chang, D. F., & Berk, A. (2009). Making cross-racial therapy work: A phenomenological study of clients' experiences of cross-racial therapy. *Journal of Counseling Psychology, 56,* 521–536. doi:10.1037/a0016905

Chao, R. K. (2001). Extending research on the consequence of parenting style for Chinese-Americans and European Americans. *Child Development, 72,* 1832–1843. doi:10.1111/1467-8624.00381

Cherlin, A. (1978). Remarriage as an incomplete institution. *American Journal of Sociology, 84,* 634–650. doi:10.1086/226830

Cherlin, A. (2004). The deinstitutionalization of American marriage. *Journal of Marriage and the Family, 66,* 848–861. doi:10.1111/j.0022-2445.2004.00058.x

Cherlin, A. (2009). The origins of ambivalent acceptance of divorce. *Journal of Marriage and the Family, 71*, 226–229. doi:10.1111/j.1741-3737.2009.00593.x

Cherlin, A., & Furstenberg, F. F., Jr. (1986). *American grandparenthood.* New York, NY: Basic Books.

Cherlin, A., & Furstenberg, F. F., Jr. (1994). Stepfamilies in the United States: A reconsideration. *Annual Review of Sociology, 20*, 259–281.

Cigoli, V., & Scabini, E. (2006). *Family identity: Ties, symbols, and transitions.* Mahwah, NJ: Erlbaum.

Clingempeel, W. G., Brand, E., & Ievoli, R. (1984). Stepparent-stepchild relationships in stepmother and stepfather families: A multimethod study. *Family Relations, 34*, 465–473. doi:10.2307/1130602

Cohan, C. L., and Kleinbaum, S. (2002). Toward a greater understanding of the cohabitation effect: Premarital cohabitation and marital communication. *Journal of Marriage and Family, 64*(1), 180–192.

Coleman, M., & Ganong, L. H. (1997). Stepfamilies from the stepfamily's perspective. *Marriage & Family Review, 26*, 107–121. doi:10.1300/J002v26n01_07

Coleman, M., Ganong, L. H., & Fine, M. (2000). Reinvestigating remarriage: Another decade of progress. *Journal of Marriage and the Family, 62*, 1288–1307. doi:10.1111/j.1741-3737.2000.01288.x

Coleman, M., Ganong, L. H., & Rothrauff, T. C. (2006). Racial and ethnic similarities and differences in beliefs about intergenerational assistance to older adults after divorce and remarriage. *Family Relations, 55*, 576–587. doi:10.1111/j.1741-3729.2006.00427.x

Comas-Díaz, L. (2006). Cultural variation in the therapeutic relationship. In C. Goodheart, A. Kazdin, & R. J. Sternberg (Eds.), *Evidence-based psychotherapy: Where practice and research meet* (pp. 81–106). Washington, DC: American Psychological Association. doi:10.1037/11423-004

Crosbie-Burnett, M. (1984). The centrality of the steprelationship: A challenge to family theory and practice. *Family Relations: Interdisciplinary Journal of Applied Family Studies, 33*, 459–463.

Crosbie-Burnett, M., & Helmbrecht, L. (1993). A descriptive empirical study of gay male stepfamilies. *Family Relations, 42*, 256–262. doi:10.2307/585554

Deal, R. (2006). *The smart stepfamily: Seven steps to a healthy family.* Minneapolis, MN: Bethany House.

Deal, R. (2010). *Marriage, family, & stepfamily facts.* Retrieved from http://www.successfulstepfamilies.com/view/24

DeGenova, M. K., & Rice, F. P. (2005). *Intimate relationships, marriages and families.* New York, NY: McGraw Hill.

DeMaris, A. (2000). Till discord do us part: The role of physical and verbal conflict in union disruption. *Journal of Marriage and the Family, 62*, 683–692. doi:10.1111/j.1741-3737.2000.00683.x

DeMaris, A., & Rao, K. V. (1992). Premarital cohabitation and subsequent marital stability in the United States: A reassessment. *Journal of Marriage and the Family, 54*, 178–190. doi:10.2307/353285

Demo, D. H., & Allen, K. R. (1996). Diversity within lesbian and gay families: Challenges and implications for family theory and research. *Journal of Social and Personal Relationships, 13*, 415–434. doi:10.1177/0265407596133007

Domenech-Rodríguez, M. M., Donovick, M. S., & Crowley, S. L. (2009). Parenting styles in a cultural context: Observations of "protective parenting" in first-generation Latinos. *Family Process, 48*, 195–210. doi:10.1111/j.1545-5300. 2009.01277.x

Dunn, J., O'Connor, T. G., & Cheng, H. (2005). Children's responses to conflict between their different parents: Mothers, stepfathers, nonresident fathers, and nonresident stepmothers. *Journal of Clinical Child and Adolescent Psychology, 34*, 223–234. doi:10.1207/s15374424jccp3402_2

Erera, P. I. (2002). *Family diversity: Continuity and change in the contemporary family.* Thousand Oaks, CA: Sage.

Fagan, J. (1998). Correlates of low-income African-American and Puerto Rican fathers' involvement with their children. *The Journal of Black Psychology, 24*, 351–367. doi:10.1177/00957984980243006

Falicov, C. J. (2009). Commentary: On the wisdom and challenges of culturally attuned treatment for Latinos. *Family Process, 48*, 292–309. doi:10.1111/j.1545-5300.2009.01282.x

Fast, I., & Cain, A. C. (1966). The stepparent role: Potential for disturbances in family functioning. *American Journal of Orthopsychiatry, 36*, 485–491. doi:10.1111/j.1939-0025.1966.tb02392.x

Fine, M. A. (1995). The clarity and content of the stepparent role: A review of the literature. *Journal of Divorce & Remarriage, 24*, 19–34.

Fine, M. A., & Kurdek, L. A. (1992). The adjustment of adolescents in stepfather and stepmother families. *Journal of Marriage and the Family, 54*, 725–736.

Fine, M. A., & Kurdek, L. A. (1995). Relation between marital quality and (step) parent–child relationship quality for parents and stepparents in stepfamilies. *Journal of Family Psychology, 9*, 216–223. doi:10.1037/0893-3200.9.2.216

Fine, M. A., & Schwebel, A. I. (1991). Stepparent stress: A cognitive perspective. *Journal of Divorce & Remarriage, 17*, 1–16. doi:10.1300/J087v17n01_01

Fine, M. A., Voydanoff, P., & Donnelly, B. W. (1993). Relationship between parental control and warmth and child well-being in stepfamilies. *Journal of Family Psychology, 7, 2*, 222–232.

Fisch, R., Weakland, J. H., & Segal, L. (1982). *The tactics of change: Doing therapy briefly.* San Francisco, CA: Jossey-Bass.

Flowers, C., Barret, R. L., & Robinson, B. E. (2000). Problems in studying gay fathers. In R. L. Barret & B. E. Robinson (Eds.), *Gay fathers: Encouraging the hearts of gay dads and their families* (pp. 153–168). San Francisco, CA: Jossey-Bass.

Foucault, M. (1980). *Power/knowledge: Selected interviews and writings*. New York, NY: Pantheon Books.

Gamache, S. (1997). Confronting nuclear family bias in stepfamily research. *Marriage & Family Review, 26*, 41–69. doi:10.1300/J002v26n01_04

Ganong, L. H. (2008). Intergenerational relationships in stepfamilies. In J. Pryor (Ed.), *The international handbook for stepfamilies* (pp. 394–422). Hoboken, NJ: Wiley.

Ganong, L. H., & Coleman, M. (1994). *Remarried family relationships*. Thousand Oaks, CA: Sage.

Ganong, L. H., & Coleman, M. (1995a). Adolescent stepchild–stepparent relationships: Changes over time. In K. Pasley & M. Ihinger-Tallman (Eds.), *Stepparenting: Issues in theory, research, and practice* (pp. 105–125). Westport, CT: Praeger.

Ganong, L. H., & Coleman, M. (1995b). The content of mother stereotypes. *Sex Roles, 32*, 495–512. doi:10.1007/BF01544185

Ganong, L. H., & Coleman, M. (1997). How society views stepfamilies. *Marriage & Family Review, 26*, 85–106. doi:10.1300/J002v26n01_06

Ganong, L. H., & Coleman, M. (2006). Obligations to stepparents acquired later in life: Relationship quality and acuity of needs. *Journal of Gerontology: Series B, Psychological Sciences and Social Sciences, 61*, 580–588.

Gerson, R., McGoldrick, M., & Petry, S. (2008). *Genograms: Assessment and intervention* (3rd ed.). New York, NY: Norton.

Giddens, A. (1992). *Transformation of intimacy: Sexuality, love and eroticism in modern societies*. Cambridge, England: Polity Press.

Goldner, V. (1982). Remarriage family: Structure, system, future. In *Therapy with Remarriage Families*, J. C. Hansen and L. Messinger (Eds.) (pp. 187–206). Rockville, MD: Aspen.

Golish, T. (2003). Stepfamily communication strengths: Understanding the ties that bind. *Human Communication Research, 29*, 41–80. doi:10.1093/hcr/29.1.41

Goodheart, C. D. (2006). Evidence, endeavor, and expertise in psychology practice. In C. D. Goodheart, A. E. Kazdin, & R. J. Sternberg (Eds.), *Evidence-based psychotherapy: Where practice and research meet* (pp. 37–62). Washington, DC: American Psychological Association. doi:10.1037/11423-002

Gottman, J. M. (1999). *The marriage clinic: A scientific based marital therapy*. New York, NY: Norton.

Gottman, J. M. (2001). What the study of relationships has to say about emotion research. *Social Sciences Information, 40*(1), 79–94. doi:10.1177/053901801040001005

Green, R. J. (2000). "Lesbians, gay men, and their parents": A critique of LaSala and the prevailing clinical "wisdom." *Family Process, 39*, 257–266. doi:10.1111/j.1545-5300.2000.39208.x

Green, R. J. (2002). Race and the field of family therapy. In E. Davis-Russell (Ed.), *CSPP handbook of multicultural education, research, intervention, and training* (pp. 221–237). San Francisco, CA: Jossey-Bass; and Hoboken, NJ: Wiley.

Green, R. J. (2008). Gay and lesbian couples: Successful coping with minority stress. In M. McGoldrick & K. Hardy (Eds.), *Re-visioning family therapy: Race, culture, and gender in clinical practice* (pp. 300–310). New York, NY: Guilford Press.

Green, R. J., Bettinger, M., & Zacks, E. (1996). Are lesbian couples fused and gay male couples disengaged? Questioning gender straitjackets. In J. Laird & R. J. Green (Eds.), *Lesbians and gays in couples and families* (pp. 185–230). San Francisco, CA: Jossey-Bass.

Green, R. J., & Mitchell, V. (2008). Gay and lesbian couples in therapy: Minority stress, relational ambiguity, and families of choice. In A. S. Gurman (Ed.), *Clinical handbook of couple therapy* (4th ed., pp. 662–680). New York, NY: Guilford Press.

Greenberg, L. S., & Goldman, R. N. (2008). *Emotion-focused couples therapy: The dynamics of emotion, love, and power.* Washington, DC: American Psychological Association. doi:10.1037/11750-000

Greenspan, S. (2006). Rethinking "harmonious parenting" using a three-factor discipline model. *Child Care in Practice, 12*(1), 5–12. doi:10.1080/13575270500526212

Grossmann, K. E., Grossmann, K., Huber, F., & Wartner, U. (1981). German children's behavior toward their mothers at 12 months and their fathers at 18 months in Ainsworth's Strange Situation. *International Journal of Behavioral Development, 4,* 157–181.

Grossmann, K. E., Grossmann, K., & Kepler, A. (2005). Universal and culture-specific aspects of human behavior: The case of attachment. In W. Friedlmeier, P. Chakkarath, & B. Schwarz (Eds.), *Culture and human development: The importance of cross-cultural research for the social sciences* (pp. 75–97). Hove, England: Taylor & Francis.

Gurman, A. S. (1991). Back to the future, ahead to the past: Is marital therapy going in circles? *Journal of Family Psychology, 4,* 402–406. doi:10.1037/0893-3200.4.4.402

Haley, J. (1973). *Uncommon therapy: The psychiatric techniques of Milton H. Erickson.* New York, NY: Norton.

Haley, J. (1976). *Problem-solving therapy: New strategies for effective family therapy.* San Francisco, CA: Jossey-Bass.

Haley, J. (1981). *Reflections on therapy.* Chevy Chase, MD: Family Therapy Institute of Washington DC.

Hamer, J. F. (1998). What African-American noncustodial fathers say inhibits and enhances their involvement with children. *The Western Journal of Black Studies, 22,* 117–127.

Hare-Mustin, R. T. (1978). A feminist approach to therapy. *Family Process, 17,* 181–194. doi:10.1111/j.1545-5300.1978.00181.x

Heider, F. (1958). *The psychology of interpersonal relations.* New York, NY: Wiley. doi:10.1037/10628-000

Herek, G. M. (2001). Homosexuality. In W. E. Craighead & C. B. Nemeroff (Eds.), *Corsini encyclopedia of psychology and behavioral science* (3rd ed., Vol. 2, pp. 683–688), New York, NY: Wiley.

Hetherington, E. M. (1988). Parents, children, and siblings six years after divorce. In R. Hinde & J. Stevenson-Hinde (Eds.), *Relationships within families* (pp. 55–79). Cambridge, England: Cambridge University Press.

Hetherington, E. M. (1989). Coping with family transitions: Winners, losers, and survivors. *Child Development, 60,* 1–14. doi:10.2307/1131066

Hetherington, E. M. (1991). Families, lies, and videotapes. *Journal of Research on Adolescence, 1,* 323–348. doi:10.1207/s15327795jra0104_1

Hetherington, E. M. (1993). An overview of the Virginia longitudinal study of divorce and remarriage with a focus on early adolescence. *Journal of Family Psychology, 7,* 39–56. doi:10.1037/0893-3200.7.1.39

Hetherington, E. M., & Clingempeel, W. G. (1992). Coping with marital transitions: A family systems perspective. *Monographs of the Society for Research in Child Development, 57*(2–3), 1–14. doi:10.1111/j.1540-5834.1992.tb00300.x

Hetherington, E. M., Cox, M., & Cox, R. (1976). Divorced fathers. *The Family Coordinator, 25,* 417–428. doi:10.2307/582856

Hetherington, E. M., & Jodl, K. (1994). Stepfamilies as settings for development. In A. Booth & J. Dunn (Eds.), *Stepfamilies: Who benefits? Who does not?* (pp. 311–331). Hillsdale, NJ: Erlbaum.

Hetherington, E. M., & Kelly, J. (2002). *For better or worse.* New York, NY: Norton.

Hetherington, E. M., & Stanley-Hagan, M. M. (1995). Parenting in divorced and remarried families. In M. H. Bornstein (Ed.), *Handbook of parenting: Vol. 3. Status and social conditions of parenting* (pp. 233–254). Hillsdale, NJ: Erlbaum.

Hetherington, E. M., & Stanley-Hagan, M. (1999a). Diversity among stepfamilies. In D. H. Demo, K. R. Allen, & M. A. Fine (Eds.), *Handbook of family diversity* (pp. 173–196). New York, NY: Oxford University Press.

Hetherington, E. M., & Stanley-Hagan, M. M. (1999b). Stepfamilies. In M. E. Lamb (Ed.), *Parenting and child development in "nontraditional families"* (pp. 137–159). Mahwah, NJ: Erlbaum.

Higgs, J., & Jones, M. (2000). *Clinical reasoning in the health professions.* London, England: Butterworth-Heineman.

Hobart (1987). The family system in remarriage: an exploratory subject. *Journal of Family Issues, 8,* 259–277.

Hoffman, L. (1981). *Foundation of family therapy.* New York, NY: Basic Books.

Holmes, T. H., & Rahe, R. H. (1967). The Social Readjustment Rating Scale. *Journal of Psychosomatic Research, 11,* 213–218. doi:10.1016/0022-3999(67)90010-4

Hong, G. K. (2009). Family diversity. In J. H. Bray & M. Stanton (Eds.), *The Wiley-Blackwell handbook of family psychology* (pp. 68–84). West Sussex, England: Blackwell. doi:10.1002/9781444310238.ch5

Ihinger-Tallman, M. (1988). Research on stepfamilies. *Annual Review of Sociology, 14*, 25–48. doi:10.1146/annurev.so.14.080188.000325

Jackson, D. (1967). The myth of normality. *Medical Opinion and Review, 3(5)*, 28–33.

Johnson, C. P., Myers, S. M., & Council on Children With Disabilities. (2007). Identification and evaluation of children with autism spectrum disorders. *Pediatrics, 120*, 1183–1215. doi:10.1542/peds.2007-2361

Johnson, S. M. (2004). *The practice of emotionally focused couples therapy: Creating connections.* New York, NY: Brunner-Routledge.

Johnson, S. M., & Bradley, B. (2009). Emotionally focused couple therapy: Creating loving relationships. In J. Bray & M. Stanton (Eds.), *The Wiley-Blackwell handbook of family psychology* (pp. 402–415). West Sussex, England: Blackwell.

Johnson, S. M., & Greenberg, L. S. (1985). Emotionally focused couples therapy: An outcome study. *Journal of Marital and Family Therapy, 11*, 313–317. doi:10.1111/j.1752-0606.1985.tb00624.x

Johnson, S. M., & O'Connor, E. (2001). *The national gay and lesbian family study.* Retrieved from http://www.mindfully.org/Reform/Gay-Lesbian-Family-Study.htm.

Karlsson, R. (2005). Ethnic matching between therapist and patient in psychotherapy: An overview of findings, together with methodological and conceptual issues. *Cultural Diversity & Ethnic Minority Psychology, 11*, 113–129. doi:10.1037/1099-9809.11.2.113

Kazdin, A. E. (2006). Assessment and evaluation in clinical practice. In C. D. Goodheart, A. E. Kazdin, & R. J. Sternberg (Eds.), *Evidence-based psychotherapy: Where practice and research meet* (pp. 153–177). Washington, DC: American Psychological Association. doi:10.1037/11423-007

Kendall, J., & Hatton, D. (2002). Racism as a source of health disparity in families with children with attention deficit hyperactivity disorder. *Advances in Nursing Science, 25(2)*, 22–39.

Kerr, D., & Beaujot, R. (2002). Family relations, low income, and child outcomes: A comparison of Canadian children in intact-, step-, and lone-parent families. *International Journal of Comparative Sociology, 43*, 134–152. doi:10.1177/002071520204300202

Kerr, M. E., & Bowen, M. (1988). *Family evaluation.* New York, NY: Norton.

Kiernan, K. (2004). Redrawing the boundaries of marriage. *Journal of Marriage and the Family, 66*, 980–987. doi:10.1111/j.0022-2445.2004.00068.x

Kleinman, A. (1988). *Rethinking psychiatry: from cultural category to personal experience.* New York, NY: Free Press.

Kornhaber, A. (1996). *Contemporary grandparenting.* Thousand Oaks, CA: Sage.

Kruk, E. (1992). Discontinuity between pre- and post-divorce father–child relationships: New evidence regarding paternal disengagement. *Journal of Divorce & Remarriage, 16*, 195–228. doi:10.1300/J087v16n03_03

Lamborn, S. D., Mount, N. S., Steinberg, L., & Dornbusch, S. M. (1991). Patterns of competence and adjustment among adolescents from authoritative, authoritarian, indulgent and neglectful families. *Child Development, 62,* 1049–1065. doi:10.2307/1131151

Layton, M. (1995). Emerging from the shadows: Looking beyond the borderline diagnosis. *The Psychotherapy Networker, 19*(1), 34–41.

Leake, V. S. (2007). Personal, familial, and systemic factors associated with family belonging for stepfamily adolescents. *Journal of Divorce & Remarriage, 47,* 135–155.

Levin, I. (1993). Family as mapped realities. *Journal of Family Issues, 14,* 82–91. doi:10.1177/0192513X93014001007

Lewin, E. (1993). *Lesbian mothers: Accounts of gender in American culture.* Ithaca, NY: Cornell University Press.

Lynch, J. M. (2000). Considerations of family structure and gender composition: The lesbian and gay stepfamily. *Journal of Homosexuality, 40*(2), 81–95. doi:10. 1300/J082v40n02_06

Lynch, J. M. (2005). Becoming a stepparent in gay/lesbian stepfamilies. *Journal of Homosexuality, 48*(2), 45–60. doi:10.1300/J082v48n02_03

MacDonald, W. L., & DeMaris, A. (1996). Parenting stepchildren and biological children: the effects of stepparent's gender and new biological children. *Journal of Family Issues, 17,* 5–25. doi:10.1177/019251396017001002

Manning, W., & Lamb, K. A. (2003). Adolescent well-being in cohabiting, married, and single-parent families. *Journal of Marriage and the Family, 65,* 876–893. doi:10. 1111/j.1741-3737.2003.00876.x

McGoldrick, M., & Carter, B. (2001). Advances in coaching: Family therapy with one person. *Journal of Marital and Family Therapy, 27,* 281–300. doi:10.1111/j.1752-0606.2001.tb00325.x

Merriam-Webster's new collegiate dictionary. (1979). Springfield, MA: Merriam-Webster.

Messinger, L. (1982). Introduction. In J. C. Hansen & L. Messinger (Eds.), *Therapy with remarriage families* (pp. xiii–xvi). Rockville, MD: Aspen.

Miller, J. A., Jacobsen, R. B., & Bigner, J. J. (1981) The child's home environment for lesbian and heterosexual mothers: A neglected area of research. *Journal of Homosexuality, 7,* 49–56.

Mills, D. (1984). A model for stepfamily development. *Family Relations, 33,* 365–372. doi:10.2307/584707

Minuchin, S. (1974). *Families and family therapy.* Cambridge, MA: Harvard University Press.

Minuchin, S., & Fishman, H. C. (1981). *Family therapy techniques.* Cambridge, MA: Harvard University Press.

Napier, A. Y., & Whitaker, C. A. (1978). *The family crucible.* New York, NY: Harper & Row.

Nealy, E. C. (2008). Working with LGBT families. In M. McGoldrick & K. Hardy (Eds.), *Re-envisioning family therapy: Race, culture, and gender in clinical practice* (pp. 289–299). New York, NY: Guilford Press.

Nichols, M. (2010). *Family therapy: Concepts and methods* (9th ed.). Boston, MA: Allyn & Bacon.

Norcross, J. C. (2001). Purposes, processes, and products of the task force on empirically supported therapeutic relationships. *Psychotherapy Theory, Research, Practice, Training, 38,* 345–356. doi:10.1037/0033-3204.38.4.345

Papernow, P. (1984). The stepfamily cycle. An experiential model of stepfamily development. *Family Relations, 33,* 355–363. doi:10.2307/584706

Papernow, P. (1993). *Becoming a stepfamily: Patterns of development in remarried families.* San Francisco, CA: Jossey-Bass.

Papernow, P. (2010). A clinician's view of "stepfamily architecture." In J. Pryor (Ed.), *The international handbook of stepfamilies* (pp. 423–454). Hoboken, NJ: Wiley.

Pasley, K. (1987). Family boundary ambiguity: Perceptions of adult remarried family members. In K. Pasley & M. Ihinger-Tallman (Eds.), *Remarriage and stepparenting: Current research and theory* (pp. 206–224). New York, NY: Guilford Press.

Pasley, K., Dollahite, D. C., & Ihinger-Tallman, M. (1993). Bridging the gap: Clinical applications of research findings on the spouse and stepparent roles in remarriage. *Family Relations, 42,* 315–322. doi:10.2307/585561

Pasley, K., & Ihinger-Tallman, M. (1982). Stress in remarried families. *Family Perspective, 16,* 181–190.

Pasley K., & Ihinger-Tallman, M. (Eds.). (1994). *Stepparenting: Issues in theory, research, and practice.* Westport, CT: Praeger.

Pasley, K., & Lee, M. (2010). Stress and coping within the context of stepfamily life. In S. Price & C. Price (Eds.), *Families and change* (4th ed., pp. 235–262). Thousand Oaks, CA: Sage.

Pasley, K., Rhoden, L., Visher, E. B., & Visher, J. S. (1996). Successful stepfamily therapy: Client's perspectives. *Journal of Marriage and the Family, 22,* 343–357. doi:10.1111/j.1752-0606.1996.tb00210.x

Patterson, C. J. (1995). Lesbian mothers, gay fathers, and their children. In A. R. D'Augelli & C. J. Patterson (Eds.), *Lesbian, gay, and bisexual identities over the lifespan* (pp. 262–290). New York, NY: Oxford University Press.

Perry, B. (1995). Step-parenting: How vulnerable are stepchildren? *Educational and Child Psychology, 12*(2), 58–70.

Pink, J. E. T., & Wampler, K. S. (1985). Problem areas in stepfamilies: Cohesion, adaptability, and the stepfather–adolescent relationship. *Family Relations, 34,* 327–335. doi:10.2307/583570

Posada, G., Gao, Y., Fang, W., Posada, R., Tascon, M., Schoelmerich, A., . . . Synnevaag, B. (1995). The secure-base phenomenon across cultures: Children's behavior, mothers' preferences, and experts' concepts. *Monographs of the Society for Research in Child Development, 60*(1–2), 27–48. doi:10.2307/1166169

Pryor, J. (2008). Children's relationships with non-resident parents. In J. Pryor (Ed.), *The international handbook of stepfamilies* (pp. 423–454). Hoboken, NJ: Wiley.

Quick, D. S., McKenry, P. C., & Newman, B. M. (1994). Stepmothers and their adolescent children: Adjustment to new roles. In K. Pasley & M. Ihinger-Tallman (Eds.), *Stepparenting: Issues in theory, research, and practice* (pp. 105–125). Westport, CT: Praeger.

Raley, R. K., & Bumpass, L. (2003). The topography of the divorce plateau: Levels and trends in union stability since 1980. *Demographic Research, 3*, Article 8. Retrieved from http://www.demographic-research.org/Volumes/Vol8/8/8-8.pdf

Rand, C., Graham, D. L., & Rawlings, E. I. (1982). Psychological health and factors the court seeks to control in lesbian mother custody trials. *Journal of Homosexuality, 8*(1), 27–39. doi:10.1300/J082v08n01_03

Rhoden, J. L., & Pasley, K. (2000). Factors affecting the perceived helpfulness of therapy with stepfamilies: A closer look at gender issues. *Journal of Divorce & Remarriage, 34*, 77–93. doi:10.1300/J087v34n01_05

Ridley, C. R., & Lingle, D. W. (1996). Cultural empathy in multicultural counseling: A multidimensional process model. In P. B. Pedersen, J. G. Draguns, W. J. Lonner, & J. E. Trimble (Eds.), *Counseling across cultures* (4th ed., pp. 21–46). Thousand Oaks, CA: Sage.

Robertson, J. (2008). Stepfathers in families. In J. Pryor (Ed.), *The international handbook of stepfamilies* (pp. 125–150). Hoboken, NJ: Wiley.

Russell, A., & Searcy, E. (1997). The contribution of affective reactions and relationship qualities to adolescents' reported responses to parents. *Journal of Social and Personal Relationships, 14*, 539–548. doi:10.1177/0265407597144008

Sager, C. J., Brown, H. S., Crohn, H., Engle, T., Rodstein, E., & Walker, L. (1983). *Treating the remarried family*. New York, NY: Brunner/Mazel.

Satir, V. M. (1964). *Conjoint family therapy*. Palo Alto, CA: Science and Behavior Books.

Satir, V. M. (1967). *Conjoint family therapy: A guide to theory and technique*. Palo Alto, CA: Science and Behavior Books.

Schenker, M. (2009). *A clinician's guide to twelve-step recovery*. New York, NY: Norton.

Schmeeckle, M. (2007). Gender dynamics in stepfamilies: Adult stepchildren's views. *Journal of Marriage and the Family, 69*, 174–189. doi:10.1111/j.1741-3737.2006.00352.x

Seltzer, J. A. (1991). Relationships between fathers and children who live apart: The father's role after separation. *Journal of Marriage and the Family, 53*, 79–101. doi:10.2307/353135

Skinner, K. B., Bahr, S. J., Crane, R., & Call, V. A. (2002). Cohabitation, marriage, and remarriage: A comparison of relationship quality over time. *Journal of Family Issues, 23*, 74–90. doi:10.1177/0192513X02023001004

Smock, P. J. (2004). The wax and wane of marriage: Prospects for marriage in the 21st century. *Journal of Marriage and the Family, 66*, 966–973. doi:10.1111/j.0022-2445.2004.00066.x

Stack, C. (1974). *All our kin*. New York, NY: Harper & Row.

Stamps, L. E. (2002). Maternal preference in child custody decisions. *Journal of Divorce & Remarriage, 37*, 1–11. doi:10.1300/J087v37n01_01

Stanton, M. (2009). The systemic epistemology of the specialty of family psychology. In J. Bray & M. Stanton (Eds.), *The Wiley-Blackwell handbook of family psychology* (pp. 5–20). West Sussex, England: Blackwell. doi:10.1002/9781444310238.ch1

Steinberg, L. (2001). We know some things: Parent–adolescent relationships in retrospect and prospect. *Journal of Research on Adolescence, 11*(1), 1–19. doi:10.1111/1532-7795.00001

Steinberg, L., Dornbusch, S., & Brown, B. B. (1992). Ethnic differences in adolescent achievement: An ecological perspective. *American Psychologist, 47*, 723–729. doi:10.1037/0003-066X.47.6.723

Sternberg, R. J. (2006). Evidenced-based practice: Gold standard, gold plated, or fool's gold. In C. D. Goodheart, A. E. Kazdin, & R. J. Sternberg (Eds.), *Evidence-based psychotherapy: Where practice and research meet.* Washington, DC: American Psychological Association. doi:10.1037/11423-011

Stewart, S. C. (2007). *Brave new stepfamilies: Diverse paths towards stepfamily living.* Thousand Oaks, CA: Sage.

Sue, D. W., & Sue, D. (1999). *Counseling the culturally different* (3rd ed.). New York, NY: Wiley.

Sullivan, H. S. (1953). *Collected works.* New York, NY: Norton.

Tangney, J. P., & Dearing, R. L. (2002). *Shame and guilt.* New York, NY: Guilford Press.

Thompson, C. A. (1992). Lesbian grief and loss issues in the coming out process. *Women & Therapy, 12*(1), 175–185. doi:10.1300/J015V12N01_14

Thompson, L., & Walker, A. J. (1989). Gender in families: Women and men in marriage, work, and parenthood. *Journal of Marriage and the Family, 51*, 845–871. doi:10.2307/353201

Thompson, R. A., & Laible, D. J. (1999). Noncustodial parents. In M. E. Lamb (Ed.), *Parenting and child development in "nontraditional" families* (pp. 103–123). Mahwah, NJ: Erlbaum.

Thomson, E., & Colella, U. (1992). Cohabitation and marital stability: Quality of commitment. *Journal of Marriage and the Family, 54*, 259–267.

Thomson, E., Mosley, J., Hanson, T. L., & McLanahan, S. S. (2001). Remarriage, cohabitation and changes in mothering behavior. *Journal of Marriage and the Family, 63*, 370–380. doi:10.1111/j.1741-3737.2001.00370.x

Thornton, A., Axinn, W. G., & Xie, Y. (2007). *Marriage and cohabitation.* Chicago, IL: The University of Chicago Press.

Thornton, A., & Young-DeMarco, L. (1996). Four decades of trends in attitudes toward family issues in the United States: The 1960s through the 1990s. *Journal of Marriage and the Family, 63*, 1009–1037. doi:10.1111/j.1741-3737.2001.01009.x

Trost, J. (1997). Step-family variations. *Marriage & Family Review, 26*, 71–84. doi:10. 1300/J002v26n01_05

van IJzendoorn, M. H., & Sagi, A. (1999). Cross-cultural patterns of attachment: Universal and contextual dimensions. In J. Cassidy & P. R. Shaver (Eds.), *Handbook of attachment: Theory, research, and clinical applications* (pp. 713–734). New York, NY: Guilford Press.

Visher, E. B., & Visher, J. S. (1979). *Stepfamilies: A guide to working with stepparents and stepchildren*. Levittown, PA: Brunner/Mazel.

Visher, E. B., & Visher, J. S. (1982). *How to win in a stepfamily*. New York, NY: Brunner/Mazel.

Visher, E. B., & Visher, J. S. (1988). *Old loyalties, new ties: Therapeutic strategies with stepfamilies*. New York, NY: Brunner/Mazel.

Visher, E. B., & Visher, J. S. (1989). Parenting coalitions after remarriage: dynamics and therapeutic guidelines. *Family Relations, 38*, 65–70. doi:10.2307/583612

Visher, E. B., & Visher, J. S. (1990). Dynamics of successful stepfamilies. *Journal of Divorce & Remarriage, 14*, 3–12. doi:10.1300/J087v14n01_02

Visher, E. B., & Visher, J. S. (1991). Therapy with stepfamily couples. *Psychiatric Annals, 21*, 462–465.

Visher, E. B., & Visher, J. S. (1996). *Therapy with stepfamilies*. New York, NY: Brunner/Mazel.

von Bertalanffy, L. (1968). *General systems theory*. New York, NY: Braziller.

Wallerstein, J. S., & Kelly, J. B. (1980). *Surviving the breakup*. New York, NY: Basic Books.

Walls, K. (2003). *Comparison of African American and Caucasian boys with ADHD*. Unpublished doctoral dissertation, Chestnut Hill College, Philadelphia, PA.

Weaver, S., & Coleman, M. (2005). A mothering but not a mother role: a grounded theory study of the nonresidential stepmother roles. *Journal of Social and Personal Relationships, 22*, 477–497. doi:10.1177/0265407505054519

Weeks, G., & Treat, S. (1992). *Couples in treatment: Techniques and approaches for effective practice*. New York, NY: Brunner/Mazel.

Weeks, J., Heaphy, B., & Donovan, C. (2001). *Same sex intimacies: Families of choice and other life experiments*. London: Routledge.

Whitaker, C. A. (1958). Psychotherapy with couples. *American Journal of Psychotherapy, 12*, 18–23.

White, M., & Epston, D. (1990). *Narrative means to therapeutic ends*. New York, NY: Norton.

Whitsett, D., & Land, H. (1992). Role strain, coping, and marital satisfaction of stepparents. *Family in Society: Journal of Contemporary Human Services, 73*, 72–92.

Whitton, S. W., Nicholson, J. M. & Markman, H. J. (2008). Research on interventions for stepfamily couples. In J. Pryor (Ed,), *The international handbook of stepfamilies* (pp. 455–484). Hoboken, NJ: Wiley.

Williams, F. (2004). *Rethinking families*. London, England: Calouste Gulbenkian Foundation.

Wintersteen, M. B., Mensinger, J. L., & Diamond, G. S. (2005). Do gender and racial differences between patient and therapist affect therapeutic alliance and treatment retention in adolescents? *Professional Psychology: Research and Practice, 36,* 400–408. doi:10.1037/0735-7028.36.4.400

Wu, Z. (1995). Stability of cohabitation relationships: The role of children. *Journal of Marriage and the Family, 57,* 231–236. doi:10.2307/353831

INDEX

Bereaved stepfamilies, *continued*
coparenting in, 160, 164
extended family in, 218–219
moral authority in, 216–218
new person in, 219–223
Berger, S. H., 20
Best practices, 18
Bernstein, A., 170, 247
Bias, 63, 83
Bicultural families, 234–235
Binuclear families
sessions with, 97–98
vulnerabilities in, 44–46
Biological subsystem
after remarriage, 36
in bereaved family case example, 148
children's fears about, 81
and complex stepfamilies'
vulnerability, 171
disciplinarian in, 109
economic concerns in, 110
holidays and traditions in, 166
maternal, 178, 188–191
paternal, 178–179, 192–195, 255
power and hierarchy in, 233
in gay/lesbian stepfamilies, 247,
248, 254
in stepfather family case example
in stepfamily therapy, 7
in stepfather families, 106
stepparents as outsiders to, 112
strengthening of, 195
stress in, 126–127
Biological subsystem support (Step 7)
in complex stepfamily case example,
187–195
in gay/lesbian case example, 254,
257–258
overview of, 94–96
in stepfather family case example,
113–114, 124–128
in stepmother family case example,
148, 155–158
Blame, 15–16, 66
Blended families, 36
Booth, A., 171
Boss, P., 251
Bouchard, G., 40
Boundaries
in African American families, 237

clarity with, 207
hierarchical, 20
permeability of, 181
in stepfamily therapy, 7
in structural model of family therapy,
16
Bowen, M., 15–16, 74, 107, 234
Bozett, F. W., 249
Brady Bunch expectation, 5
Brandt, Carolyn, 24
Bray, J. H., 20, 25
Brown S. L., 40
Browning, S. W., 8–9, 26, 30, 68, 246
Bumpass, L. L., 42

Caretaker role, 5
Carter, E. A., 22–23
Change, 14
Chaos, 76, 80, 206
Cherlin, A., 40–42
Children. *See also* Stepchildren
in African American stepfamilies,
237
anger of, toward stepparent, 81
behavioral disturbances in, 6
of bereaved families, 216–218
at binuclear family meetings, 97–98
born into complex stepfamilies,
172–173, 199
in cohabiting couple relationships,
42, 43
in complex stepfamily biological
subsystem, 187
daughters, after remarriage, 115,
181–182
in dysfunctional hierarchies, 20
from first-union families, 58
in gay/lesbian stepfamilies, 249
individual session with, 81–82, 95
loyalty binds of, 56–57
as mediators, 207
parent connection with, 64
parent empathy for, 25–26
passive-aggression of, 199
pushed to bond with stepparent,
80–81
rejection of stepparent by, 47–49,
216, 220–222
reunion fantasies of, 113–114
sons, after remarriage, 116, 181–182

Efficacy of practice models, 67
Egalitarian relationships, 238, 241, 249
Emotional disengagement, 62–63, 65
Emotionally focused couples therapy,
    84
Emotionally focused model, 17
Emotional outbursts, 62, 63
Emotions
    conflicted, 74
    and differentiation, 15–16
    in family therapy models, 17
    guilt as, 51
Empathic understanding (Step 5)
    in complex stepfamily case example,
        182–186
    in gay/lesbian case example, 256–257
    overview of, 85–88
    in stepfather family case example,
        116–121
    in stepmother family case example,
        151–154
Empathy, 7
    capacity for, 78–79
    cognitive, 227
    cultural, 227
    for divergent points of view, 116
    and feeling understood, 226–227
    between parent and child, 25–26
    of stepparent, 56
Enactments, 21
Entire family sessions
    in family therapy movement, 15
    with first-union families, 76
    for integration, 101, 136
    in stepfamily therapy, 19–20
Erickson, M. H., 16, 87
Ethnic groups. See Diverse populations
Evidence-based practice, 66–68
Evidence-based practice in psychology
    (EBPP), 66–67
Exclusion of stepparent, 72
Ex-partners
    conflict between, 165
    conjoint session with, 200
    continual conflict between, 106
    goals of therapy session with, 131
    importance of, 44
    in stepfamily functioning, 5–6
    as subsystem, 179

Expectations
    after remarriage, 180–181
    of Brady Bunch type of stepfamily, 5
    in fantasy stage of stepfamily cycle, 30
    in gay/lesbian stepfamilies, 247
    as problematic, 112
    for stepfather role, 121–122
    in stepmother family case example,
        154–155
    for structure of stepfamily, 63–64
Explosive outbursts, 65
Extended families, 205–223
    in stepmother family case example,
        148–150, 160–165
    in bereaved stepfamilies, 218–219
    in gay/lesbian case example,
        255–256, 259
    with remarriage after bereavement,
        213–223
    in stepfather family case example, 115
    stepgrandparents in, 207–213
    structural complexity in, 205–207
Externalization, 17

Fairy tale myths, 140
Family diagram, 16
Family of choice, 249
Family of origin, 249
Family rules
    establishment of new, 124
    implementation of, 134
    in stepfamily therapy, 21–22
    in stepfather family case example, 109
    in stepmother family case example,
        160
The Family Therapy Collections on
    Therapy With the Remarried Family
    (L. Messinger), 22
Family therapy movement, 13–19
Family typologies, 14
Fathers
    African American, 238
    in biological subsystem, 178–179
    and children from first-union
        family, 58
    and child support payments, 106, 134
    in custody cases, 248
    gay, 249, 250
    role of, 38

ABOUT THE AUTHORS

Scott Browning, PhD, is a professor in the Department of Professional Psychology at Chestnut Hill College in Philadelphia. He received his master's degree from Boston University, and his doctorate from the California School of Professional Psychology, Berkeley. Dr. Browning completed his postdoctoral internship at Philadelphia Child Guidance Clinic. He is a noted authority on psychological treatment with stepfamilies. As a scholar, teacher, and clinician, Dr. Browning has explored the intricacies of treating stepfamilies and has provided advanced training in the treatment of stepfamilies to clinicians and graduate students both nationally and abroad. He is the author of numerous chapters and articles on the topics of stepfamilies, empathy, codependency and family therapy training practices.

Elise Artelt is a licensed marriage and family therapist and works for Carson Valley Children's Aid, a school and community mental health agency with offices in Philadelphia and Montgomery County, Pennsylvania. She is currently assigned to work in schools as a student assistance program counselor doing group and individual counseling. She received her MEd from Penn State University in secondary school guidance and her MS in counseling psychology from Chestnut Hill College. Her interest in stepfamily work began with her experience as a stepgrandchild and as a stepmother with three stepchildren and four stepgrandchildren. She also has a daughter, Maya. Ms. Artelt has a private practice in Wayne, Pennsylvania, specializing in stepfamily therapy.